Somos así
EN SUS MARCAS B
Second Edition

James F. Funston
Alejandro Vargas Bonilla
Daphne Sherman

Contributing Writers

Rolando Castellanos
Dana Cunningham
Toni Theisen
Robert Headrick
Sarah Vaillancourt

CONSULTANTS

Lourdes C. Adams
Niceville High School
Niceville, Florida

Sandra Martin Arnold
Palisades Charter High School
Palisades, California

Washington B. Collado
Broward County Public Schools
Ft. Lauderdale, Florida

Nancy S. Hernández
Simsbury High School
Simsbury, Connecticut

Paul J. Hoff
University of Wisconsin—Eau Claire
Eau Claire, Wisconsin

Emily S. Peel
Wethersfield High School
Wethersfield, Connecticut

Jane S. Stevens
Niceville High School
Niceville, Florida

EMC/Paradigm Publishing, Saint Paul, Minnesota

Credits

Assistant Editors
Amy Dorn-Fernández
Yuri M. Guerra Guerra

Editorial Consultants
Karin D. Fajardo
Christine Gensmer
Sharon O'Donnell
Steve Patterson
Isabel Picado
Rubi Borgia Pinger
Eliana Silva Premoli
David Thorstad
Michael A. Webb

Editorial Assistance
Glenndell Larry

Illustrators
Tune and Khet Insisiengmay
Hetty Mitchell

Cartoon Illustrator
Steve Mark

Photo Research
Jennifer Anderson

Design and Production
Joan D'Onofrio
Jennifer Wreisner

We have attempted to locate owners of copyright materials used in this book. If an error or omission has occurred, EMC/Paradigm Publishing will acknowledge the contribution in subsequent printings.

ISBN 0-8219-1958-X

Published by EMC/Paradigm Publishing
875 Montreal Way
St. Paul, Minnesota 55102
800-328-1452
www.emcp.com
E-mail: educate@emcp.com

Printed in the United States of America
4 5 6 7 8 9 10 X X X 05 04 03

About the Cover

In *Capítulo 8* of *Somos así EN SUS MARCAS–B*, you will learn about some traditions of the people of Spain. A well-known, ancient Spanish cultural institution is *la Tuna*, the musical group featured in the painting on the cover of this textbook. The original acrylic by Kelly Stribling Sutherland focuses on a group of four singing musicians that recalls the traveling minstrels of thirteenth century Spain. Back then, poor university students gathered to play folk songs in local inns to earn money for their education. They also played these songs to court their girlfriends. Today, members of *la Tuna* keep alive traditions from the past by dressing in period costumes, performing on the streets and in restaurants, and singing songs accompanied by the same musical instruments that their predecesors used–the guitar and the *bandurria* (similar to a mandolin).

The artist adds a woman to the traditional, male group along with a tambourine player. The man in the center is dressed in the traditional costume of *la Tuna*: a black, fitted jacket; a white shirt with lace at the collar and cuffs; black, puffy pants; and long, black stockings. He wears a long, black cape not only for protection from the elements, but to display his love of travel and women. The badges on his cape come from the different cities and countries in which he has performed. Other ribbons and streamers sewn to his cape are in honor of the young women whose hearts he has won. Notice how the artist has collaged various pieces of fabric over the heads of the performers. Can you identify which Spanish artist painted the scene at the top of the tambourine player's hat? It's representative of the whimsical, imaginative work of Miró, a famous Spanish artist of the twentieth century. In her painting Ms. Sutherland combines contemporary Spanish art with the traditions of the past to portray one of the musical, romantic customs of Spain.

Table of Contents

BRIDGE PROGRAM B1

Etapa 1 En clase B2

Vocabulario Los cognados **B4**
Saludos **B4**
En la clase **B5**
La hora **B5**
Idioma *Ser* vs. *estar* **B6**
Gustar **B8**
Los verbos que terminan en *-ar* **B9**
Comunicación B10
Conexión cultural B11
Proyectos B13

Etapa 2 En casa B14

Vocabulario La familia **B16**
El transporte **B17**
Idioma Los adjetivos **B18**
Los adjetivos posesivos **B18**
El verbo *ir* **B19**
Los pronombres de complemento indirecto **B20**
Comunicación B20
Conexión cultural B21
Proyectos B22

Etapa 3 En ruta B24

Vocabulario ¿Qué tienes? **B26**
Las palabras interrogativas **B27**
Los números y los meses **B27**
Idioma Los verbos que terminan en *-er* y en *-ir* **B28**
Los verbos irregulares **B29**
Comunicación B30
Conexión cultural B31
Proyectos B32

Etapa 4 En Mérida B34

Vocabulario Los colores **B36**
Las comidas **B36**
Las comidas y los precios **B37**
Idioma Exclamaciones **B38**
Repaso de los verbos regulares **B39**
Comunicación B39
Conexión cultural B40
Proyectos B41

Etapa 5 En Chichén Itzá B42

Vocabulario Las actividades **B44**
Los precios **B44**
Idioma Los pronombres de complemento directo **B45**
Repaso de los verbos irregulares **B46**
Comunicación B47
Conexión cultural B48
Proyectos B49

CAPÍTULO 6 **El hogar 1**

Lección 11 2

En la cocina 2
Para ti Más cosas de la cocina 3
Conexión cultural Venezuela 5
Algo más *Tener que* y *deber* 6
Idioma El presente de los verbos con el cambio *e* → *ie* 7

Para ti Proverbios y dichos 8
Algo más *Pensar:* un poco más 9
Oportunidades ¿Piensas viajar a otro país? 10
En el comedor 11
Para ti Más sobre la comida 11
Conexión cultural La comida venezolana 12
Para ti Una clave 14
Algo más Para hablar de cantidades 15
Idioma Los adjetivos demostrativos 16
Autoevaluación 19
¡La práctica hace al maestro! 20
Vocabulario 21

Lección 12 22

Una carta de Jorge 22
Para ti Las palabras *e* y *u* 23
Conexión cultural Colombia 23
Algo más Para expresar deseos 24
Idioma El presente del verbo *decir* 25
Algo más Usando *que* para reportar 26
El dibujo de Jorge 28
Para ti La planta baja y el primer piso 28
Estrategia Para hablar mejor: *recognizing words in context* 29
No quiero salir de casa 31
Idioma El presente de los verbos con el cambio *e* → *i* 32
Algo más *Pedir* y *preguntar* 33
¿Qué tienen? 35
Repaso rápido Adjetivos y expresiones con *tener* 36
Repaso rápido Los verbos regulares 37
Autoevaluación 37
¡La práctica hace al maestro! 38
Vocabulario 39

A leer

Estrategia para leer: *using graphics to understand a reading* 40
La casa ideal de Jorge 41

A escribir

Estrategia para escribir: *connecting phrases* 42

Repaso 43

CAPÍTULO 7 Los pasatiempos 45

Lección 13 46

Quiero poner el televisor 46
Conexión cultural ¡Gol! ¡Qué buen partido de fútbol! 47
Conexión cultural La Argentina 48
Idioma El presente de los verbos con el cambio *o* → *ue* y *u* → *ue* 49
Los pasatiempos 51
Conexión cultural Damas y caballeros 51
El tiempo libre 53
Algo más Expresiones con *hace* 54
Algo más Para hablar del tiempo 55
Alquilamos una película 56
Idioma El presente progresivo 57
Idioma Los gerundios con irregularidades 59
Repaso rápido El complemento directo 60
Algo más Más sobre los pronombres de complemento directo 61
Para ti Comparando el inglés con el español 62
Autoevaluación 63
¡La práctica hace al maestro! 64
Vocabulario 65
Estrategia Para aprender mejor: *learning vocabulary* 65

Lección 14 66

¿Cómo son las estaciones en Chile? 66
Conexión cultural ¿Puedes esquiar en verano? 68
Conexión cultural Chile 69
Idioma El presente de los verbos *dar* y *poner* 70
Una carta electrónica 71
Algo más ¿Dónde pongo un acento? 72
¿Qué tiempo hace? 73
Conexión cultural ¿Qué temperatura hace? 74
Para ti Proverbios y dichos 75
Algo más Para deportistas 78
Oportunidades El español y los deportes 78
Idioma Los números ordinales 79
Conexión cultural Los deportes olímpicos en el mundo hispano 80
Autoevaluación 81
¡La práctica hace al maestro! 82
Vocabulario 83

A leer

Estrategia para leer: *previewing* 84
Los deportes más populares 84

A escribir

Estrategia para escribir: *questioning* 86

Repaso 87

CAPÍTULO 8 **¿Qué haces en casa?** 89

Lección 15 90

Preparando una fiesta 90
Conexión cultural La paella 91
Arreglando la casa 92
Repaso rápido Los pronombres de complemento directo 93
Para ti El verbo *colgar* 93
Algo más La expresión *acabar de* 94
Idioma El complemento indirecto 95
Los quehaceres 97
Algo más El cambio de *g* → *j* 98
Algo más Para aclarar y para dar énfasis 99
Idioma El presente de los verbos *oír* y *traer* 100
Después de la fiesta 102
Para ti El uso de *vosotros,-as* 102
Idioma El pretérito de los verbos regulares *-ar* 102
Conexión cultural España 104
Autoevaluación 105
¡La práctica hace al maestro! 106
Vocabulario 107

Lección 16 108

En el supermercado 108
Conexión cultural Receta de la paella valenciana 110

Algo más *Hacer falta, parecer* e *importar* 111
Para ti Proverbios y dichos 111
Idioma Para comparar 112
Conexión cultural Imágenes de España 115
En el mercado 116
Buscando el mejor precio 119
Oportunidades Regatear 120
Estrategia Para aprender mejor: *survival skills* 120
Repaso rápido El pretérito de los verbos regulares *-ar* 121
Idioma El pretérito de *dar* y *estar* 122
Autoevaluación 123
¡La práctica hace al maestro! 124
Vocabulario 125

A leer

Estrategia para leer: *gathering meaning from context* 126

Las tapas: una tradición española 126

A escribir

Estrategia para escribir: *using graphic organizers* 128

Repaso 129

CAPÍTULO 9 **En la tienda** 131

Lección 17 132

La ropa 132

Algo más ¿Uso un artículo? 134

Para ti Los colores 134

Conexión cultural Panamá 135

Conexión cultural Palabras diferentes para decir lo mismo 136

Estrategia Para comunicar mejor: *asking questions* 137

Julia compró ropa 138

Para ti Proverbios y dichos 139

Repaso rápido El pretérito de los verbos regulares *-ar* 140

Idioma El pretérito de los verbos regulares *-er* e *-ir* 140

Idioma El pretérito de los verbos *ir* y *ser* 143

Idioma Las expresiones afirmativas y negativas 145

Autoevaluación 147

¡La práctica hace al maestro! 148

Vocabulario 149

Lección 18 150

Un regalo para Carmencita 150

Algo más Los diminutivos 151

Conexión cultural Ecuador 152

Idioma El pretérito de *leer, oír, ver, decir, hacer* y *tener* 153

En el departamento de regalos 155

Para ti Diciéndolo de otra manera 156

¿En efectivo o a crédito? 157

Oportunidades En el mercado internacional 158

Repaso rápido Las preposiciones 159

Idioma Usando las preposiciones 159

Algo más Para hablar de dinero 162

Autoevaluación 163

¡La práctica hace al maestro! 164

Vocabulario 165

A leer

Estrategia para leer: *using visual format to predict meaning* 166

Encuesta de la Plaza Paitilla 166

A escribir

Estrategia para escribir: *indicating sequence* 168

Repaso 169

CAPÍTULO 10 **De vacaciones** 171

Lección 19 172

¿Qué hiciste el fin de semana pasado? 172

Para ti Expresiones de emoción 172

Conexión cultural El Perú 174

Oportunidades En otro país 175

Repaso rápido *Tener que* 176

Estrategia Para aprender mejor: *the importance of reviewing* 176

Conexión cultural La arqueología de las civilizaciones indígenas 178

Para ti Proverbios y dichos 179

Autoevaluación 179

¡La práctica hace al maestro! 180

¿Qué recuerdas? 181

Lección 20 182

El correo electrónico 182

Para ti Me gustaría 183

Conexión cultural Guatemala 184

Oportunidades Carreras en las que se puede usar el español 187

Autoevaluación 191

¡La práctica hace al maestro! 192

¿Qué recuerdas? 193

A leer

Estrategia para leer: *identifying the main idea of each paragraph* 194

Los Pasofinos: caballos de los conquistadores 195

A escribir

Estrategia para escribir: *defining your purpose for writing* 196

Repaso 197

Appendices

Appendix A Grammar Review 198

Appendix B Verbs 200

Appendix C Numbers 205

Appendix D Syllabification 206

Appendix E Accentuation 207

Vocabulary

Spanish-English 208

English-Spanish 222

Index 234

Credits 236

Nº	PAIS	Nº	PAIS
1	ST. CRISTÓBAL Y NEVIS	20	ALBANIA
2	SAN VICENTE Y LAS GRANADINAS	21	LÍBANO
3	DOMINICA	22	JORDANIA
4	BARBADOS	23	LESOTHO
5	PAÍSES BAJOS	24	SWAZILANDIA
6	BÉLGICA	25	BAHREIN
7	LUXEMBURGO	26	ESTONIA
8	REP. CHECA	27	LETONIA
9	AUSTRIA	28	LITUANIA
10	SUIZA	29	MOLDAVIA
11	MÓNACO	30	GEORGIA
12	SAN MARINO	31	ARMENIA
13	LIECHTENSTEIN	32	AZERBAIDZHAN
14	HUNGRÍA	33	KIRGUIZISTÁN
15	ESLOVENIA	34	TADZHIKISTÁN
16	CROACIA	35	ESLOVAQUIA
17	BOSNIA-HERZEGOVINA	36	DJIBOUTI
18	YUGOSLAVIA	37	RUANDA
19	MACEDONIA	38	BURUNDI

GLACIAL ÁRTICO
RUSIA
Alaska (EE.UU.)
KAZAJSTÁN
MONGOLIA
UZBEKISTÁN
TURKMENISTÁN
TURQUÍA
SIRIA
CHIPRE
ISRAEL
IRAK
IRÁN
AFGANISTÁN
PAKISTÁN
REP. POP. CHINA
COREA DEL NORTE
COREA DEL SUR
JAPÓN
OCÉANO PACÍFICO
KUWAIT
QATAR
EMIRATOS ÁRABES UNIDOS
ARABIA SAUDITA
OMÁN
YEMEN
EGIPTO
ERITREA
SUDÁN
ETIOPÍA
SOMALIA
UGANDA
KENYA
TANZANIA
MALAWI
MOZAMBIQUE
MADAGASCAR
COMORES
SEYCHELLES
MAURICIO
MALDIVAS
SRI LANKA
NEPAL
BHUTAN
BANGLADESH
INDIA
BIRMANIA
LAOS
VIETNAM
THAILANDIA
CAMBOYA
TAIWÁN
Manila
FILIPINAS
REP. DE PALAOS
BRUNEI
MALASIA
SINGAPUR
INDONESIA
PAPÚA NUEVA GUINEA
SALOMÓN
OCÉANO ÍNDICO
Trópico de Capricornio
AUSTRALIA
NUEVA ZELANDA
Línea internacional de cambio de hora
UNDI
a en el mundo
AL ANTÁRTICO
RTIDA
Países donde el español es la lengua oficial o co-oficial
Zonas donde el español es hablado por una parte de la población
Madrid Ciudad de más de 1 millón de hab.
Panamá Ciudad de 100.000 a 1 millón de hab.
Malabo Ciudad de menos de 100.000 hab.
Límite de Estado
Capital de Estado
Otras ciudades

MÉXICO
©edigol ediciones,s.a.
ESTADOS UNIDOS
Golfo de México
OCÉANO PACÍFICO
Golfo de California
Golfo de Tehuantepec
Cabo San Lucas
Trópico de Cáncer
Sierra Madre Occidental
Sierra Madre Oriental
Sierra Madre del Sur
Sierra Madre de Chiapas
MISSISSIPPI
BRAZOS
COLORADO
RÍO GRANDE
SONORA
YAQUI
RÍO DEL FUERTE
USUMACINTA
COLOTOPEC
BELICE
GUATEMALA
HONDURAS
EL SALVADOR
Tijuana
San Diego
Mexicali
Las Cruces
El Paso
Ciudad Juárez
Chihuahua
Hermosillo
La Paz
Culiacán
Mazatlán
Houston
San Antonio
Corpus Christi
Nueva Orleans
Laredo
Nuevo Laredo
Brownsville
Matamoros
Monterrey
Saltillo
Ciudad Victoria
Tampico
Zacatecas
Aguascalientes
San Luis Potosí
Guanajuato
Querétaro
León
Guadalajara
Tepic
Puerto Vallarta
Colima
Morelia
Toluca
Ciudad de México
Cuernavaca
Tlaxcala
Puebla
Jalapa Enríquez
Veracruz
Chilpancingo
Acapulco
Oaxaca
Villahermosa
Palenque
Campeche
Mérida
Uxmal
Chichén Itzá
Tulum
Cancún
Chetumal
Belmopán
Guatemala
San Salvador
Tegucigalpa
30°
20°
90°
100°
110°

AMÉRICA CENTRAL Y EL CARIBE

ESPAÑA

MAR CANTÁBRICO
FRANCIA
OCÉANO ATLÁNTICO
PORTUGAL
MAR MEDITERRÁNEO
GOLFO DE CÁDIZ
Estrecho de Gibraltar
MARRUECOS
GALICIA
ASTURIAS
CANTABRIA
PAÍS VASCO
NAVARRA
LA RIOJA
ARAGÓN
CATALUÑA
ANDORRA
Andorra la Vella
CASTILLA Y LEÓN
MADRID
CASTILLA-LA MANCHA
EXTREMADURA
COMUNIDAD VALENCIANA
MURCIA
ANDALUCÍA
ISLAS BALEARES
MALLORCA
MENORCA
IBIZA
FORMENTERA
CABRERA
Palma de Mallorca
La Coruña
Lugo
Pontevedra
Orense
Oviedo
Santander
Bilbao
San Sebastián
Vitoria
Pamplona
Logroño
León
Burgos
Palencia
Soria
Valladolid
Zamora
Salamanca
Segovia
Ávila
Madrid
Guadalajara
Cuenca
Toledo
Cáceres
Badajoz
Ciudad Real
Albacete
Huesca
Zaragoza
Teruel
Lérida
Gerona
Barcelona
Tarragona
Castellón de la Plana
Valencia
Alicante
Murcia
Córdoba
Jaén
Sevilla
Huelva
Cádiz
Granada
Málaga
Almería
Gibraltar (R.U.)
Ceuta
Melilla
Lisboa
Cordillera Cantábrica
Pirineos
Sistema Central
Montes Ibéricos
Sierra Morena
Sierra Nevada
Mulhacén 3478
MIÑO
DUERO
EBRO
TER
TAJO
GUADIANA
TURIA
JÚCAR
SEGURA
GUADALQUIVIR
CANARIAS
LA PALMA
LA GOMERA
EL HIERRO
TENERIFE
Santa Cruz de Tenerife
Teide 3715
GRAN CANARIA
Las Palmas de Gran Canaria
FUERTEVENTURA
LANZAROTE
OCÉANO ATLÁNTICO
10°
6°
2°
42°
38°
28°
18°
16°
14°
©edigol ediciones,s.a.

AMÉRICA DEL SUR
MAR CARIBE
G. de Venezuela
BARRANQUILLA
CARTAGENA
MARACAIBO
L. de Maracaibo
CARACAS
Delta del Orinoco
MÉRIDA
VENEZUELA
ORINOCO
BUCARAMANGA
ARAUCA
MEDELLÍN
MAGDALENA
SANTA FE DE BOGOTÁ
VILLAVICENCIO
CALI
PASTO
COLOMBIA
QUITO
Cotopaxi 5896
Chimborazo 6267
ECUADOR
GUAYAQUIL
Golfo de Guayaquil
CUENCA
CAQUETÁ
IQUITOS
PERÚ
Pta. Negra
CHICLAYO
TRUJILLO
Los Andes
CALLAO
LIMA
Machu Picchu
CUZCO
ICA
JULIACA
L. Titicaca
LA PAZ
BOLIVIA
COCHABAMBA
L. de Poopó
SUCRE
POTOSÍ
ARICA
GEORGETOWN
PARAMARIBO
CAYENA
GUYANA
SURINAM
GUAYANA FRANCESA (Fra.)
OCÉANO ATLÁNTICO
Estuario del Amazonas
Ecuador
AMAZONAS
FORTALEZA
B R A S I L
RECIFE
SAN FRANCISCO
SALVADOR
PARAGUAY
BRASILIA
BELO HORIZONTE
PARANÁ
SÃO PAULO
RÍO DE JANEIRO
Gran Chaco
PARAGUAY
CONCEPCIÓN
PILCOMAYO
Itaipú
Cataratas del Iguazú
ASUNCIÓN
URUGUAY
RESISTENCIA
CORRIENTES
OCÉANO PACÍFICO
Trópico de Capricornio
ANTOFAGASTA
CHILE
SAN MIGUEL DE TUCUMÁN
ARGENTINA
Aconcagua 6959
CÓRDOBA
SAN JUAN
PARANÁ
SALTO
URUGUAY
IS. JUAN FERNÁNDEZ (Chile)
VIÑA DEL MAR
VALPARAÍSO
SANTIAGO DE CHILE
MENDOZA
ROSARIO
BUENOS AIRES
LA PLATA
MONTEVIDEO
RÍO DE LA PLATA
SALADO
Pampas
TALCA
CONCEPCIÓN
COLORADO
BAHÍA BLANCA
MAR DEL PLATA
Pta. Norte
NEUQUÉN
NEGRO
VALDIVIA
SAN CARLOS DE BARILOCHE
PUERTO MONTT
Patagonia
C. Tres Puntas
Golfo de Penas
Bahía Grande
Estr. de Magallanes
ISLAS MALVINAS (R.U.)
PUERTO STANLEY
PUNTA ARENAS
TIERRA DEL FUEGO
USHUAIA
Cabo de Hornos
Estr. de Drake
GEORGIA DEL SUR (R.U.)
©edigol ediciones,s.a.
80°
60°
40°
20°
0°

Introducción

Nuestro proyecto

Etapa 3
En ruta

Etapa 4
En Mérida

Etapa 2
En casa

Etapa 5
En Chichén Itzá

Etapa 1
En clase

¡Bienvenidos! Soy la señora Mendoza, la profesora de español. Me gusta bailar y viajar.
¡Hola! Soy Selena. Tengo 13 años. Me gusta ir de compras.
¡Buenos días! Me llamo Soledad. Tengo 14 años. Me gusta jugar al básquetbol.
¡Hola! ¿Qué tal? Me llamo Beto. Tengo 12 años. Me gustan las computadoras.
¡Buenos días! Soy Diego. Tengo 13 años. Me gustan la música salsa y el fútbol.
¡Buenos días! Me llamo Quique el quetzal. Tengo 80 años. Me gusta leer.
¡Hola! Soy Juana la iguana. Tengo 5 años. Me gusta comer insectos.

Etapa 1

En clase

¡Buenos días! Tengo un proyecto para Uds. ¡Vamos a visitar Chichén Itzá! Allá hay un secreto.
CHICHÉN ITZÁ
¿Está muy lejos de aquí?
¡Sí, claro! Está en la península de Yucatán.
Los mayas son de Chichén Itzá, ¿verdad?
¡Fantástico! ¡Vamos ahora!
Aquí está Chichén Itzá.
MÉXICO
CHICHÉN ITZÁ
¿Hablan español en Chichén Itzá?
¿Hay un secreto? ¿Qué vamos a buscar allá?
¿Cuándo salimos?
¿Cómo vamos?
¿Quieren Uds. ir con nosotros?
¡Vamos a Chichén Itzá!

Vocabulario

Los cognados

You will often find Spanish words that look similar to English ones and have the same meaning. These words are called cognates (*cognados*).

1 En inglés, por favor

Look again at some words that you saw in *Etapa 1*. What do you think they mean in English?

1. excelente
2. proyecto
3. visitar
4. secreto
5. península
6. mayas

Saludos

2 ¿Buenos días, buenas tardes o buenas noches?

What should Selena say to the following people when she greets them?

la señora Mendoza
Buenos días, señora Mendoza.

el señor Alicante
Buenas tardes, señor Alicante.

1. Beto

2. doña Luisa

3. la señorita Ramos

4. tía Alicia

5. Soledad y Diego

En la clase

3 ¿Qué tienes en la mochila?

Everyone is getting ready for the first day of school. Choosing several items from the illustration, tell a classmate what each person has in his or her backpack.

Soledad
En su mochila Soledad tiene una regla, un libro, su cuaderno y un lápiz.

1. Beto
2. Selena
3. Diego
4. la señora Mendoza
5. yo

La hora

4 ¿A qué hora tienes...?

Working with a partner, take turns asking and telling each other at what time you have certain classes.

biología
A: ¿A qué hora tienes la clase de biología?
B: Tengo la clase de biología a las nueve. ¿Y tú? ¿A qué hora tienes la clase de biología?
A: Tengo la clase de biología a las dos y media.

1. español
2. matemáticas
3. historia
4. inglés

IDIOMA

Ser vs. *estar*

The Spanish verbs *ser* and *estar* both mean "to be."

ser		estar	
yo	**soy**	yo	**estoy**
tú	**eres**	tú	**estás**
Ud. / él / ella	**es**	Ud. / él / ella	**está**
nosotros / nosotras	**somos**	nosotros / nosotras	**estamos**
vosotros / vosotras	**sois**	vosotros / vosotras	**estáis**
Uds. / ellos / ellas	**son**	Uds. / ellos / ellas	**están**

5 ¿De dónde eres?

The students in Sra. Mendoza's Spanish class have chosen Spanish names for themselves and a Spanish-speaking country for their birthplace. Tell where the following people come from by completing each sentence with the appropriate present-tense form of the verb *ser*.

Maribel <u>es</u> de Ecuador.

1. Yo...de Cuba.
2. Nicolás y Paco...de México.
3. Rico y yo...de Panamá.
4. Uds....de Guatemala, ¿verdad?
5. ¿Y tú? ¿De dónde...?

The verbs *ser* and *estar* are used in very different situations.

ser	estar
* origin **Los mayas son de Chichén Itzá.** * characteristic or distinguishing trait **Ella es la profesora.**	* temporary condition **Estoy muy bien.** * location **¿Dónde está mi mochila?**

Looking at the chart of the different uses of *ser* and *estar* on page B6, which verb do you use to...

1. tell where something is located?
2. tell where you are from?
3. describe someone's size, personality and profession?
4. describe someone's health?

estar
ser
ser
estar
¡Felicitaciones!

6 ¿La señora Mendoza es o está...?

Diego is writing a brief description of his Spanish teacher, Sra. Mendoza. Complete each sentence with the appropriate form of *ser* or *estar*.

La señora Mendoza...de Mérida. Mérida...en la península de Yucatán. Ella...la profesora de español. También, ella...muy inteligente.

7 ¿Quién es?

Find a picture of a well-known person (sports figure, politician, actor, community leader, musician) in a newspaper or magazine. Attach the picture to a sheet of paper and write four sentences to describe your person. Tell...

1. his or her name.
2. where he or she was born.
3. where he or she is living now.
4. what he or she is like.

Se llama Sammy Sosa. Es de la República Dominicana. Ahora está en los Estados Unidos. Es muy popular.

amable
bonito
cariñoso
divertido
egoísta
cómico
generoso
fantástico
importante
inteligente
interesante
popular
simpático

Gustar

The verb *gustar* ("to like") is always used with an indirect object pronoun.

8 ¿Qué te gusta?

Just like the students in the *Etapas*, you are going to be put in teams to work on your group projects. To get to know a little more about your teammates and their likes and dislikes, interview two of them, using a word from Column A and an appropriate expression from Column B for each question. Make a grid like the one that follows and jot down your partners' responses.

A	B
tocar	por los exámenes
cantar	al fútbol
tomar	la salsa
estudiar	la guitarra
hablar	español
jugar	en junio, julio y agosto
bailar	con un grupo de rock
nadar	mucho tiempo con la computadora
pasar	el almuerzo en la cafetería

Miranda, ¿te gusta tocar la guitarra?
Sí, me gusta mucho tocar la guitarra.

Carlos, ¿te gusta tocar la guitarra?
No, no me gusta ni un poco tocar la guitarra.

¿Te gusta...?		
	Miranda	Carlos
tocar la guitarra	mucho	no, ni un poco

Los pronombres de complemento indirecto con *gustar*

me gusta/gustan	**nos** gusta/gustan
te gusta/gustan	**os** gusta/gustan
le gusta/gustan	**les** gusta/gustan

Nos gusta la música.
Me gustan las canciones de amor.

Looking at the chart on page B8, what do you say if...

1. you like only one thing?
2. you like more than one thing?
3. you and your friend like only one thing?
4. your friends like more than one thing?

Me gusta....
Me gustan....
Nos gusta....
Les gustan....
¡Qué bueno!

9 ¿Me gusta o no me gusta?

Now tell about your likes and dislikes, using the choices listed in Activity 8. Don't forget to use the plural form of *gustar* if you name more than one activity in a sentence.

Los verbos que terminan en *-ar*

To form the present tense of a regular *-ar* verb, remove the *-ar* and add the endings that correspond to each of the subject pronouns. Here is the present tense of the verb *comprar* ("to buy").

comprar	
yo	compr**o**
tú	compr**as**
Ud. / él / ella	compr**a**
nosotros / nosotras	compr**amos**
vosotros / vosotras	compr**áis**
Uds. / ellos / ellas	compr**an**

Looking at the chart of the verb *comprar*, what is the ending...

1. when you ask your friend a question?
2. when you answer your friend?

-as
-o
¡Magnífico!

10 ¿Hablas español?

To find out more information about your team members, write appropriate questions. Follow the model.

estudiar en la biblioteca
¿Estudias en la biblioteca?

1. hablar español con tus padres
2. entrar a la escuela a las ocho de la mañana
3. necesitar más cuadernos
4. buscar un mapa de México
5. mirar las fotos de México

11 Una encuesta

Now ask your teammates the questions you prepared in Activity 10. Make a grid like the one that follows and note your teammates' responses.

	Miranda	Carlos
estudiar en la biblioteca	sí	
hablar español con tus padres		
entrar a la escuela a las ocho de la mañana		
necesitar más cuadernos		
buscar un mapa de México		
mirar las fotos de México		

Miranda, ¿estudias en la biblioteca?
Sí, estudio en la biblioteca.

Comunicación

12 ¡Hablemos!

Pick one of the members of your team and get to know this person better. Spend several minutes talking to him or her. In the course of your conversation:

1. greet each other.
2. ask and tell each other how you are.
3. ask and give your new Spanish name.
4. ask and tell which Spanish-speaking country you come from.
5. ask and tell your age.
6. tell each other several activities that you like to do.
7. exchange phone numbers in case you need to work on a team assignment together.
8. tell each other "good-bye."

13 ¡Escribamos!

One of the requirements for the project is to keep a notebook or folder that contains important information about yourself and your team as well as details about the project. Your first notebook entry is an autobiography. Write an introductory paragraph about yourself in which you include:

1. your new Spanish name.
2. the Spanish-speaking country you come from.
3. at what time you have Spanish class.
4. your age.
5. several activities that you like and don't like to do.
6. a brief description of your personal qualities.

14 ¿Qué necesitamos?

With one of your teammates, make a list of school and travel supplies that you need to put in your *mochila* for your trip to Chichén Itzá.

Conexión cultural

Many people think that the Mayans disappeared shortly after the arrival of the Spanish in the sixteenth century. But the modern-day Mayans still live within the boundaries of their ancient world: Guatemala, Belize, El Salvador, Honduras and the Yucatán Peninsula of Mexico. The Mayan people work hard to preserve their traditions, arts, food and culture. Rigoberta Menchú, a powerful Mayan woman from Guatemala, focused the world's attention on the difficult plight of modern Mayans and the many human rights injustices they have suffered when she received the Nobel Peace Prize in 1992.

The ancient Mayan civilization is filled with facts, stories, myths and legends about a very powerful, intelligent culture. The major religious centers of Chichén Itzá, Uxmal and Palenque contain evidence of people who constructed buildings in which they could chart the stars, sports arenas in which they could play a special game to honor the Mayan gods and pyramids where they could celebrate important cultural ceremonies. The Mayans created a series of 17 calendars. The two main calendars, the Haab (solar calendar) and the Tzolkin (sacred religious calendar) correspond to the movement of the stars and the other planets in a way that is more accurate than any calendar to date. The Mayans were also gifted in math. Their number system is called a "vigesimal" system. It uses a base number of 20, unlike our decimal system based on 10. Dots and bars make up the main number system. A dot represents one and a bar stands for five.

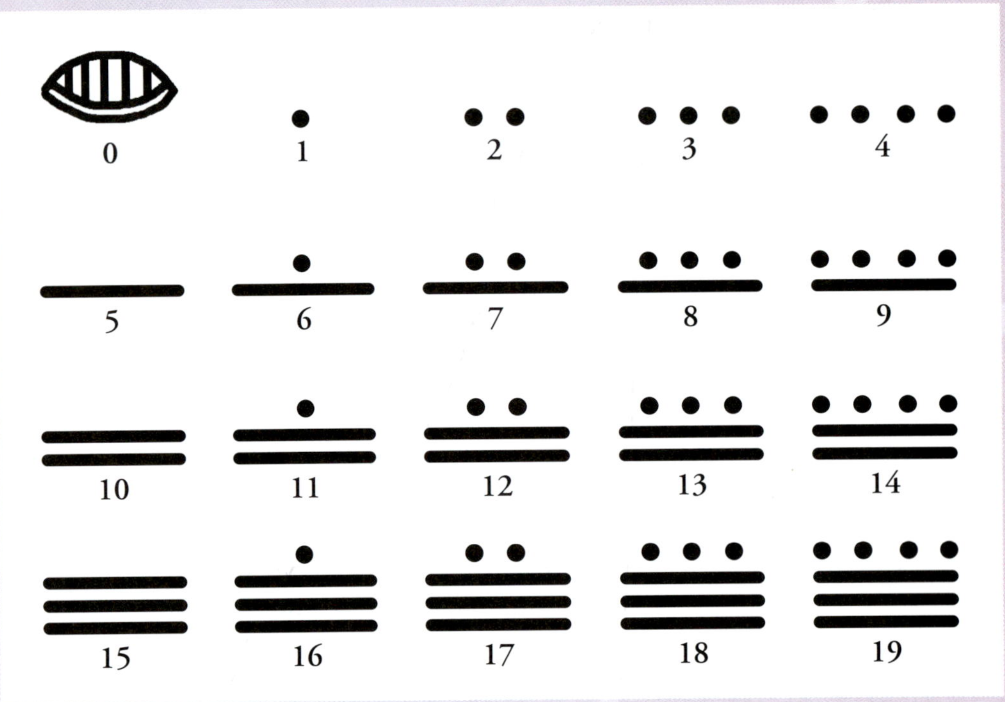

Animals played an important part in the Mayan culture and can be identified in both legends and art. Stories of serpents, jaguars, iguanas, quetzal birds and dogs were just as important to people as stories about the heroic deeds of their gods. Archeologists tell us that the glyphs (designs) on buildings, on columns called "stelae" and on pottery portray a culture in which animals taught the lessons of the day. We have much to learn from the secrets of the Mayans. Are you ready to discover your secret?

Proyectos

15 Mi cosa favorita

Create a picture poem in Spanish about you and one of your favorite things or activities. Write the words of your poem in the shape of someone or something that is central to your description, for example, a dog, a soccer ball, a piano, etc.

16 Una ciudad maya

With the other members of your team, design and construct an ancient Mayan city. Before you begin, you might want to do some research on this topic on the Internet or in your school's instructional materials center. You might use tagboard, clay or sugar cubes as possible building materials. Make sure your city has a big sun pyramid, a small moon pyramid, an observatory in which to watch the stars, a sports arena, a sacred well, a marketplace and houses for nobles and priests.

17 Mis amigos

The Mayan "stelae" were columns that contained images or designs to tell stories. Make your own "stela" with crayons or brightly colored markers so that it looks like a totem pole. Begin by gathering the information you need: ask five classmates their name, how old they are and what they like. Then, draw a grid with four rows like the one that follows and add the information you obtained for each person.

1. In the first row, write the person's name.
2. In the second row, draw a symbol to represent what this person likes. For example, if the person likes horses, draw a horse.
3. In the third row, write this person's age using Spanish words.
4. In the fourth row, represent this person's age in the Mayan numbering system with the appropriate number of bars and dots.

Beto	Rafael	Marisol	Diego	Luisa

doce				

Etapa 2

En casa

¡Oye, hermano, tengo una sorpresa! Te presento a mi amiga, Juana. Ella es muy bonita y simpática.
¡Mucho gusto, Juana!
Ella es la mascota del equipo.
¿Adónde vas?
Voy a jugar al fútbol en el parque.
¿Vas con tu primo en su carro?
No, voy a pie.
Selena y yo vamos a buscar unos libros para estudiar la historia de los mayas.
¿Es para su proyecto? ¿Y qué más necesitan?
¿Y Uds.?
¿Qué necesitan para su proyecto?

Vocabulario

La familia

1 ¿Cómo es la familia de Soledad?

Soledad is going to describe her family members to her classmates. Look at her family tree and then help her complete the chart with the list of words that she will use to describe each person.

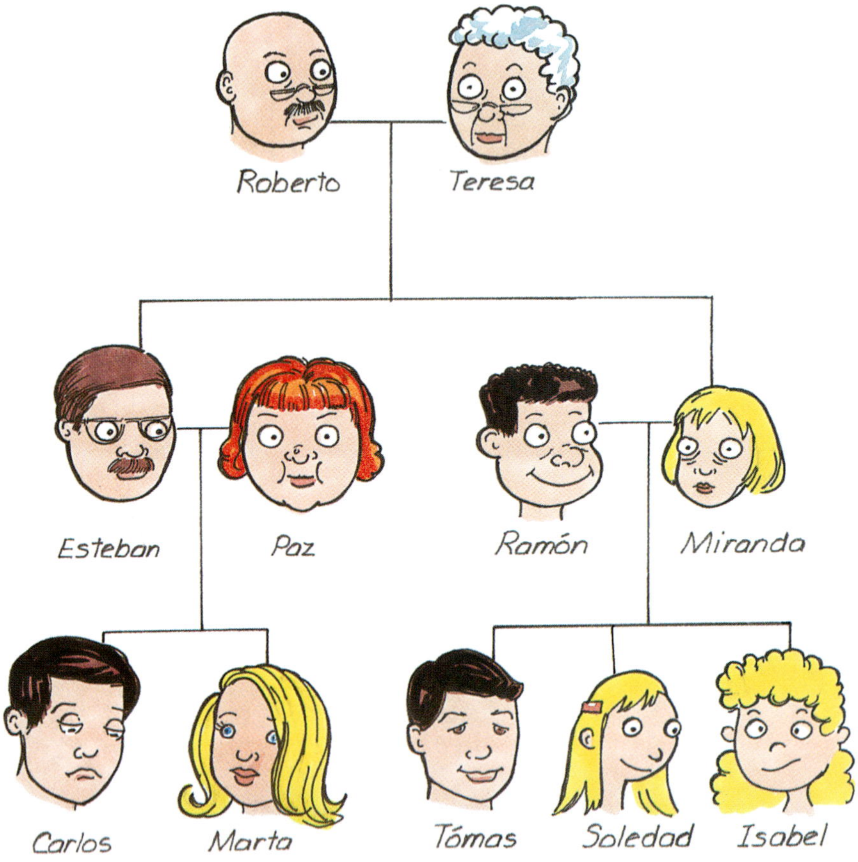

Name	Relationship to Soledad	Hair	Appearance/Personality
Miranda	su madre	rubia	delgada

El transporte

2 ¿Adónde vamos? ¿Cómo vamos?

To work on your class project with your teammates, you may want to go to the illustrated places. State the best means of transportation to take in order to get to each place.

Remember that a + el = al.

en metro	a pie
en carro	en autobús
en bicicleta	en avión

Vamos al parque en autobús.

1. 

2. 

3. 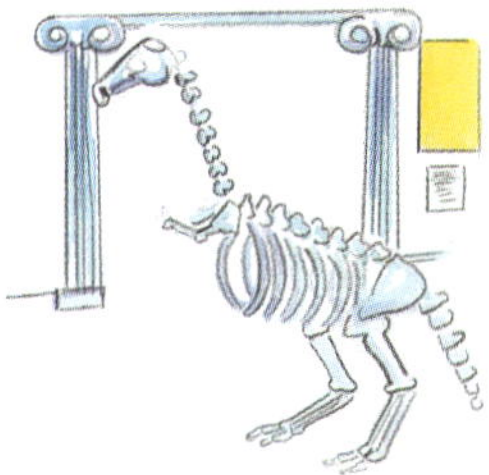

4. 

5. 

6. 

IDIOMA

Los adjetivos

Do you remember that adjectives must match the gender (masculine or feminine) and number (singular or plural) of the nouns they describe? Look at the following examples for a quick review.

Mi hermano es **alto.**	*My brother is tall.*
Mi hermana es **alta.**	*My sister is tall.*
Mis hermanos son **altos.**	*My brothers (and sisters) are tall.*
Mis hermanas son **altas.**	*My sisters are tall.*

3 ¿Cómo es?

Let's look at our four friends at the beginning of *Etapa 2.* Using adjectives that you already know, describe some of Beto, Selena, Soledad and Diego's family members.

1. Selena es.... Su padre es.... Su abuela es.... Su madre es....
2. Beto es.... Su hermano es....
3. Diego es.... Su padre es....
4. Soledad es.... Su madre es....

Los adjetivos posesivos

Don't forget that possessive adjectives, like other adjectives, also agree in gender and number with the nouns they describe. For example, "my parents" in Spanish is *mis padres.*

mi, mis	**nuestro, nuestra, nuestros, nuestras**
tu, tus	**vuestro, vuestra, vuestros, vuestras**
su, sus	**su, sus**

4 ¿Es como o no es como?

Tell whether or not the first person mentioned looks like the second one, according to the illustrations in *Etapa 2.* Follow the model.

Selena/la madre de Selena
Selena es como su madre.

1. Selena/la abuela de Selena
2. Beto/el hermano de Beto
3. Diego/el padre de Diego
4. Soledad/la madre de Soledad
5. Diego y Selena/la mascota del equipo
6. la madre de Selena/la señora Mendoza
7. yo/los padres

El verbo *ir*

The verb *ir* means "to go."

ir	
yo	**voy**
tú	**vas**
Ud. / él / ella	**va**
nosotros / nosotras	**vamos**
vosotros / vosotras	**vais**
Uds. / ellos / ellas	**van**

The present tense of *ir* followed by *a* and an infinitive tells what is going to happen.

Selena y Soledad **van a estudiar**. *Selena and Soledad are going to study.*

5 ¿Qué van a hacer?

Selena and Diego are talking about what some of their classmates are going to do after school today. Complete each sentence with the appropriate form of the verb *ir*.

1. Tomás...a ver la televisión.
2. Margarita y José...a comprar unos mapas.
3. Pedro y Roberto...a tomar refrescos.
4. Nosotros...a buscar unos libros en la biblioteca.
5. Y tú, Diego, ¿...a jugar al fútbol?

Remember that you can invite someone to do something by using *vamos a* and an infinitive.

6 ¡Vamos a...!

Invite a friend to do each of the following activities with you.

1. study at the library
2. eat in the cafeteria
3. buy notebooks
4. play baseball
5. dance

Los pronombres de complemento indirecto

You have used indirect object pronouns to tell what various people like.

Me gusta la escuela.	*I like school.*
Le gusta la música.	*He/she/you like(s) music.*
Nos gusta la playa.	*We like the beach.*

Now we will use indirect object pronouns to introduce people. How would Beto introduce his brother to Juana?

Juana, **te presento a** mi hermano.	*Juana, this is my brother.*

las presentaciones
te (to 1 person, informal) name + **le** (to 1 person, formal) + verb + **a** + person being introduced **les** (to 2 or more people)

7 Las presentaciones

After you have formed teams for your project, you will want to introduce your teammates, other people in your class and your family members to each other. How would you introduce the following people?

1. a male teammate to your dad
2. a female friend to Soledad
3. your sister to Sra. Mendoza
4. a male friend to your parents

Comunicación

8 ¡Hablemos de nuestras familias imaginarias!

To form an imaginary family, use back issues of magazines or newspapers to find 15 people of various ages. (You may also want to include some animals.) Next, cut them out and arrange them in small groups on a large piece of paper. Then, decide which person you are going to be. After you have determined how you are related to all the others, give each person a Spanish name. Finally, take turns with a partner describing your "new" family members (giving their name, relationship to you and one descriptive adjective) before making a presentation to the entire class.

9 ¡Escribamos sobre qué vamos a hacer!

With a partner, play the roles of two friends who each have a lot of things to do this weekend. You've decided to do together the things you have in common. Begin by each writing a list of five things that you're going to do, for example, *voy a buscar unos libros para nuestro proyecto.* Then, share your list with your partner. After hearing what you both plan to do, make a pair of intersecting circles. In the left circle, write the things that Partner A is going to do; in the right circle, write the things that Partner B is going to do. Where the circles intersect, write the things that both of you can do together. Hand in this diagram to your teacher.

Conexión Cultural

You remember that animals, such as rabbits, monkeys, dogs, frogs, tigers, pumas, iguanas, eagles and turtles, played important roles in many Mayan folktales and myths. The Mayans passed on legends about these animals so that future generations could learn about their surroundings, cultural values and beliefs, and basic lessons about life.

Twice a year you can see the image of a giant snake coming down the steps of the pyramid.

Snakes, jaguars and quetzal birds are the three animals that are most often portrayed in the Mayan culture. Kukulcán, the plumed serpent, was the representation of the main Mayan god. Even today, visitors to Chichén Itzá still see the powerful image of this giant snake coming down the famous pyramid. The jaguar represented night to the Mayans. According to legend, the jaguar followed a path to the west all night long to bring back the day to Kukulcán, who symbolized the sun. Mayan warriors often dressed as jaguars or wore jaguar masks since this animal exemplified strength and power. At Chichén Itzá the Temple of Jaguars is next to the famous ball court. The quetzal bird with its three-foot-long blue and green tail feathers and its bright crimson body and emerald-green head

signified freedom and wealth. Mayan priests and nobles wore headdresses made of quetzal feathers. This bird's feathers were so valuable that they were also used in trading at the ancient Mayan markets.

Not only were legends and ceremonies central to Mayan culture, sports played an important role as well. A game called *pok ta pok* served not only as a sacred religious rite but also as entertainment. The largest playing field was located at Chichén Itzá. Even though the rules of the game are still not totally clear, experts believe that the sport resembled basketball. Two teams of four to six players moved a hard rubber ball the size of a basketball up and down the court using only their legs, arms, hips and heads. They could not use their hands. The object was to get the ball through a stone hoop attached to a wall on the side of the field.

The king sat in the temple at the end of the ball court.

Proyectos

10 ¡Vamos a adoptar una mascota maya!

You've learned that the Mayans used many animals in their stories and folktales as well as in their carvings and designs on their buildings. Choose a popular Mayan animal (jaguar, monkey, turtle, dog, quetzal bird, snake, eagle, iguana or rabbit) as your adopted pet. First, draw it. Then, create a profile of your pet so that you can introduce it to your class. In your presentation:

1. give your pet's name.
2. tell your pet's age.
3. describe the color, appearance and personality of your pet.
4. say what your pet likes and dislikes.
5. tell how you feel about your pet.

11 Una historia maya

With the other members of your team, do research on Mayan folktales, myths or legends that focus on animals and their human characteristics. You can find many interesting sites on the Internet, or you can use your school's instructional materials center. After reading some of these tales, create your own story in English with your teammates. Be sure to include typical Mayan animals and sites in your story. Then tell your team's tale orally and act it out for the entire class. Also submit the written version of your team's story to be published for the class. Remember that the purpose of many of these Mayan tales was to teach and inform members of the community about their common culture. The animals in the original Mayan legends and myths took on human characteristics, so use your imagination!

12 ¡Juguemos al bingo!

To play adjective bingo in Spanish, make a 20-square bingo board. In each square write both the masculine and feminine form of an adjective, for example, *rubio/rubia*. When you have completed your bingo board, ask a classmate, *"¿Eres rubio/rubia?"* If the person answers affirmatively, get his or her signature in the block. Then ask a second person a question using a different adjective. Continue asking classmates questions until someone calls out *"¡Bingo!"* or your teacher ends the game.

Etapa 3

En ruta

448 MERIDA
aeromexico
Salimos por la puerta veinticinco a las diez y media.
¡Mira, la bandera de México!
¡Sí, y tiene una serpiente!
¿A qué hora es la película?
En veinte minutos. Es una película en español.
¡Ay! ¡No comprendo mucho español!
¡Por favor, señorita, quiero ver GODZILLA!
Estamos en ruta a Mérida y Chichén Itzá. ¿Están Uds. listos?

Vocabulario

¿Qué tienes?

1 Una encuesta

Choose five objects from those in the illustration. Then interview five of your classmates to find out whether or not they have each of the five objects. Mark their responses on a form like the one that follows. After you have finished your interview, be prepared to report your findings to the entire class, using your completed survey form.

Tomás: ¿Tienes una mochila?
Soledad: Sí, tengo una mochila.
Tomás: ¿Y tienes una bicicleta?
Soledad: No, no tengo una bicicleta.
* *
Tomás: Soledad tiene una mochila, pero no tiene una bicicleta....

To make a sentence negative, put *no* in front of the verb.

	Soledad	Ángel	Carolina	Gerardo	Lucía
una mochila	✓				
una bicicleta					

Las palabras interrogativas

In order to ask for information, you need to know some interrogative expressions. Do you remember these question words?

a qué hora
dónde
cómo
quiénes
qué
por qué
cuántos

2 ¡Muchas preguntas!

Complete each question with the appropriate expression from those that are listed above.

1. ¿...estás?
2. ¿...años tienes?
3. ¿...tienes la clase de español?
4. ¿...está tu mochila?
5. ¿...necesitas para tu proyecto?
6. ¿...vas a estudiar a la biblioteca?
7. ¿...van con Ud.?

Los números y los meses

Do you remember the numbers in Spanish? With a partner, practice counting aloud in Spanish from 0 to 31. Then, with your partner, see if you know the months of the year, taking turns naming them in order.

3 ¿Cuándo es tu cumpleaños?

Write the name of each month in Spanish on a small piece of paper. Next circulate around your classroom asking at least 10 students *¿Cuándo es tu cumpleaños?* Marta, for example, might answer *Mi cumpleaños es el dieciséis de febrero.* Then on your piece of paper for February, write "Marta — 16." Be prepared to share your results with the whole class.

IDIOMA

Los verbos que terminan en *-er* y en *-ir*

In Spanish there are three types of regular verbs: *-ar* verbs, *-er* verbs and *-ir* verbs. In *Etapa 1*, you reviewed *-ar* verbs. Now let's take a look at *-er* and *-ir* verbs. Remove the *-er* or *-ir* from the infinitive, and then add the endings that correspond to each of the subject pronouns. Here are the present-tense forms of *comer* ("to eat") and *vivir* ("to live").

comer	
yo	**como**
tú	**comes**
Ud. / él / ella	**come**
nosotros / nosotras	**comemos**
vosotros / vosotras	**coméis**
Uds. / ellos / ellas	**comen**

vivir	
yo	**vivo**
tú	**vives**
Ud. / él / ella	**vive**
nosotros / nosotras	**vivimos**
vosotros / vosotras	**vivís**
Uds. / ellos / ellas	**viven**

Note that the endings of *-ir* verbs are the same as those of *-er* verbs, except for *-imos* and *-ís*.

4 Después de las clases

Diego is leaving school and practicing his Spanish as he sees some of his classmates. Finish each of his sentences by writing the appropriate form of the *-er* or *-ir* verb indicated.

1. Nosotros...en español todos los días. (leer)
2. Mis amigos y yo...mucho en español. (comprender)
3. Oye, Beto, ¿...con tu tío y tus sobrinos? (comer)
4. Tú y tus hermanos...cerca de aquí, ¿verdad? (vivir)
5. Mi padre...la puerta del carro. (abrir)

5 ¡Más preguntas!

With a partner, take turns asking and answering questions using the indicated cues.

where you live
A: ¿Dónde vives?
B: Vivo en Louisville, Kentucky.

1. if you read a lot in English
2. who is eating in the cafeteria
3. why you open your Spanish book
4. how many questions you understand in Spanish

Los verbos irregulares

Some verbs ending in *-er* and *-ir* do not follow the pattern described above. Here are four important irregular verbs in Spanish: *tener* ("to have"), *hacer* ("to do, to make"), *salir* ("to go out") and *venir* ("to come").

	tener	hacer	salir	venir
yo	tengo	hago	salgo	vengo
tú	tienes	haces	sales	vienes
Ud. / él / ella	tiene	hace	sale	viene
nosotros / nosotras	tenemos	hacemos	salimos	venimos
vosotros / vosotras	tenéis	hacéis	salís	venís
Uds. / ellos / ellas	tienen	hacen	salen	vienen

6 Una entrevista

With a partner, find out as much as you can about each other by asking for and giving the following information.

your age
A: ¿Cuántos años tienes?
B: Tengo catorce años. ¿Y tú? ¿Cuántos años tienes?
A: Tengo trece años.

1. where you come from
2. how many brothers you have
3. if your family has a dog
4. at what time you leave for school
5. if you ask a lot of questions in class

7 Una presentación

With the information you found out about your partner in Activity 6, prepare an oral presentation introducing and describing him/her to the class. Remember to begin your presentation by giving your partner's name, for example, *Mi compañero/a se llama....*

Comunicación

8 ¡Hablemos del viaje a Chichén Itzá!

Imagine that you have been chosen to go along on Sra. Mendoza's class trip to Chichén Itzá. She has given you a list of suggested items to take in your backpack. Get together with a partner to talk about preparations for the trip and shopping together for the things that you need. In the course of your conversation:

1. greet each other.
2. tell each other how you feel about the trip to Mexico.
3. ask and tell each other if you're ready for the trip.
4. tell each other three things that you already have for the trip.
5. ask and tell each other what you need to buy this weekend.
6. decide what day and what time you're going shopping this weekend.
7. using your list of what you need to buy, decide on what stores you're going to visit together.
8. tell each other "good-bye."

Para el viaje....

una regla
dos revistas para el viaje
tres bolígrafos
un diccionario (español-inglés)
un reloj
un libro para el avión
cinco lápices
un mapa de México
un mapa de la Yucatán
un libro de la historia de los mayas
dos cuadernos
mucho papel
un mapa de Mérida

9 ¡Escribamos!

Pretend that you are a Mayan astronomer. Record the sunrises and sunsets for one week, beginning with today. (The Internet or a newspaper can give you the data that you need.) Draw a picture of the sun with seven rays. In each ray, write the day, the date, the time of the sunrise and the time of the sunset, for example, ***lunes, el 25 de enero, a las ocho menos veinte, a las cinco y diez.***

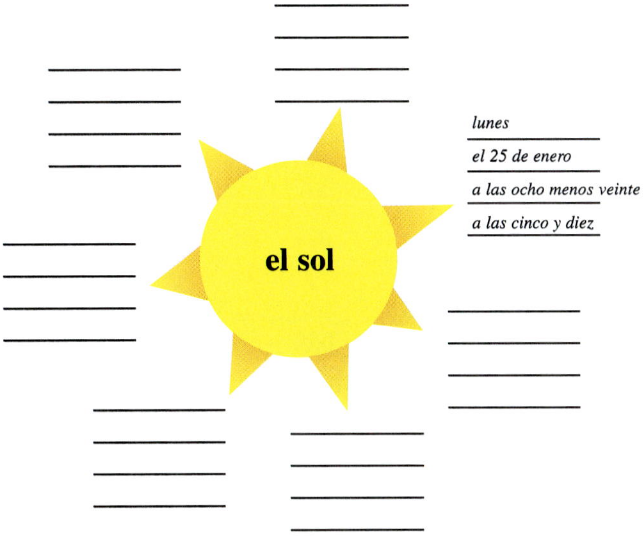

Conexión cultural

Telling time and using calendars have been a challenge to every culture throughout history. The calendar used by most of the world today is the Gregorian calendar, established by Pope Gregory XIII in 1582. The Gregorian calendar has a leap year for every year that can be divided by four, with the restriction that years divisible by 100 are leap years only when they are also divisible by 400. That means that the year 2000 is a leap year, but the year 1900 was not.

The Mayans were skilled astronomers who turned telling time into an exact science by scrutinizing the sky from some of the first observatories ever built. Many years before the introduction of leap year and the Gregorian calendar, the Mayans had established a method to make up for the extra time needed to complete the solar year. They also created accurate calendars that predicted solar and lunar eclipses, cycles of the planet Venus, the movement of the constellations, and solstices and equinoxes. With this information they could suggest accurate dates for planting and harvesting as well as plan specific holidays and religious events central to their culture.

Two of the most important Mayan calendars were the Haab and the Tzolkin calendars. The Haab (or solar) calendar had 365 days divided into 18 months of 20 days and one month of five days. This short month was considered to be very unlucky. The architecture at Chichén Itzá reflected the Haab calendar. El Castillo, the pyramid, has one set of 91 stairs on all four sides. The top platform is considered to be the final step, so the total number of steps is 365. The Tzolkin (or religious) calendar consisted of 260 days: 20 day signs (glyphs) were combined with a Mayan dot/bar number from 1 to 13. Note that the number of days in the Tzolkin calendar (260) is the same as the number of days in a year that the moon is visible in the sky. This calendar, with its nine moon cycles of 28 or 29 days each, possibly represented the gestation period of a human. Notice how the Mayans cleverly linked their science of astronomy with the life cycle of the planet.

Proyectos

10 Para comprender el calendario Tzolkin

Make a copy of each of the 20 day signs (glyphs) that are part of the Tzolkin calendar. (You can either draw them or print them from an Internet site.) Put each glyph on a small card along with its name. Then make 13 small cards that each have one of the 13 Mayan numbers. Remember to use the combination of dots and bars that represents these numbers. (You may want to return to *Etapa 1* to review them.) Next lay out the day glyphs in order and place the numbers from one to thirteen under the appropriate glyphs. Since there are 20 day glyphs and only 13 numbers, once you get to 13 you will need to reuse the numbers. Notice that each day, or Kin, of the 260-day calendar has a name and a number, for example, Kin 4 and Kin 11. How long will it take to get back to the original formation that you started with?

11 Un calendario nuevo

Imagine that you and your teammates are in charge of designing an innovative calendar to reflect the new millennium. In planning your group's calendar, you should keep several facts in mind: ancient cultures used the sun as well as the moon and stars to calculate time, whereas today we use clocks, watches and technology; throughout the ages, different cultures marked the passage of time by referring to important events, geography and famous people. Now, with these ideas in mind, create your team's own calendar. First, determine how your calendar will be set up, or how time will be divided in your system. Decide how many days each week will have and how many weeks and months will be in a year. Choose names for the months and the days. Also include any holidays that you feel are important. Remember to use as many Spanish words as you can. Your team should be ready to explain your calendar to the class and the reasons for its unique design. Then display it for everyone to examine.

12 Un día en la vida

Create a storyboard in which you draw six boxes that tell a story about a typical day in your real or imaginary life. First, draw a picture in each box. Then, write a caption in Spanish to accompany it. Here are the subjects of the pictures in your six boxes:

1. who you are
2. where you live
3. where you are now
4. where you go
5. at what time you leave and how you get there
6. what you do there

Etapa 4

En Mérida

Aquí está la catedral de San Idelfonso. Es muy vieja y famosa.
Señora, ¡quiero comer!
¡Yo también!
Diego, en diez minutos. En esta plaza, hay muchos edificios antiguos.
A las tres vamos al Museo del Arte Popular.
¡Qué divertido!
Hay un restaurante típico en la Avenida Montejo. ¡Vamos!
¿Dónde está el mesero? ¿Comemos tacos?
La especialidad es el pollo pibil. Es un pollo de Yucatán con una salsa roja.
Voy a tomar un jugo de naranja.
Quiero comer una comida mexicana. ¿Cuánto cuesta?
¡Mira, en ese edificio está la bandera de México!
Me gustan sus colores— el verde, el blanco y el rojo.
Mañana vamos a hacer un viaje a Chichén Itzá. ¿Están Uds. listos?

Vocabulario

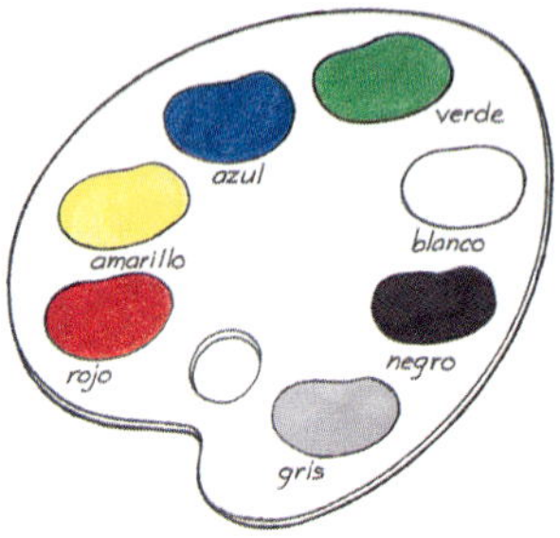

Los colores

Do you remember how to say the names of the colors in Spanish?

1 ¿De qué color?

When you think about the following things, what colors come to mind? Answer in Spanish.

1. a banana
2. ink
3. snow
4. an iguana
5. the sky
6. a cloudy day
7. a traffic light

2 La bandera de México

What are the colors of the Mexican flag?

Las comidas

3 ¿Qué te gusta comer?

Imagine that you are going to prepare a meal for two of your friends. Practice saying the names of the pictured foods and beverages.

Then, in order to know what to serve your friends, survey them. Ask them whether or not they like each illustrated food item or beverage.

Francisco: ¿Te gustan los tacos?
Teresa: Sí, me gustan los tacos.
Francisco: ¿Y el pollo?
Teresa: No, no me gusta el pollo.

	Teresa	Sergio
los tacos	sí	
el pollo	no	

Finally, using the results of the survey you conducted, write the menu for the meal you intend to serve your friends.

Las comidas y los precios

4 ¿Cuánto cuesta tu comida favorita?

Imagine that you and your teammates are going to eat at La Fogata restaurant. Here is part of their menu with prices indicated in pesos. First, write down what you want to eat and drink, along with the price of each item. Then, total your bill. Finally, report to your classmates what you have chosen to eat and drink and how much it will cost.

Yo quiero comer una ensalada de aguacate de 26 pesos, un pollo en mole poblano de 55 pesos y una limonada de 9 pesos. Mi comida cuesta 90 pesos.

La Fogata

Ensaladas	
Ensalada Chef	$30.00
Ensalada de Aguacate	$26.00
Ensalada de Camarón	$45.00
Ensalada de Atún	$27.00
Carnes	
Bistec Ranchero (trocitos de filete)	$59.00
Fajitas a la Fogata	$59.00
Filete Mignon	$79.00
Filete Cordón Bleu	$79.00
Aves	
Pollo en Mole Poblano	$55.00
Filete de Pollo a la Tampiqueña	$65.00
Filete de Pollo a la Plancha	$55.00
Combinaciones Mexicanas	
Taco de carne, enchilada de queso	$41.00
Dos enchiladas (queso ó carne)	$43.00
Chiles Rellenos	$49.00
Quesadilla, enchilada y taco de carne	$48.00
Bebidas Preparadas y Tropicales	
Bebidas y Refrescos	$12.00
Limonada	$ 9.00
Naranjada	$ 9.00
Te Helado	$ 8.00
Club Soda	$ 8.00
Leche	$ 9.00
Te Caliente	$ 8.00

IDIOMA

Exclamaciones

Do you remember that you can put the word *qué* before an adjective or a noun to make an exclamation?

¡*Qué* + adjective / noun = exclamation!

¡**Qué** interesante!	*How interesting!*
¡**Qué** proyecto!	*What a project!*

5 ¡Qué divertido!

You are looking at your friend Carmen's photo album of her summer vacation. As you look at each picture, make an appropriate enthusiastic comment, using *qué* and an adjective or a noun.

Repaso de los verbos regulares

Let's review the endings of regular *-ar, -er* and *-ir* verbs one more time.

	hablar	leer	cumplir
yo	hablo	leo	cumplo
tú	hablas	lees	cumples
Ud. / él / ella	habla	lee	cumple
nosotros / nosotras	hablamos	leemos	cumplimos
vosotros / vosotras	habláis	leéis	cumplís
Uds. / ellos / ellas	hablan	leen	cumplen

6 ¿Qué pasa?

Now that Sra. Mendoza and her students have left on their trip to Mexico, the students' parents are curious to know what their children are doing. The parents call each other to see who has information. Complete each question with the appropriate form of the indicated verb.

1. ¿...los estudiantes español? (hablar)
2. ¿...ellos del hotel al centro? (caminar)
3. ¿A qué hora...las puertas del museo? (abrir)
4. ¿...Selena mucho? (comprar)
5. ¿Dónde...los estudiantes? (comer)
6. ¿Quién...con la profesora en la plaza? (bailar)

Comunicación

7 ¡Hablemos en el restaurante!

With two partners, play the roles of two customers and a server at a Mexican restaurant in Mérida. The two customers are anxious to try some Mexican foods and are interested in some specialties from the Yucatán Peninsula. The server suggests some typical dishes that the customers might like. During the course of your conversation:

1. The server greets the customers and asks what they would like.
2. The customers greet the server and ask what the typical foods of the region are.
3. The server suggests some popular Mexican foods and several specialties of the region.

4. Each customer says what he or she likes and doesn't like and then orders something to eat and drink.
5. The server brings the food and verifies each customer's choice.
6. The customers thank the server.
7. The server returns to the table and asks if everything is all right.
8. Each customer expresses his or her opinion.
9. After the customers finish eating, the server brings the bill. The customers ask how much each item costs, since they want to pay separately.
10. The server indicates the prices.
11. The customers pay the bill and thank the server.
12. The server says, "You're welcome."
13. The customers and the server tell each other "good-bye."

8 ¡Escribamos sobre un día en Mérida!

Pretend that it's midnight on one of the days of your Mexican trip to Mérida. Because you don't have enough time to write a complete entry in your journal for today, you jot down some notes for an outline you can write from later on. Using the Spanish you already know, write a summary for one day of your trip. Give the day, times, locations, events or sights, and your reaction to each one. For example, you might write:

sábado:	9:00	hacer el viaje a Mérida
		¡Qué avión!
	2:00	ir al Hotel Turista
		en el número 368 con Alicia
		¡Qué bonito!
	4:00	ver la ciudad con el grupo
		la catedral de San Idelfonso — muy vieja
		¡Qué famosa!
	6:00	ir de compras — tarjetas postales y una bandera de México
		¡Qué colores!
	8:00	comer en el restaurante
		pollo pibil
		¡Qué bueno!
	10:00	bailar en la plaza con el grupo
		¡Qué fiesta!

Conexión cultural

Modern Mayan cuisine still uses many of the same ingredients that were so important to the ancient Mayans. Corn, beans, chili peppers (especially the *habanero*), seafood, chicken and pork make up some of the basic foods. Plentiful tropical fruits, such as mangoes, papayas, guavas, bananas and pineapples, accent many of the local dishes.

Mayan specialties include chicken *pibil* and pork *pibil*, a type of barbecue that is seasoned with *achiote* spice (similar to paprika), then marinated in orange juice and baked in a pit. *Sopa de lima* (lime soup), also called *sopa de tortilla*, is made from chicken broth, *tortilla* strips and lime. *Panuchos* and *papdzules* are other Yucatán favorites. *Panuchos* consist of refried beans pocketed between two deep-fried *tortillas*. *Papdzules* are rolled *tortillas* stuffed with hard-boiled eggs and covered with pumpkin seeds and *chiltomate* sauce. Pickled onions often garnish this popular dish.

You can also find common Mexican dishes in the Yucatán Peninsula. Since the Mayan people believe that humans were created out of corn husks, this vegetable plays an important part in many foods. *Tamales*, *enchiladas* and many *tortilla* dishes, including *tacos*, are prepared with corn. Three typical *taco* dishes are *carnitas*, *tacos sudados* and *tacos dorados*. Carnitas feature baked pork. *Tacos sudados*, *tortillas* stuffed with refried beans, red *mole*, green *mole* and pork rinds, are often garnished with pickled vegetable sticks and chili peppers. *Tacos dorados*, deep-fried *tacos*, contain shredded pork, chicken or beef that is served on lettuce and topped with sour cream and grated cheese.

Proyectos

9 En el restaurante

Picture what the menu of a small neighborhood restaurant in Mérida looks like. With the other members of your team, design this restaurant's menu in Spanish, including at least four beverages and ten food items. Indicate the price in *pesos* for each menu item. Give your restaurant a Spanish name. Then take your team's menu and attach it to one of the walls in your classroom. Imagine that you and your teammates are in Mérida and plan to eat at a restaurant. Check out all the various options as you walk around your classroom, examining the different menus. Discuss what your teammates like and don't like about the food and beverage choices at each restaurant. Also compare the prices. Then agree on the restaurant where your team is going to eat.

10 El país y la bandera

For this project on any Spanish-speaking country of your choice and its flag, you need to do some research either in your school's instructional materials center or on the Internet. You should also have some poster board and colored markers on hand.

1. Find the name of your country's capital city. Using about two-thirds of your poster board, draw your country and write its capital in the correct location.
2. Determine the colors and design of the country's flag. Using your colored markers and about one-third of your poster board, make an exact replica of this flag.
3. Research the name of the country's money and what its current value is in relation to the American dollar.
4. Choose two famous people from the country's history.

Share what you have learned by giving an oral presentation in Spanish to your classmates as you show the map and flag you have drawn.

Etapa 5

En Chichén Itzá

¡Una foto, por favor, para nuestro proyecto!
¿Qué buscamos?
¿El secreto?
¡Mira, Beto, el jaguar!
¿Cuál es el secreto?
Señora, ¡todavía no comprendemos el secreto!
Ahora es el momento. ¡Mira la estatua roja! El jaguar tiene el secreto.
Amigos..., amigos..., ¡escuchen! ¡Qué sorpresa! El secreto es... ¡QUE UDS. SON MUY IMPORTANTES!

Vocabulario

Las actividades

1 ¿Qué va a hacer nuestro equipo?

Do you recall what the various members of our team intend to do once they get to Mérida and Chichén Itzá? Reread all the conversations in the *Etapas* and then match the letter of the teammate with what he or she is going to do on the trip.

1. va a comprar una serpiente de plástico
2. va a bailar
3. va a buscar su mochila
4. va a ser la mascota del equipo
5. va a subir a la pirámide
6. va a ir a la playa
7. va a escuchar sus discos compactos
8. va a ir al museo
9. va a comer unas comidas mexicanas
10. va a sacar muchas fotos
11. va a escribir a sus parientes

A. Diego
B. Beto
C. Selena
D. Soledad
E. la señora Mendoza
F. Juana
G. Quique

Los precios

2 En el mercado

While you are sightseeing in Chichén Itzá, you decide to stop at a local *mercado* (market) to buy some souvenirs for your friends and family. You have set aside 150 *pesos* for these gifts. First, look at the various items on display. Decide what you are going to buy for each person on your list. Then, write down your choices on a piece of paper, along with whom each item is for and its price in *pesos*. Finally, total your purchases. Remember to stay within your budget!

3 ¿Cuánto cuesta?

With a partner, take turns playing the roles of the customer in Activity 2 and a vendor at the market. The customer names each item he or she wants, and the vendor confirms its price in *pesos*. The vendor has a calculator, adds up all the prices and annonces the total. Does it correspond to the total the customer came up with?

IDIOMA

Los pronombres de complemento directo

A direct object is the person or thing that receives a verb's action and answers the question "what" or "whom." The direct object may be replaced by a pronoun.

me	**nos**
te	**os**
lo, la	**los, las**

¿Quién tiene el secreto? — *Who has the secret?*
El jaguar **lo** tiene. — *The jaguar has it.*

4 ¿Qué o a quién buscas?

Now that you're all in Chichén Itzá, there are so many things to see and do that you don't know where to begin. First, prioritize them by listing what you're going to look for in order of importance. (Only ten items in the box should be on your list.) For example, if looking for a restaurant is the most important to you, your first sentence will be *Yo busco el restaurante.*

las estatuas	las tiendas	la playa
los refrescos	los museos	la catedral de San Idelfonso
la comida mexicana	los edificios antiguos	el pollo pibil
el mapa	el secreto	la pirámide
el arte	los caballos	las tarjetas postales
el restaurante	los discos compactos	el jaguar
la sorpresa	la serpiente	

Next, get into your teams. Have your team leader call out each of the 20 items under consideration and say whether or not it is on your top ten list. Follow the model.

Daniel: ¿El restaurante?
Enrique: Yo lo busco.
Carlos: Yo no lo busco.

5 ¿Qué tienes en tu mochila?

With a partner, play the roles of two roommates who are packing their backpacks before going out for a day of sightseeing in Chichén Itzá. Using the accompanying list, the first student asks if the second student has each item in his or her backpack. The second student answers, according to what he or she sees in the hotel room. Follow the model.

el mapa
los cuadernos
el bolígrafo
el reloj
el diccionario
el lápiz
los libros
la mascota

Pilar: ¿Tienes el mapa?
Yolanda: No, no lo tengo.

Repaso de los verbos irregulares

Irregular verbs do not follow the pattern of regular *-ar*, *-er* and *-ir* verbs. How well do you know the present-tense forms of the common irregular verbs that are listed here? With a partner, take turns giving the present-tense forms of each one.

estar	hacer	ir	saber	salir	ser	tener	venir	ver

6 ¿Cuál es el secreto?

You have been assigned to write an article in Spanish for your school's newspaper. You are going to tell about your team's trip to Chichén Itzá and what you discovered. Complete each blank with the appropriate form of the indicated verb.

¿...(saber) Uds. el secreto? ¡Yo lo...(saber)! El secreto...(estar) en Chichén Itzá. Si Uds....(hacer) un viaje a la pirámide El Castillo, Uds....(ir) a la puerta abierta. Allí hay una estatua roja de dónde...(venir) el secreto. Uds. miran la estatua, y luego Uds....(salir) de México con el secreto. Ahora si Uds....(estar) con sus amigos, en casa o en clase, Uds. lo...(saber). ¡El secreto...(ser) que Uds....(ser) muy importantes! Ahora Uds....(tener) el secreto para siempre.

Comunicación

7 ¡Hablemos en el mercado!

With a partner, play the roles of a tourist at a souvenir stand in Chichén Itzá and a vendor who works there. The tourist wants to buy some postcards and a more expensive item, hoping to bargain for a better price. In the course of your conversation:

1. The tourist and vendor greet each other.
2. The vendor asks the tourist what he or she would like.
3. The tourist says which postcards he or she likes and asks some questions about the scenes on the postcards.
4. The vendor answers the tourist's questions.
5. The tourist asks how much the postcards cost, and the vendor answers.
6. Then the tourist picks out a more expensive souvenir and asks its price.
7. The vendor replies.
8. The tourist offers a lower price.
9. The tourist and vendor continue to discuss the price until they arrive at one that is agreeable to both of them.
10. The vendor totals the tourist's bill.
11. The tourist pays the vendor and thanks him or her.
12. The tourist and vendor tell each other "good-bye."

8 ¡Escribamos una tarjeta postal!

Instead of buying a postcard, you have decided to design an original one. On one side, draw something that you found interesting at one of your favorite sites in Chichén Itzá. On the other side, write a message to a friend or family member in which you:

1. address your card appropriately.
2. indicate the date and greet the person.
3. write about where you are and what you see. Specifically tell about the subject of your drawing and express how you feel about it.
4. describe several other sites and tell what you think about each one.
5. describe some Mexican food that you like.
6. close, say "good-bye" and sign your name.

Conexión Cultural

Located about 75 miles east of Mérida, Chichén Itzá is by far the biggest and most famous of all the Mayan archeological and cultural sites. Chichén Itzá means "mouth of the well of Itzá." This well, or *cenoté*, furnished part of the Mayans' daily supply of fresh water, since there were few rivers and lakes in the region. Sacred wells served as sacrificial sites for the Mayans, and scores of human skeletons have been uncovered in them. The *Cenoté Sagrado* at Chichén Itzá measures 195 feet wide by 120 feet deep and was a constant site of pilgrimage, worship and offerings to the gods and goddesses. Not far from Chichén Itzá lies a dark underground world filled with different kinds of wells. Inside these murky, water-filled limestone sinkholes there is a blaze of color. Stalactites of blood-red limestone ooze from the walls. Roots of trees hang from the ceiling, reaching for the green pools of glowing water below.

Sacrificial victims were drowned in the *Cenoté Sagrado* as offerings to the rain gods.

The many archeological sites at Chichén Itzá are powerful symbols of the Mayans who constructed them. The central pyramid, called El Castillo by the Spanish because it reminded them of a castle, served as a large solar calendar. The main sculpture on this pyramid is the feathered serpent, Kukulcán. During the equinoxes in March and September the sun casts seven triangular shadows over the left side of the pyramid, forming the shape of a serpent that seems to be writhing down the stairs. So precise were Mayan mathematics that the tens of thousands of spectators who come twice a year to see this snake's diamond-backed body slowly move down the pyramid are never disappointed. Inside the pyramid a narrow, dark, secret staircase leads visitors to a small room. There on a pedestal sits the statue of the red jaguar covered with jade dots.

We have already noted some of the other important sites at Chichén Itzá. At the observatory, El Caracol, Mayan astronomers studied the sun's travels across the sky, the stars and the moon so they could create their different calendars. The ball court, 545 feet long by 225 feet wide, was the site of the sacred game called *pok ta pok*. A Mayan king sat in a temple at one end of the field presiding over the games. Legend says that the winning captain presented his head to the losing captain. This may not seem like much of a prize for the winner, but the Mayans believed this to be the ultimate honor. The winning captain earned a direct ticket to heaven instead of going through the 13 steps that were required of ordinary Mayans. All these features of Chichén Itzá represent some of the most important historical sites in all of Mexico.

In the Mayan archeological center of Bonampak, brilliant murals were discovered in the early part of the twentieth century that give us insight into their daily life, special ceremonies and important battles. Codices, or accordion-like books made of bark, told their histories, prophecies, songs, sciences and genealogies. Unfortunately, the Spanish destroyed most of these codices and only several remain today. We still have many secrets about the Mayans left to discover.

Proyectos

9 Un modelo de El Castillo

With the other members of your team, design and construct an accurate model of El Castillo. Before beginning, you might want to do additional research on this topic on the Internet or in your school's instructional materials center so that you can find more detailed photographs and descriptions. You might use tagboard, cardboard, sugar cubes, clay or Legos® as construction materials. Be creative! Display your model for the whole class to examine.

10 La importancia de Kukulcán

Conduct a research project on the vernal and autumnal equinoxes and their importance to the Mayans. Examine the many reasons why they celebrated these two times of the year and what they did to observe these days. Also find out about and explain what happens every March and September at the pyramid of El Castillo. What is the importance of Kukulcán, and what role does this serpent play in the ceremony?

11 Un mapa de Chichén Itzá

With the other members of your team, create a map of Chichén Itzá that is drawn to scale. Before you start, investigate the layout of all the major sites, specifically those that were described in the various *Etapas*: the pyramid, the ball court, the observatory, the sacred well and the Temple of the Jaguar. Add any other sites you read about as you conduct your research. Be sure to label all the major attractions accurately in Spanish. Then compare your map with those of other teams.

12 ¿Cuál es la importancia del secreto?

In the first *Etapa* you read that Beto, Selena, Soledad, Diego, Sra. Mendoza, Juana and Quique were going to Chichén Itzá and that their project involved discovering a secret. During this project, as our friends prepared for the trip, landed in Mérida and finally arrived at Chichén Itzá, the search to uncover the secret was always on their minds. Upon visiting El Castillo, they finally learned the secret. Write a paragraph in English of six to eight sentences in which you explain why this secret is an important message for you and for everyone.

El hogar

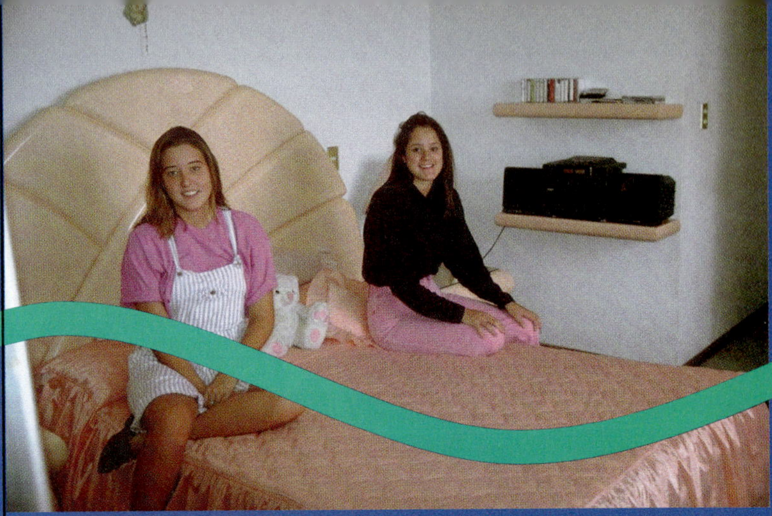

CAPÍTULO 6

In this chapter you will be able to:

- talk about everyday activities
- talk about the future
- express opinions
- state wishes and preferences
- identify items in the kitchen and at the dinner table
- express quantity
- state location
- write a letter
- describe a household
- express feelings

Lección 11

Contexto cultural
VENEZUELA

En la cocina

MARISOL: Hola, mamá. ¿Qué haces?

SRA. VEGA: Hago un almuerzo **especial** porque Uds. **viajan** mañana **otra vez**° a ver a su primo en Colombia.

JORGE: ¡Qué bueno, mamá! Te **queremos** ° **ayudar.**°

SRA. VEGA: ¿Sí? Pues, hay muchas **cosas**° que **tienen que**° hacer.

MARISOL: ¿Qué tenemos que hacer?

SRA. VEGA: Para **empezar,**° Marisol, **debes**° **cerrar**° la puerta del refrigerador y **después**° **encender**° las **luces** del **comedor.**

MARISOL: De acuerdo, mamá. ¿Qué más quieres?

SRA. VEGA: **Pienso**° hacer más arepas porque no hay muchas.

MARISOL: Muy bien, yo las hago. Y, Jorge, ¿por qué no ayudas a **poner la mesa?**°

JORGE: ¿La debo poner con **estos**° **platos** y **esas**° **servilletas?**

SRA. VEGA: No, esos platos son **de todos los días.**° **Prefiero aquellos**° platos que están **allá.**°

JORGE: ¡Ah, **ya**° los veo!

otra vez *again* **queremos** *we want* **ayudar** *to help* **cosas** *things* **tienen que** *you have to* **empezar** *to start* **debes** *you should* **cerrar** *close* **después** más tarde, luego **encender** *turn on* **Pienso** *I am thinking* **poner la mesa** *to set the table* **estos** *these* **esas** *those* **de todos los días** *everyday* **aquellos** *those* **allá** *over there* **ya** *already*

1 ¿Qué comprendiste?

1. ¿Dónde están la Sra. Vega, Jorge y Marisol?
2. ¿Por qué hay un almuerzo especial?
3. ¿Quiénes van a ayudar a la Sra. Vega?
4. Para empezar, ¿qué debe hacer Marisol? ¿Y después?
5. ¿Qué tiene que hacer Jorge?
6. ¿Qué platos prefiere la Sra. Vega?
7. ¿Qué ves en la cocina?

2 Charlando

1. ¿Ayudas mucho en la cocina?
2. ¿Qué cosas haces para ayudar en la cocina?
3. ¿Tiene tu familia platos para días especiales? Explica.
4. ¿Qué hay en la cocina de tu casa?

PARA ti

Más cosas de la cocina

el horno	*oven*
la licuadora	*blender*
el microondas	*microwave oven*
la sartén	*frying pan*

3 En la cocina

Look at these classified ads for kitchen appliance repair from the Venezuelan newspaper *El nacional.* Then answer these questions.

ATENCION, FRIOMAX garantizado a domicilio, reparamos refrigeradores, lavadoras, secadoras, estufas, cualquier marca, precio solidario. Información: 443.7695 Sr. Luis Manzano.

REFRIGERACION LOS RUICES
Reparamos todo tipo de refrigeradores, lavaplatos y microondas. Venta de repuestos filtros de campanas. Más de 20 años de experiencia. Atendemos emergencias. Telf. 682.1746, 24 horas al día.

REFRICOM reparación a domicilio: lavaplatos, fregaderos, hornos. Garantía, fiel cumplimiento conforme Ley Protección Consumidor, Avenida Sucre, cerca del Banco Provincial, Caracas. Teléfono: 284.1087

1. What phone numbers could you call to have your refrigerator repaired?
2. Whom would you speak to for information about repairing your stove?
3. What does Refrigeración Los Ruices repair?
4. What does Refricom repair?
5. Where is Refricom located?
6. Which company would you call in an emergency?
7. Which company repairs dishwashers?
8. Which repair company has a consumer protection guarantee?

¿Cómo es la cocina donde vives?

Conexión cultural

En el lago Maracaibo hay petróleo.

Venezuela

Venezuela has an extensive coastline along the Atlantic Ocean and borders Colombia, Brazil and Guyana. European explorers were inspired to name the area Venezuela (Little Venice) because the homes that were located along the shores of Lake Maracaibo reminded them of Venice, Italy. The country's capital and largest city, Caracas, is a fast-growing, modern city that was named after the Caracas Indians who originally inhabited the land.

At one time Venezuela had one of the highest standards of living in South America due to its many natural resources, especially the vast abundance of oil found near Lake Maracaibo. The country is one of the world's major producers of oil and an important member of OPEC (in Spanish, *OPEP,* or *Organización de Países Exportadores de Petróleo*). In more recent years, fluctuating oil prices have caused increased inflation and political instability.

Simón Bolívar, a native of Venezuela, was an important figure in attaining Venezuela's independence, as well as the independence of Bolivia, Colombia, Ecuador and Peru. Bolívar is considered a national hero throughout Latin America, and most Venezuelan cities have a plaza named after him.

La Plaza Bolívar en Mérida, Venezuela.

In addition to their national hero, the Venezuelan people are also very proud of the beauty of their country. One of the most sensational attractions is Angel Falls *(el Salto del Ángel),* the highest waterfall in the world. When Venezuelans gather, they enjoy talking, laughing and sharing good food, such as *arepas, ropa vieja* and *cachapas.*

Find out more about this South American country. What you learn may surprise you.

4 Venezuela

Complete the following statements about Venezuela. There may be some words that you do not know.

1. El nombre *Venezuela* quiere decir....
2. La capital y ciudad más grande es....
3. El héroe nacional de Venezuela se llama....
4. El producto principal de exportación de Venezuela es....
5. Una de las atracciones más importantes de Venezuela es....
6. Tres platos de comida famosos de Venezuela son ropa vieja, cachapas y....

Algo más

Tener que y deber

The expressions *tener que* (+ infinitive) and *deber* (+ infinitive) have similar uses. However, *tener que* (+ infinitive) indicates a need to do something, whereas *deber* (+ infinitive) implies more of a moral obligation or what someone should do.

***Tengo que** poner la mesa.*	I have to set the table.
***Debo** ayudar a mi madre.*	I should help my mother.

Debo ayudar a mi abuela.

5 ¿Debo o tengo que?

Decide whether a form of *deber* or a form of *tener que* would be more appropriate in a sentence that contains the following phrases. Then use each phrase in a sentence, according to the indicated cues.

poner la mesa todos los días (Ana)
Ana tiene que poner la mesa todos los días.

hacer la tarea primero y ver televisión después (los estudiantes)
Los estudiantes deben hacer la tarea primero y ver televisión después.

1. poner los platos sucios en el lavaplatos (yo)
2. leer el periódico todos los días (Uds.)
3. llamar a nuestra abuela (mi hermana)
4. viajar a Caracas mañana a las diez (nosotros)
5. cerrar siempre la puerta del refrigerador (tú)
6. ayudar a su madre (ellos)

6 Estamos ocupados

In groups of three or four, discuss what you have to do or ought to do today, tomorrow and next week. List at least two things you must do and two things you should do. Compare your busy schedule with members of your group.

A: Mañana tengo que ayudar a mi padre.
B: La semana que viene yo debo llamar a mi abuela.

IDIOMA

El presente de los verbos con el cambio *e* → *ie*

Some verbs in Spanish may require the spelling change *e* → *ie* in all forms of their present-tense stem except for *nosotros* and *vosotros.* The verb *pensar (ie)* is one example of this type of verb. (The letters in parentheses after the infinitive are to help you identify these verbs and to indicate the change that occurs in the stem.) **Note:** The stem changes do not affect the regular verb endings.

pensar			
yo	pienso	nosotros nosotras	pensamos
tú	piensas	vosotros vosotras	pensáis
Ud. él ella	piensa	Uds. ellos ellas	piensan

Other *e* → *ie* stem-changing verbs you have already seen include *cerrar (ie), empezar (ie), encender (ie), preferir (ie), querer (ie)* and *sentir (ie).* The verbs *tener* and *venir* have this same change except for the *yo* irregular forms of these two verbs *(tener: tengo; venir: vengo).*

*¿Qué **piensas**?*
*Jorge no **cierra** la puerta del refrigerador.*
*Yo **empiezo** a hacer las tareas en casa a las tres.*
*¿**Enciendo** la luz?*
*¿Qué platos **prefieres**?*
***Quieren** las servilletas blancas.*
*Lo **siento** mucho.*

but:

***Tengo** una casa bonita.*
***Vengo** mañana.*

Note: The verb *empezar* is used with *a* when an infinitive follows, as in *Empiezo a estudiar* (I am beginning to study).

Empiezo a estudiar.

Pienso poner la mesa.

7 ¿Qué piensas?

Create at least six sentences to say what the following people are planning to do, trying to use all the words in each column. Verb forms may be repeated.

I	II	III
Marisol	pensamos	buscar los platos de todos los días
tú	piensan	ayudar en la cocina después de llamar a un amigo
las chicas	pienso	comer en el comedor
Jorge y Pepe	piensas	tener arepas para un almuerzo especial
yo	piensa	viajar a Caracas otra vez
mi amiga y yo		encender la luz de la cocina
		hacer unas cosas especiales para tu fiesta

8 Los padres son diferentes

Marisol and Jorge realize how different their tastes are from those of their parents. Use the cues that follow to create sentences that compare and contrast how they differ from Sr. and Sra. Vega. Follow the model.

querer ir al cine/querer ver una película en casa
Si nosotros queremos ir al cine, ellos quieren ver una película en casa.

1. tener que hacer la tarea/tener que ver televisión
2. empezar a oír música/empezar a leer
3. encender el estéreo/encender el tocadiscos viejo
4. preferir salir a bailar/preferir salir a caminar
5. querer comer en un restaurante/querer comer en casa otra vez
6. pensar viajar a otra ciudad/pensar ir a un museo
7. cerrar la puerta/abrir las ventanas

PARA ti

Proverbios y dichos

Knowing a language means more than memorizing a lot of words and learning grammar. It is just as important to learn what is appropriate to say and when you should speak. Anytime you use the languages you know, it is always a good idea to consider carefully what you say: *Antes de hablar es bueno pensar* (Think before you speak).

Algo más

Pensar: un poco más

The verb *pensar* has several different uses when combined with other words.

- When followed immediately by an infinitive, *pensar* indicates what someone plans or intends to do.

Pienso hacer *un viaje a Caracas.*	I plan to take a trip to Caracas.
¿Cuándo ***piensas ir?***	When do you intend to go?

- When combined with *en, pensar* is used to indicate whom or what someone is thinking about.

¿En qué ***piensas?***	What are you thinking about?
Pienso en *estudiar español en Venezuela.*	I am thinking about studying Spanish in Venezuela.

- *Pensar* may be combined with *de* to ask for an opinion. As a response, *pensar* is used with *que* to express an opinion or thought.

¿Qué ***piensas de*** *la lámpara nueva?*	What do you think of the new lamp?
Pienso que *es muy bonita.*	I think it is very pretty.
Mamá ***piensa que*** *debes poner la mesa.*	Mom thinks you ought to set the table.

9 ¿En qué piensan?

Imagine you are planning a party and have asked several friends to help. Everyone will be responsible for different tasks. Working with a partner, take turns asking and answering questions about what your friends are thinking about as they prepare for the party, according to the illustrations.

A: ¿En qué piensa tu amiga Rosa?
B: Piensa en los amigos que vienen a la fiesta.

tu amiga Rosa

1. Marta y Carmen

2. nosotros

3. otros amigos que vienen a la fiesta

4. Jorge

5. yo

6. tu madre

7. tú

10 Piensan tener una fiesta

Hay una fiesta de despedida para Marisol y Jorge porque van a pasar el verano en Colombia con su primo Martín. Completa el siguiente párrafo con la forma correcta de los verbos.

Hoy los amigos de Marisol y Jorge *1. (pensar)* tener una fiesta porque ellos van a pasar el verano en Colombia con su primo. La fiesta *2. (empezar)* a las siete. Ana y Lucía *3. (venir)* y Paco *4. (pensar)* venir también. Marisol lo *5. (sentir)* mucho, pero no *6. (querer)* ir a la fiesta porque está muy cansada. Jorge *7. (pensar)* que Marisol *8. (deber)* venir a la fiesta también. Javier y Ana *9. (preferir)* venir a las cuatro porque *10. (querer)* estar más tiempo con Marisol y con Jorge. Y tú, ¿qué *11. (pensar)* de tener una fiesta? ¿Es una buena idea?

11 ¿Qué piensan Uds.?

Working in groups of three, say what each of you is thinking about doing after school tonight or next weekend. The student with the funniest or most imaginative answer will report to the class what the three of you think you will be doing.

A: Pienso ir a mi casa a comer.
B: Yo también pienso ir a mi casa a comer.
C: Pienso cantar con Enrique Iglesias en un concierto.

Pienso cantar con Enrique Iglesias.

Oportunidades

¿Piensas viajar a otro país?

Have you ever thought about traveling to another country? Where would you like to go? Do you have relatives that live in a different country? Have you ever visited them? What opportunities do you think there might be to use your language skills while traveling?

En el comedor

MARISOL: Papá, **pásame** las arepas, por favor.
SR. VEGA: Cómo no. Aquí las tienes.
SRA. VEGA: Jorge, ¿cómo está **la sopa**? ¿Te gusta?
JORGE: No sé, mamá. ¡No tengo **cuchara**! Mari, una cuchara, por favor.
SRA. VEGA: Lo siento, Jorge. Yo tengo dos. Aquí está.

12 ¿Qué comprendiste?

1. ¿Qué quiere Marisol?
2. ¿Le gusta a Jorge la sopa? ¿Por qué?
3. ¿Qué hay sobre la mesa?
4. ¿Piensas que van a comer postre?
5. ¿Tiene comedor tu casa?

13 ¡Pásame el pan, por favor!

Working in pairs, take turns asking what your partner needs while pointing at an item shown in the illustration titled *En el comedor.* Your partner then must ask you to pass the item to him or her.

A: ¿Qué necesitas? ¿Qué quieres?
B: Pásame el pan, por favor.

PARA ti

Más sobre la comida

el arroz	*rice*
el café	*coffee*
la carne	*meat*
el flan	*caramel custard*
la leche	*milk*
el panecillo	*roll*
el pastel (la torta)	*cake*
el té	*tea*
las verduras	*vegetables*

Conexión Cultural

La comida venezolana

Venezuela has a variety of traditional dishes. One of them, the *hallaca,* is prepared in nearly every Venezuelan home during Christmas. This is a popular dish that consists of a corn-flour pie filled with pork, chicken, vegetables and spices. It is cooked wrapped in plantain leaves from a variety of banana called *plátano.* Plantains are used often in Venezuelan kitchens and are common ingredients for many national foods.

The *arepas* are perhaps the most popular food in Venezuela. They can be eaten alone or as a kind of bread to accompany a meal. They can also be stuffed with meat, cheese, scrambled eggs or other fillings. *Arepas* are easy to make and have only three ingredients: corn flour, salt and water. Originally *arepas* were prepared from freshly husked and ground corn, but today, using precooked white corn flour can save time.

Mamá hace buenas arepas.

CONEXIONES 14 Cruzando fronteras

Look at the following recipe for *arepas* and answer the questions. Then prepare the recipe at home for a taste of this typical Venezuelan food.

LAS AREPAS

2 tazas de harina de maíz
2 cucharitas de sal
2 tazas de agua caliente

Preparación

Para empezar, poner la harina de maíz en una taza grande y poco a poco poner el agua con sal. Luego, **mezclar** el agua con la harina hasta que se convierta en masa. Después, **dejar** la masa **en reposo** por cinco minutos. Ahora, hacer con la masa unos **rollos** de 3" de diámetro y de 1" a 2" de **ancho**. En una **sartén** con un poquito de aceite, **cocinar** las arepas hasta ver los rollos **dorados**. Después, poner las arepas en el horno a 350 grados para cocinar por aproximadamente 30 minutos, hasta tener arepas **crujientes**.

mezclar *mix* **dejar** *leave* **en reposo** *rest* **rollos** *rolls* **ancho** *thick* **sartén** *frying pan* **cocinar** *cook* **dorados** *golden* **crujiente** *crunchy*

1. ¿Cuáles son los tres ingredientes para hacer arepas?
2. ¿Cuánta sal, harina y agua necesitas para la receta?
3. ¿Qué debes hacer para empezar?
4. ¿Por cuánto tiempo tienes que dejar la masa en reposo?
5. Después de hacer rollos con la masa, ¿qué debes hacer?
6. ¿Por cuánto tiempo deben estar las arepas en el horno?

15 En la mesa

Completa las siguientes oraciones, según las ilustraciones.

Necesito la sal.

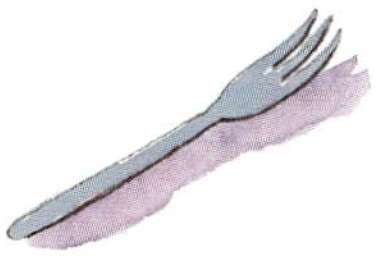
1.

2.

3.

4.

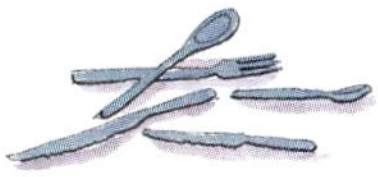
5.

6.

7.

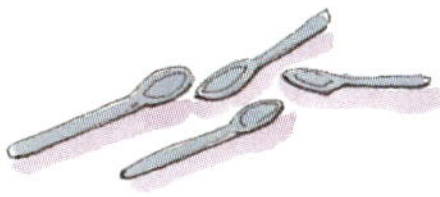
8.

9.

10.

1. Necesito un (1).
2. Pásame el (2), por favor.
3. Son las (3) de todos los días.
4. Quiero un (4) de agua muy fría.
5. Estos (5) están sucios.
6. Prefiero la (6) bien caliente.
7. Quiero más (7) para la ensalada.
8. Necesitan unas (8) para el postre.
9. El (9) es de nuestra abuela.
10. Pásame la (10), por favor.

16 En el comedor

Find the phrase that completes or describes the idea. Some answers may be used more than once.

1. Necesito la pimienta y la...
2. Me gusta el pan...
3. Quiero tener...
4. Quiero un plato...
5. Por favor, pásame...
6. No quiero café, gracias. Prefiero un vaso...
7. Para la sopa necesito...
8. Por favor, pásame un...

A. una taza limpia.
B. de agua mineral.
C. caliente.
D. un plato de sopa y una cuchara.
E. sal.
F. tenedor.
G. de sopa.
H. el postre.

17 ¿Qué no hay en mi ilustración?

Create a sketch of a table place setting that is similar to the one in the illustration titled *En el comedor,* but with three items missing. Then working with a partner, take turns asking one another what is not in your illustration and write in Spanish the name of each missing object you find in your partner's illustration. Finally, check to see if you guessed which objects were missing and whether you spelled them correctly.

18 Tienes que buscar

With a partner, look at the following illustration and decide what seems wrong or makes no sense. Then prepare a list in Spanish of all the things you discover.

El gato está sobre la lámpara.

PARA ti

Una clave

In addition to the model there are at least fourteen more things that are wrong with the illustration. How many did you find?

¿Cómo es el comedor de tu casa?

19 En casa de los Vega

The following questions and statements are part of a conversation the Vega family had during lunch. Match each question or statement to the most appropriate response. Then in pairs, play the roles of two members of the Vega family. Take turns reading the questions and responses from their conversation.

¿Qué hay de postre?

1. ¿Quién necesita la pimienta?
2. ¿Te gusta el pan?
3. ¿Por qué no abres la puerta?
4. ¿Qué hay de postre?
5. Por favor, pásame el azúcar.
6. ¿Quieres un vaso de agua mineral?
7. ¿Dónde debo poner estos cubiertos?
8. ¿El mantel está sucio?
9. ¿La luz del refrigerador no se enciende?
10. ¿La comida está caliente?

A. Ensalada de frutas.
B. Sí, y también está muy buena.
C. Sí, me gusta con mantequilla.
D. No, prefiero jugo.
E. No debe estar sucio. Es nuevo.
F. Porque ya está abierta.
G. No. Tengo que comprar otra.
H. Yo la necesito para la sopa.
I. En el fregadero, por favor.
J. Cómo no. Aquí lo tienes.

Algo más

Para hablar de cantidades

¿Cuánto?

Uno. (Una.)	One.
Más./Menos.	More./Less.
Mucho. (Mucha.)/Poco. (Poca.)	A lot./A little.
Un poco de (sal, etc.).	A little (salt, etc.).
Un poquito.	A very little.
Un poco más/menos.	A little more/less.

¿Cuántos?

Unos. (Unas.)	Some.
Muchos. (Muchas.)/Pocos. (Pocas.)	Many./Few.

¿Quieres un poquito más?

Note: Whereas *uno, mucho* and *poco* have masculine, feminine, singular and plural forms, *más, menos, un poco (de)* and *(ni) un poquito* require no additional changes in their forms.

20 ¿Cuánto quieres?

Working with a partner, imagine you are in the kitchen preparing a meal. Take turns asking and answering questions based upon the information given.

sal
A: ¿Cuánta sal quieres?
B: Un poquito.

agua
B: ¿Cuántos vasos de agua necesitamos?
A: Un vaso de agua.

1. platos de sopa
2. cucharitas
3. pan
4. azúcar para el postre
5. servilletas de papel
6. mantequilla
7. aceite para la ensalada
8. pimienta

21 ¿Qué comes hoy?

With a classmate, prepare a dialog that occurs at the dinner table. Include at least five questions or statements each. You may wish to include any of the following: requests for items at the table (Pass me the salt and pepper.), questions about what your partner thinks (What do you think of the *arepas*?), questions about your partner's needs (Do you want more soup?), comments about the food (The salad needs more oil.) and so on. Be sure to be polite (use *por favor* and *gracias*).

IDIOMA

Los adjetivos demostrativos

Place a demonstrative adjective *(adjetivo demostrativo)* before a noun to draw attention to where someone or something is located in relation to yourself ("this house," "that car," etc.). Demonstrative adjectives, like the other adjectives you have learned, must agree in gender and number with the nouns they modify.

los adjetivos demostrativos			
singular		**plural**	
masculino	**femenino**	**masculino**	**femenino**
este	esta	estos	estas
ese	esa	esos	esas
aquel	aquella	aquellos	aquellas

When pointing out people or objects that are nearby, use *este, esta, estos* or *estas* (this/these).

Pienso comprar uno de ***estos*** *platos.*
Pues, ***este*** *plato es bonito.*

Use *ese, esa, esos* or *esas* (that/those) to call attention to people or objects that are farther away.

¿Qué piensas de ***esas*** *casas?*
Esas *casas que están allí son grandes.*

Draw attention to people or objects that are even farther away ("over there") by using *aquel, aquella, aquellos* or *aquellas* (that/those over there).

Aquellas *casas que están allá son bonitas.*
Mi amiga vive en ***aquella*** *casa grande.*

¿Qué piensas de estos platos?

22 ¡Quiero otra casa!

Completa las siguientes oraciones con la forma apropiada de *este*.

Quiero otra casa porque (1) casa tiene pocas ventanas y hay muy poca luz. (2) ventanas no cierran muy bien. No me gusta (3) cocina. ¿Por qué? Pues, (4) fregadero no tiene agua caliente. La puerta de (5) refrigerador no abre bien y la puerta de (6) lavaplatos no cierra. (7) luces no encienden y el comedor está tan lejos de la cocina. No me gusta (8) mesa del comedor y (9) sillas son pequeñas. (10) tarde quiero empezar a buscar otra casa.

23 Ponemos la mesa

Imagine you are preparing the table for dinner guests. Working in pairs, take turns asking if your partner needs the items you are offering. Your classmate must answer each question negatively. Follow the model.

plato
A: ¿Quieres este plato?
B: No, no quiero ese plato.

1. mantel amarillo
2. cucharitas
3. tazas
4. servilletas azules
5. vaso nuevo
6. tenedores
7. silla
8. platos de postre

24 ¿Pienso ir...?

Imagine you and a friend are looking out an observatory window from which you can see several places in Caracas, Venezuela. Point out where you intend to go this week, using the given cues. Follow the model.

restaurante venezolano
Pienso ir a aquel restaurante venezolano.

1. casa amarilla
2. museo de arte
3. parques interesantes
4. calles con muchas tiendas
5. cine allá cerca del teatro
6. plaza grande

Pienso ir de compras al centro de Caracas.

25 ¿Este, ese o aquel?

Use the appropriate form of *este, ese* or *aquel* to answer the following questions, based upon the cues shown in the illustration.

¿Qué vaso prefieres?
Prefiero este vaso.

1. ¿Qué lámpara prefieres?

2. ¿Qué plato prefieres?

3. ¿Qué tazas prefieres?

4. ¿Qué pan prefieres?

5. ¿Qué servilletas prefieres?

6. ¿Qué postre prefieres?

26 De compras

Imagine you have rented your first apartment and you are at a store with a friend buying various items for the kitchen and dining room. Working with a partner, create a dialog in which you choose items to purchase from the illustration below. Express your preferences, ask each other's opinion and try to decide which things you want to, have to or ought to buy.

A: ¿Qué piensas de aquella mesa?
B: Prefiero esa mesa porque es más grande.

Autoevaluación. As a review and self-check, respond to the following:

1. Imagine you are preparing dinner for your family. How can you tell a sister and brother five things they have to do or should do to help you get ready?
2. What should they do first to start? After that?
3. How would you ask a friend what he or she is thinking about?
4. Ask two classmates what they are thinking about doing this Saturday.
5. Your aunt has prepared a special dessert and wants to know how much you would like. How do you respond?
6. Imagine you are seated at the diningroom table and the glass and silverware you need are far away from you, near your brother. How can you ask your brother politely to pass you that glass and that silverware?
7. Imagine you are eating lunch at *La Estancia,* one of Caracas' best restaurants. Name some of the items you might see on the table when the server seats you.
8. Name two typical Venezuelan dishes that you read about.

¡La práctica hace al maestro!

A Comunicación

Imagine you and two friends are having lunch at the restaurant *La Vía Emilia* in Caracas, Venezuela. You are discussing your plans for the week and talking about what you want to do, ought to do, have to do or prefer to do in the next seven days. As you converse, you may politely interrupt each other to ask for the things you need passed to you. You may also comment on things and people around the restaurant. Make the conversation as realistic as you can.

A: Tengo que ir a la biblioteca mañana.
B: Yo también. Perdón, por favor, pásame....

B Conexión con la tecnología

Using the Internet, do research about Venezuela. Find out what you can about the following: the history of Venezuela; important cities (attractions, population and so forth); food; lodging; customs; transportation to Venezuela and within the country; and attractions that a visitor might be interested in seeing. Prepare a summary of your research. Present some of the more interesting findings to the class, including maps or pictures you were able to download and print, information about airfares and any other details you think the class may find appealing.

VOCABULARIO

En la cocina

el aceite
el azúcar
la cocina
los cubiertos
la cuchara
la cucharita
el cuchillo
la estufa
el fregadero
el lavaplatos
la luz
el mantel
la mantequilla
la mesa
el pan
la pimienta
el plato
el plato de sopa
el postre
el refrigerador
la sal
la servilleta
la sopa
la taza
el tenedor
el vaso

Expresiones y otras palabras

allá
aquel, aquella (aquellos, aquellas)
el comedor
la cosa
de todos los días
después
ese, esa (esos, esas)
especial
este, esta (estos, estas)
la lámpara
menos
otra vez
pensar de/en/que
un poco (poquito) de
poner la mesa
ya

Verbos

ayudar
cerrar (ie)
deber
empezar (ie)
encender (ie)
pásame
pensar (ie)
poner
preferir (ie)
querer (ie)
sentir (ie)
tener que
viajar

¿Te gusta el flan de postre?

Papá hace la comida en la estufa.

Pongo las servilletas de Navidad.

Lección 12

Contexto cultural COLOMBIA

Una carta de Jorge

Queridos papás, Cartagena, 2 de junio

Estamos aquí en Cartagena **desde**° el jueves. Esta ciudad es muy bonita **e** interesante, ¿saben? **Cada**° día a Marisol le gusta más la idea de pasar el verano aquí, pero a mí **me gustaría** estar con Uds. en Caracas.

La casa del primo Martín es grande y **cómoda.**° Voy a hacer un **dibujo**° para Uds. Sus amigos son simpáticos y muy divertidos. El mes que viene, **dicen que**° vamos a pasar siete **u** ocho días en Bucaramanga con la tía Bárbara y allá vamos a nadar en su **piscina**° y **aprender a**° montar a caballo. Marisol y yo **tenemos ganas de**° ir.

Saben que a Marisol no le gusta **escribir cartas.**° Entonces, el viernes que viene ella los quiere llamar **por** teléfono a las nueve de la noche.

Un **abrazo** de su hijo,

Jorge

desde *since* **Cada** *Each* **cómoda** *comfortable* **dibujo** *drawing* **dicen que** *they say that* **piscina** *swimming pool* **aprender a** *to learn to* **tenemos ganas de** *want* **escribir cartas** *to write letters*

1 ¿Qué comprendiste?

1. ¿Dónde están Marisol y Jorge desde el jueves?
2. ¿Cómo es la ciudad?
3. ¿A quién escribe Jorge esta carta?
4. ¿Cómo es la casa en Cartagena?
5. ¿Cuánto tiempo piensan pasar en Bucaramanga?
6. ¿Qué van a hacer los muchachos allá?

2 Charlando

1. ¿Te gusta estar lejos de tu casa? ¿Por qué?
2. ¿Cómo es tu casa?
3. ¿Qué te gustaría hacer cada verano?
4. ¿Qué tienes ganas de hacer este fin de semana?
5. ¿A quién llamas mucho por teléfono?

PARA ti

Las palabras *e* y *u*

The word *y* becomes *e* before words that begin with *i* or *hi*. Similarly, the word *o* changes to *u* before words that begin with *o* or *ho*.

*Juan **e** Isabel viven en la capital de Colombia.*

*Dicen que van a nadar en la piscina hoy **u** otro día.*

Cartagena, Colombia.

Conexión cultural

Colombia

Colombia is located at the juncture between Central and South America. This Spanish-speaking country contains some of the most spectacular and varied terrain in the world including mountains, plains, lowlands, tropical jungles and an extensive coastline that touches on both the Atlantic and the Pacific Oceans. Also, its climate does not change with the seasons but rather is determined by Colombia's elevations. For example, the lowlands and the coastal areas offer a tropical climate such as you might experience if you travel to the beautiful city of *Cartagena*. *Santa Fe de Bogotá*, the capital, and other parts of the country that are located in mountainous regions of Colombia have a mild climate all year long.

La muralla de Cartagena.

The Spaniards founded *Cartagena de Indias* on Colombia's northwest coast in 1533. Pirates frequently attacked the port seeking gold and other valuables, so a wall was constructed around the city as a means of defense. The wall *(muralla)* remains today, along with the entire city, a symbol of colonial times in Colombia.

Santa Fe de Bogotá was founded in 1538. The city is vibrant and modern. However, you may catch a glimpse into Colombia's past by visiting the exceptional and unique *Museo del Oro* (Gold Museum), which holds over 30,000 pieces of pre-Columbian gold.

Everyone knows Colombia produces large quantities of excellent coffee, but not everyone knows it is the world's major source of emeralds. Colombia is also famous for its music, including the distinctive dance rhythms of *la cumbia, el porro, el merecumbé* and the accordion accompaniment of songs known as *vallenatos*. Colombia is indeed one of the jewels of South America.

Colombia

Las esmeraldas son importantes en Colombia.

3 ¿Qué sabes de Colombia?

Read the following statements about Colombia. There may be some words that you do not know. Then tell whether the statements are *verdad* or *falso*.

1. Colombia está en la América Central.
2. Hablan español en Colombia.
3. Colombia no tiene costas en el Pacífico.
4. Cartagena es un símbolo del período colonial español.
5. El clima es determinado por la elevación.
6. Santa Fe de Bogotá es la capital del país.
7. Colombia es famosa por el café, las esmeraldas y la música.

¿Te gustaría viajar a Santa Fe de Bogotá?

Algo más

Para expresar deseos

To express your wishes you may use *quiero* or the more polite and less emphatic *me gustaría* plus an infinitive. Compare the following:

***Quiero** viajar a Colombia.*	I want to travel to Colombia.
***Me gustaría** viajar a Colombia.*	I would like to travel to Colombia.

4 ¿Qué te gustaría hacer?

Completa lógicamente las siguientes oraciones de una manera original.

Me gustaría viajar....
Me gustaría viajar a Cartagena, Colombia.

1. Me gustaría ir....
2. Me gustaría comprar....
3. Me gustaría vivir....
4. No me gustaría vivir....
5. Me gustaría tener....
6. No me gustaría ir....

5 Comparaciones

Compare and contrast the wishes, intentions and obligations of various people you know, using the following verbs: *gustaría, pensar, preferir* and *querer.* Use a variety of subjects and write at least one sentence for each verb. Then exchange your paper with a partner and take turns asking and answering questions about what each of you wrote.

A mis padres les gustaría ir a Venezuela cada verano. Yo prefiero ir a Colombia. Un día pienso hacer un viaje a Santa Fe de Bogotá.

A: ¿Adónde les gustaría ir a tus padres?
B: A mis padres les gustaría ir a Venezuela.

6 ¡A escribir!

Help Jorge's parents write him a short note, including the following information: They are pleased to hear from their dear son; they know that he is far from home in Caracas, but not far from his family; they would like to see the photos of the trip to Bucaramanga when he and his sister are home again. Be sure to include the city and the date and use appropriate greetings and farewells, such as *Querido Jorge, hasta pronto* or *un abrazo.*

IDIOMA

El presente del verbo *decir*

The present tense of *decir* has an irregular *yo* form and requires a stem change for all forms except *nosotros/as* and *vosotros/as.* Use *decir* for reporting what is said.

decir	
digo	decimos
dices	decís
dice	dicen

Yo digo "Hola".

¿Qué dices tú?

7 ¿Qué dicen?

What would the people indicated say in reaction to the corresponding illustrations?

Marisol

Marisol dice "Aló".

1. tú

2. mi amigo

3. ellas

4. nosotros

5. yo

6. Uds.

Algo más

Usando *que* para reportar

You have already used the word *que* to connect two parts of a sentence: *Pienso* ***que*** *Jorge quiere estar en Caracas.* When you summarize what someone says, it is necessary to use *que* between *decir* and the expression or phrase that follows:

¿Qué dicen los amigos de Martín? Dicen ***que*** *van a pasar una semana en Bucaramanga.*	What do Martín's friends say? They say (**that**) they are going to spend a week in Bucaramanga.

¿Qué dice Ud.?

8 ¿Reportando los resultados?

Imagine you are reporting the results of a poll about whether students from your school would like to participate in an exchange program with a high school in Santa Fe de Bogotá, Colombia, that would require them to be away from home for the school year. Report your findings based upon the following information.

Isabel
Isabel dice que no.

1. Eva
2. Miguel y yo
3. la señora Barrera e Isabel
4. Pedro y la señorita Alba
5. Ud.
6. el señor Sánchez y Daniel

9 ¿Qué hacen?

Trabajando en parejas, haz mini-diálogos usando la forma apropiada del verbo *decir*.

tú/escribir cartas a la familia
A: ¿Qué dices?
B: Digo que escribo cartas a la familia.

1. Jorge y Marisol/aprender a montar a caballo
2. Uds./pensar viajar a Colombia
3. tú/estudiar español e inglés
4. ellas/empezar a comprender
5. Ud./salir a comer ahora
6. tus amigas/llamar por teléfono a las siete

¿Dices que piensas visitar a Colombia?

10 Encuesta

Survey your classmates about activities they enjoy and places they want to visit. In groups of three, compare the information each of you has obtained. Finally, select one person in your group to present a summary of your survey results to the class.

A: ¿Te gusta estar lejos de tu casa?
B: Sí, me gusta estar lejos de mi casa porque me gusta viajar.
C: No, no me gusta estar lejos de mi casa. Prefiero estar cómodo/a en mi casa.
A: *B* dice que le gusta estar lejos de su casa pero *C* dice que prefiere estar cómodo/a en su casa.

El dibujo de Jorge

Aquí tienes el dibujo de la casa **donde** vive el primo Martín. No tiene **primer piso**° y, claro, no hay **escalera.**° Todo está en la **planta baja.**° Entramos en la casa **por**° una puerta en el **patio**, donde hay una mesa, sillas y muchas **plantas.** El **cuarto** de Marisol está **al lado de**° la cocina. Tiene unas ventanas **pequeñas.**° Yo estoy en el cuarto de Martín que está al lado del cuarto de sus padres. **Cuando** Martín y yo estamos aburridos, vamos a la **sala** a ver televisión u oír música. A veces, nos gusta jugar en la computadora. **Por las noches**° comemos en el comedor, pero los domingos comemos en el patio. Y claro, cada tarde a las cuatro vamos a la playa de Bocagrande.

primer piso *first floor above (the main floor)* **escalera** *stairs* **planta baja** *main floor* **por** *through* **al lado de** *next to* **pequeñas** *small* **Por las noches** *At night*

11 ¿Qué comprendiste?

1. ¿De quién es la casa?
2. ¿El cuarto de Jorge está en el primer piso?
3. ¿Qué hay en el patio?
4. ¿Qué hacen Jorge y Martín cuando están aburridos?
5. ¿Tiene una escalera la casa? ¿Un baño?
6. ¿Qué cuarto está al lado del garaje?

PARA ti

La planta baja y el primer piso

Some people refer to *la planta baja* as *los bajos* (downstairs). The expression *los altos* is roughly equivalent to the English **upstairs** or **upper floor(s).** The term *primer piso* (first floor) often identifies the second floor of a building, although many people also use the term to refer to the main floor.

Yo vivo en ***los bajos*** *y mis padres viven en* ***los altos****.*
Yo vivo en ***la planta baja*** *y mis padres viven en* ***el primer piso****.*

Here are several more words to talk about your home:

el apartamento	apartment
el condominio	condominium
el jardín	garden, yard
el sótano	basement, cellar
el ático/el desván	attic
el techo	roof

12 Charlando

1. ¿Cómo es la casa donde vives? ¿Hay una escalera? ¿Hay un patio?
2. ¿Cuántos pisos tiene la casa?
3. ¿Dónde está tu cuarto? ¿Es grande o pequeño?
4. ¿Tienes plantas en tu casa? ¿Dónde?
5. ¿Qué haces por las noches? ¿Comes? ¿Estudias? ¿Sales con amigos?

Estrategia

Para hablar mejor: *recognizing words in context*

You may notice how differently people express themselves in Spanish. Words and expressions you hear may be different from those you have learned. For example, *cuarto, habitación* and *pieza* are all used for **room.** For the word **bedroom** you may encounter the Spanish words *alcoba, dormitorio, habitación, pieza, recámara* and *cuarto de dormir* (literally, a **room for sleeping**), which is sometimes shortened to *cuarto.* However, do not confuse this shortened form of *cuarto* for the expression *cuarto de baño* (bathroom), which is usually shortened to *baño.*

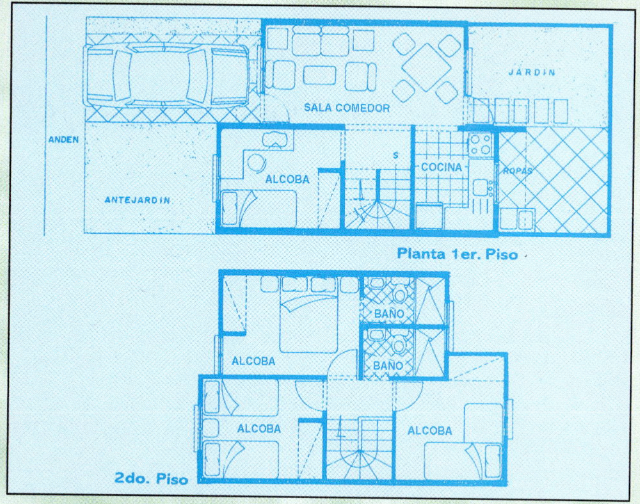

Knowing that these differences exist will be invaluable in your effort to communicate with others. Remember that the important result of your effort is communication, which depends upon the people involved, the place and the context. Use the words and expressions you have learned and take note of new expressions along the way that will help you understand others while you express yourself in Spanish.

13 ¿Adónde necesitan ir en la casa?

Tell where in the house each of these people needs to go, based upon the following statements.

Estoy muy cansada.
Necesitas ir a tu cuarto.

1. Mi mamá tiene ganas de mirar fotos y oír la radio.
2. Mi hermana viene de jugar al tenis.
3. Mis tíos están aquí para comer con nosotros.
4. Mi hermano está aburrido y va a ver televisión.
5. Mi papá necesita el carro.
6. Quiero un vaso de agua.
7. Voy a leer un libro muy interesante.

¿Hablas por teléfono en tu cuarto?

14 En la casa del primo Martín

Relatives of Jorge and Marisol in Cartagena, Colombia, are involved in various activities this morning somewhere in their house. Tell what everyone is doing, and where, according to the illustrations.

Su tío lee un libro en la sala.

1. 

2. 

3. 

4. 

5. 

CONEXIONES 15 Cruzando fronteras

Imagine you are studying to be an architect. Your first major assignment is to draw a blueprint of the floor plan of your house or apartment (you may even choose to make a pop-up version of the home if you like) and label the rooms in Spanish. Make the plan as detailed as you can. Then write at least five statements in Spanish that summarize the architectural plan you have created. For example, state whether the blueprint is of a house *(casa)* or an apartment *(apartamento)*, how large it is, the number and type of rooms, where the rooms are located, how many doors, windows and floors there are and any other information you can give. Make up any details you wish.

16 Habla de tu casa

Working in pairs, talk with your classmate about your house and some of the things that members of your family do during the week. Discuss similarities and differences in your lives at home *(casa* or *apartamento)*, your weekly routines and your lives in general. Discuss at least seven activities, including some of the following: *caminar, comer, escribir cartas, ir en autobús, leer* and *ver televisión.* You can make up the information if you wish. Write down what your partner says and report what you discussed to the class.

A: ¿A qué hora come tu familia?
B: Bueno, comemos muchas veces a las siete.
A: Pues, en mi casa comemos a las seis o a las siete, pero no los domingos. Los domingos comemos a las tres o a las cuatro. ¿Ven televisión en tu casa por la mañana o por la noche?

No quiero salir de casa

MARISOL: Jorge, ¿por qué no vas al parque a **correr?°** Estás con tu música desde las ocho y quiero leer el periódico.
JORGE: La **verdad°** es que no quiero salir de casa y no quiero correr. ¿Por qué no vas tú al patio?
MARISOL: Porque Martín está allí con unos amigos. Y, ¿por qué no **pides prestado°** el carro al tío Paco y vas a la playa? ¡Es divertido!
JORGE: Marisol, lo voy a **repetir** por última vez: no quiero salir de casa.
MARISOL: **Lo que°** **quieres decir°** es que tú prefieres estar aquí en la sala donde estoy yo y oír tu música.
JORGE: No, eso es una **mentira.°** Lo que yo digo es que si no te gusta mi música, tienes que ir a otro cuarto de la casa.
MARISOL: Pues, bien, voy a leer el periódico en mi cuarto.

correr *to run* **verdad** *truth* **pides prestado** *(ask to) borrow* **Lo que** *What* **quieres decir** *you mean (to say)* **mentira** *lie*

17 ¿Qué comprendiste?

1. ¿Qué quiere hacer Marisol?
2. ¿Desde qué hora está Jorge con la música?
3. ¿Qué es la verdad para Jorge?
4. ¿Por qué no va Marisol al patio?
5. ¿Por qué no pide prestado Jorge el carro al tío Paco?
6. ¿Qué repite Jorge por última vez?
7. ¿Es verdad o es mentira que cuando Jorge dice que no quiere salir de casa, quiere decir que prefiere estar en la sala con Marisol y oír su música?
8. ¿Qué va a hacer Marisol?

18 Charlando

1. ¿Te gusta pedir favores? Explica.
2. ¿Qué te gusta hacer cuando estás en casa?
3. ¿Sales a correr al parque? ¿A la playa?
4. ¿Siempre dices la verdad o a veces dices mentiras?

IDIOMA

El presente de los verbos con el cambio *e* → *i*

You have seen that some verbs require the spelling change *e* → *ie* for some of their present-tense forms: *yo cierro, nosotros cerramos*. Similarly, some verbs in Spanish may require the spelling change *e* → *i* in all forms of their present-tense stem except for *nosotros* and *vosotros*. The verbs *pedir (i, i)* and *repetir (i, i)* are two examples of this type of verb.

Pedimos ayuda al profesor.

pedir	
pido	pedimos
pides	pedís
pide	piden

repetir	
repito	repetimos
repites	repetís
repite	repiten

Note: With the exception of the irregular *yo* form *(digo)*, the verb *decir* follows the same pattern: *dices, dice, decimos, decís, dicen.*

19 ¿Quién pide mucho?

Completa el siguiente párrafo con la forma apropiada de los verbos *pedir, repetir* o *decir*.

Carlos siempre (1) cosas. Un día (2) prestado un bolígrafo; otro día (3) un libro. A veces tiene que (4) prestado unos pesos para el almuerzo y siempre (5) ver mis tareas. Sabes, es porque él nunca las hace. A mí no me gusta cuando otros estudiantes me (6) la tarea. Claro, no debo (7) esas cosas, ¡pero (8) la verdad! Nunca (9) una cosa que es mentira. Mmm, ¿qué opinas si nosotros le (10) unas cosas a Carlos? ¿Qué va a decir?

Algo más

Pedir y preguntar

The equivalent of *pedir* in English is "to ask for, to request, to order (in a restaurant)." For asking a question, use *preguntar* or *hacer una pregunta.* ***Pedir permiso (para)*** is "to ask for permission (to do something)," although sometimes people use the abbreviated expression *con permiso,* which is "excuse me" or "with your permission." Use ***pedir perdón*** to excuse yourself and to ask for forgiveness for having done something wrong; however, the word *Perdón* can be used for "Excuse me" or "Pardon me." ***Pedir prestado/a*** is "to ask for a loan" or "to borrow something."

20 ¿Pedir o preguntar?

Estas personas están en casa. Completa lo que dicen con la forma apropiada de *pedir* o *preguntar*.

Pido ayuda a mi mamá.

1. ¿Siempre (1) Uds. ayuda con su tarea a su mamá?
2. David siempre (2) dónde está su mochila.
3. Mi amigo y yo (3): ¿cuándo vamos a viajar a otro país?
4. ¿Siempre (4) tú quiénes son?
5. Mis padres siempre (5) ayuda en la cocina.
6. ¿Siempre (6) tú permiso para nadar en la piscina?
7. Siempre (7) perdón cuando no comprendemos lo que dice nuestro abuelo.
8. A veces tengo que (8) dinero a mi papá.

21 ¿Qué debes decir o hacer en las siguientes circunstancias?

Match the circumstances in column A with the most appropriate response in column B.

A	B
1. No comprendes a tu mamá.	A. Pido ayuda.
2. Quieres salir del cuarto.	B. Pido perdón.
3. Necesitas diez dólares para ir al cine.	C. Digo "con permiso".
4. Dices lo que no debes decir a tu papá.	D. Hago una pregunta.
5. Necesitas ayuda con la tarea.	E. Pido prestado el dinero.

22 En nuestra casa....

¿Qué dices o haces en estas situaciones? Sigue el modelo.

Sales para ir al colegio y ves que no tienes dinero.
Pido prestado dinero.

1. Repites lo que no es verdad.
2. Necesitas hacer una pregunta a tu abuelo/a, pero está en su cuarto con la puerta cerrada.
3. Quieres ir a nadar en la piscina de tu primo/a.
4. Vas al cine con tu hermana. Hay un grupo de personas en la puerta y no pueden pasar.
5. No tienes un bolígrafo para escribir una carta a tu amiga. Tu hermana tiene un bolígrafo.

El médico dice que no debo caminar.

Ella pide prestado el teléfono.

¿Qué tienen?

Tengo ganas de correr.
Mario
Tengo sueño.
Raúl
Tengo miedo.
la prima pequeña
Tengo mucha sed.
la abuela
Tengo mucho calor.
También tengo mucho calor.
los tíos
Tengo frío.
el abuelo
Tengo prisa.
Marta
Tengo poca hambre.
Jaime
Tengo mucha hambre.
Julia

23 ¿Qué tienen?

Working with a partner, take turns asking and answering the following questions, according to the preceding illustration.

A: ¿Qué tiene Raúl?
B: Raúl tiene sueño.

1. ¿Qué tiene Mario?
2. ¿Quién tiene mucha hambre?
3. ¿Quiénes tienen mucho calor?
4. ¿Quién tiene mucha sed?
5. ¿Quién tiene frío?
6. ¿Qué tiene Marta?
7. ¿Qué tiene Jaime?
8. ¿Quién tiene miedo?
9. ¿Qué tienes tú?

Repaso rápido

Adjetivos y expresiones con *tener*

The verb *tener* may be combined with a noun *(sustantivo)* to ask about or to express physical or emotional conditions. As you have already learned, any accompanying adjectives must agree with the noun they modify. Thus, masculine adjectives such as *mucho* and *poco* are used with the masculine nouns *miedo, frío, calor* and *sueño,* whereas feminine adjectives such as *mucha* and *poca* accompany the feminine nouns *hambre, prisa* and *sed.*

24 ¿Mucho o poco?

Working with a partner, take turns asking and answering the following questions.

A: ¿Cuánto sueño tienes?
B: Tengo mucho (poco) sueño.

1. ¿Cuánto calor tienes?
2. ¿Cuánta hambre tienes?
3. ¿Cuánto miedo tienes?
4. ¿Cuánta prisa tienes?
5. ¿Cuánta sed tienes?
6. ¿Cuánto frío tienes?
7. ¿De qué tienes muchas ganas?
8. ¿De qué tienes pocas ganas?

25 De vacaciones en Cartagena

Imagine you are going to go on vacation in Cartagena. Use the library or the Internet to investigate tourist attractions in Cartagena. Then working in pairs, tell one another three things you feel like doing during the weekend.

A: El viernes por la noche tengo ganas de ir a bailar a la Ciudad Vieja.
B: El viernes por la noche tengo ganas de visitar el Castillo San Felipe.

Repaso *rápido*

Los verbos regulares

You have recently seen verbs with spelling changes *(e → ie, e → i)*. Earlier you saw many regular verbs. Do you remember which endings to use for them?

hablar		comer		vivir	
habl**o**	habl**amos**	com**o**	com**emos**	viv**o**	viv**imos**
habl**as**	habl**áis**	com**es**	com**éis**	viv**es**	viv**ís**
habl**a**	habl**an**	com**e**	com**en**	viv**e**	viv**en**

26 Una prima vive en la capital

Completa el siguiente párrafo con las formas apropiadas de los verbos indicados.

Me llamo Mónica y soy otra prima de Jorge y Marisol. *1. (vivir)* con mis padres en Santa Fe de Bogotá, la capital de Colombia. Nosotros *2. (tener)* una casa cómoda. Mi cuarto es pequeño pero *3. (preferir)* estudiar allí. El año que viene *4. (querer)* estudiar en la Universidad Javeriana. Mi madre *5. (ser)* colombiana y es una profesora en la universidad. Mi padre es de Newark, New Jersey, pero él también *6. (saber)* español. Entonces, en nuestra casa, nosotros *7. (hablar)* español e inglés. Mis padres *8. (decir)* que yo hablo muy bien el inglés y ahora mis amigos *9. (tener)* ganas de aprender el inglés también. Tengo más familia en Estados Unidos—un hermano, Alejandro, dos tíos, dos tías y cuatro primos. Yo les *10. (escribir)* muchas cartas a ellos. Mi hermano Alejandro *11. (escribir)* muy poco y *12. (deber)* escribir más. Él *13. (pensar)* que no necesito saber de él porque estoy muy lejos, pero no es verdad. *14. (Querer)* a mi hermano.

***Autoevaluación.* As a review and self-check, respond to the following:**

1. How can you greet someone in Spanish when you write a letter?
2. Tell a friend one thing you would like to learn to do in the future.
3. Imagine you are telling a friend about various things that others say. Tell your friend five things that five different people say, including yourself.
4. Describe your house by listing the rooms, floors and location of as many items as you can in Spanish.
5. Imagine that your brother or sister needs to borrow a pen and paper to write a letter. How can you say that they should ask to borrow the items from someone else because you do not have them?
6. How can you politely ask someone to repeat what they say?
7. Say how you feel in the following situations: you have not eaten anything all day, it is very hot and your mouth is dry, you studied all night long for an exam and did not sleep, you are late for school.

¡La práctica hace al maestro!

A Comunicación

¿Cómo es tu cuarto?

Working in groups of three, talk in Spanish about your home. (Make up any details you wish.) Each student must describe his or her home *(tiene una sala grande)*, say why he or she does or does not like the home *(no me gusta porque mi cuarto es pequeño)* and then mention who lives there *(vivo con...)*. Members of the group should try to add any details necessary to complete the description *(comemos en la mesa grande del comedor)*, mentioning any items the person would like to buy for his or her home *(me gustaría comprar...)*. *¡Sean tan creativos como sea posible!* (Be as creative as possible!)

¿Tiene tu casa una sala como esta sala?

B Conexión con la tecnología

Write a short e-mail in Spanish to someone you know about your home and family. Use Jorge's letter as a model, if necessary.

VOCABULARIO

La casa
- el baño
- el cuarto
- la escalera
- el garaje
- el patio
- la piscina
- el piso
- la planta
- la planta baja
- el primer piso
- la sala

¿Vas a la sala a ver televisión?

Para describir
- al lado de
- cada
- cómodo,-a
- cuando
- desde
- donde
- el lado
- pequeño,-a
- poco,-a
- por
- por la noche
- primer

¿Cómo estás?
- el calor
- el frío
- la gana
- el hambre *(f.)*
- el miedo
- la prisa
- ¿Qué *(+ tener)?*
- la sed
- el sueño
- tener (calor, frío, ganas de, hambre, miedo de, prisa, sed, sueño)

Expresiones y otras palabras
- el abrazo
- la carta
- el dibujo
- e
- lo que
- me/te/le/nos/les gustaría
- la mentira
- pedir (perdón, permiso, prestado,-a)
- el permiso
- por teléfono
- querer decir
- u
- la verdad

Verbos
- aprender a
- correr
- decir *(+ que)*
- escribir
- gustaría
- pedir
- repetir

Ella tiene mucha sed.

¿Te gustaría tener una piscina?

a leer

Estrategia

Preparación

Estrategia para leer: ***using graphics to understand a reading***

Before reading a selection, it is helpful to look over any graphics, artwork, photographs and so forth that accompany what you are about to read. These visuals can help you predict the content or main idea of the reading.

Mira el dibujo para contestar las siguientes preguntas como preparación para la lectura.

1. ¿De qué es el dibujo?
2. ¿Cuántos pisos tiene la casa?
3. ¿Qué hay en el centro de la casa?
4. ¿Qué piensas que vas a leer?

La casa ideal de Jorge

Este dibujo es de mi casa ideal. Aquí está la sala, donde está el piano, y en este cuarto yo pienso ver televisión y escribir en la computadora. Pienso que este cuarto va a ser mi cuarto favorito. Al lado de la sala están mi cuarto y el cuarto de mis padres. Yo sé que mis padres prefieren tener un cuarto lejos de la sala, pero en mi casa ideal su cuarto está un poquito más cerca de la sala.

Entro a esta casa por la puerta principal o por la puerta del garaje. Camino por el patio hasta el comedor y al lado está la cocina. Mi madre piensa tener los platos en la cocina, pues a ella no le gusta tener los platos en el comedor. Aquí hay un cuarto grande donde tengo mi gimnasio y ese cuarto que ves al lado es un cuarto de baño.... Ah, y hay una piscina también. Es una casa grande y cómoda. Me gustan las casas cómodas y bonitas, con muchas ventanas.

¿Cómo es tu casa ideal?

A ¿Qué comprendiste?

1. ¿Dónde están el piano y la computadora?
2. ¿Qué cuarto piensa Jorge va a ser su favorito?
3. ¿Qué está al lado de la sala?
4. ¿Por dónde entra Jorge a su casa ideal?
5. ¿Cómo va Jorge al comedor?
6. ¿Qué piensa tener en la cocina la madre de Jorge?
7. ¿Qué cuarto está al lado del gimnasio?
8. ¿Cómo es la casa?

B Charlando

1. ¿Son diferentes la casa ideal de Jorge y tu casa? Explica.
2. ¿Vives ahora en tu casa ideal?
3. ¿Qué cuartos tiene tu casa ideal?
4. ¿Dónde te gustaría vivir? ¿Por qué?

a escribir

Estrategia

Estrategia para escribir: *connecting phrases*

To avoid a choppy writing style, include some of the following transition words to make your sentences flow from one to another: *a causa de* (because of), *como* (since, like, as), *después* (later), *entonces* (then), *pero* (but), *por eso* (therefore), *sin embargo* (however), *también* (also), *y* (and). These words will act as the glue that binds together the ideas in a paragraph as a connected unit.

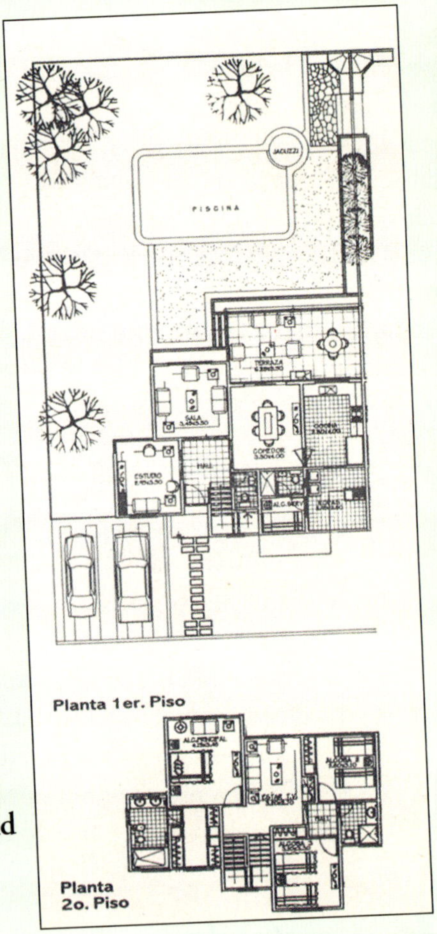

A. Design a basic floor plan of *la casa de mis sueños* and label the rooms and contents in Spanish. Be creative! You may also want to add color and graphics to your floor plan to make your drawing visually appealing.

B. Write one or two paragraphs in Spanish to describe your *casa ideal.* Tell how large the house is, where it is located, the number and type of rooms it has, the number of windows and doors it has, where the rooms are located (i.e., *en la planta baja, al lado de la cocina*) and any other details you wish to include. Be sure to use some transition words to make your sentences flow more smoothly.

La casa de mis sueños está en Cartagena. Como tiene cuatro pisos, es muy grande....

repaso

Now that I have completed this chapter, I can...

- ✓ talk about everyday activities.
- ✓ talk about the future.
- ✓ express opinions.
- ✓ state wishes and preferences.
- ✓ identify items in the kitchen and at the dinner table.
- ✓ express quantity.
- ✓ state location.
- ✓ write a letter.
- ✓ describe a household.
- ✓ express feelings.

¿Prefieres comer en la cocina o en el comedor?

I can also...

- ✓ talk about life in Venezuela and Colombia.
- ✓ discuss typical foods from Venezuela.
- ✓ identify and describe the rooms of my house.
- ✓ recognize words in context to help improve my speaking ability.
- ✓ recognize when to use *pedir* or *preguntar* to ask for something.

¿le gustaría comer arepas?

Los pasatiempos

CAPÍTULO 7

In this chapter you will be able to:

- indicate a length of time
- talk about everyday activities
- offer an invitation
- apologize and make excuses
- discuss pastime activities
- talk about how often something is done
- state what is happening right now
- describe the seasons and weather
- use ordinal numbers

Lección 13

Quiero poner el televisor

MAMÁ: ¡Pepe...! **¿Cuánto tiempo hace que°** ves televisión? Ya es la hora de ***Vidas°*** *nuevas*, mi **telenovela** favorita. Son **casi°** las tres.

JOSÉ: No, **todavía°** no. Tengo unos **minutos.** Son las tres menos nueve y los **equipos** de Argentina y Estados Unidos juegan un partido de fútbol....

MAMÁ: Cuando quiero **poner°** el **televisor** para ver mi **programa** favorito, no **puedo.**

JOSÉ: Mamá, salgo a las cuatro **después del°** partido y **esta noche** no voy a **volver°** hasta las nueve. ¿No **recuerdas°** que el mes que viene es mi cumpleaños? Los televisores no **cuestan** mucho dinero. Me puedes **dar°** uno, ¿no? ¡Ja, ja, ja!

¿Cuánto tiempo hace que...? *How long have you been...?* **Vidas** *Lives* **casi** *almost* **todavía** *yet* **poner** *to turn on* **después del** *after* **volver** *to return* **recuerdas** *you remember* **dar** *give*

Conexión cultural

¡Gol! ¡Qué buen partido de fútbol!

El fútbol is a very popular sport in Argentina and in most other Spanish-speaking countries. It is one of the most preferred pastimes for people of all ages: nearly everyone has *la fiebre del gol* (goal fever).

1 ¿Qué comprendiste?

1. ¿Cómo llama la madre a José?
2. ¿Qué programa ve José?
3. ¿Qué equipos juegan en el partido de fútbol?
4. ¿Qué quiere ver la madre? ¿Cómo se llama el programa?
5. ¿A qué hora empieza la telenovela?
6. ¿Qué quiere José para su cumpleaños?

2 Charlando

1. ¿Te gusta ver televisión?
2. ¿Te gusta ver telenovelas? ¿Cuáles?
3. ¿Cuántos programas de televisión ves en un día?
4. ¿Cuántos televisores hay en tu casa? ¿Dónde están?
5. ¿Qué vas a hacer esta noche?

Conexión cultural

Un gaucho en Las Pampas.

La Argentina

Argentina is the largest Spanish-speaking country in the world. The country occupies an area about one-third the size of the United States and extends from the frigid regions near the South Pole to the northern tropical regions of the central part of South America.

The southern plains of Patagonia are the center of the sheep-raising industry. In the central plains, *las pampas,* there are large cattle ranches *(estancias)* where cowboys known as *gauchos* tend the herds of cattle. Argentina produces beef that is sold and shipped throughout the world.

The country also offers many beautiful lakes and forests. The plentiful national parks and ski resorts, such as Bariloche, are popular with tourists throughout the world. In addition, some of the finest beaches in the world are located along Argentina's extensive coastline.

Buenos Aires es la capital de Argentina.

The capital, Buenos Aires, is located on the shores of the *Río de la Plata* estuary (the point where the tide meets a river current). This modern city combines skyscrapers *(rascacielos),* lovely plazas and parks, excellent food and interesting old buildings into what is often called the "Paris of the Spanish-speaking world." The population blends just about every ethnic and racial group imaginable and includes large populations from Germany, Italy, Great Britain, Poland and numerous other countries.

Argentina is fascinating for its variety. In cosmopolitan Buenos Aires, you may dance the tango in the colorful neighborhood called *La Boca,* or you may be invited to sip a wonderful tea-like hot drink called *mate.* You may find yourself alone at the top of a mountain (Aconcagua), skiing the famous slopes of the Andes, viewing the breathtaking Iguazú waterfalls or walking along the streets of the largest Spanish-speaking city south of the equator (Buenos Aires). You also may join the Argentine people in the enjoyment of their national sport—*el fútbol.*

¿Verdad o Falso?

1. La Argentina es el país más grande de gente de habla hispana.
2. Los gauchos viven en las estancias de las pampas.
3. A los turistas no les gusta pasar tiempo en los parques nacionales.
4. Bariloche es "El París del mundo hispano."
5. El baile famoso de la Argentina es el tango.
6. *Mate* es un programa famoso de la televisión en la Argentina.
7. El deporte nacional de la Argentina es el fútbol.

Argentina en Sudamérica

CONEXIONES 3

Cruzando fronteras

Create a map of Argentina, its surrounding countries and bodies of water. Locate and label as many of the geographical features mentioned in the *Conexión cultural* as you can.

IDIOMA

El presente de los verbos con el cambio *o → ue* y *u → ue*

As you have already learned, some verbs may require a change from *e → ie* or *e → i* in all forms of their present-tense stem except for *nosotros* and *vosotros.* Similarly, some verbs require the change *o → ue* *(poder)* or *u → ue (jugar)* in all forms of their present-tense stem except for *nosotros* and *vosotros.* These stem changes do not interfere with regular verb endings.

poder	
puedo	podemos
puedes	podéis
puede	**pue**den

jugar	
juego	jugamos
juegas	jugáis
juega	**jue**gan

Mi equipo favorito ***juega*** *al fútbol mañana a las tres.*
Yo no ***puedo*** *ir, pero voy a ver el partido en la televisión.*

Other *o → ue* stem-changing verbs include *costar (ue), recordar (ue)* and *volver (ue).*

¿Cuánto ***cuesta*** *un televisor nuevo?*
Recuerda *poner el televisor a las tres.*
David y Rosa ***vuelven*** *a casa para ver su programa favorito.*

¿Puedes jugar al tenis?

¿Recuerdas cómo bailar el tango?

4 Las actividades preferidas

Completa las siguientes oraciones con la forma apropiada de los verbos.

1. A Mónica no le gusta la televisión. Ella *(jugar)* al tenis con sus amigos.
2. Enrique *(poder)* ver televisión todas las tardes.
3. Ella todavía no *(tener)* un televisor nuevo.
4. Roberto va a una tienda donde los televisores no *(costar)* mucho.
5. Mario y yo no *(jugar)* al tenis, nosotros preferimos jugar al fútbol.
6. Gloria *(pensar)* que el fútbol es divertido.
7. Sonia y Rocío no *(volver)* a jugar partidos de fútbol.
8. Nosotros *(poder)* jugar otro deporte.
9. ¿Qué *(poder)* jugar yo?

5 ¿Puedes?

Working with a partner, take turns inviting one another to do various activities. You may refuse or accept each invitation, giving an excuse if you refuse or changing the suggested time if you accept.

jugar al fútbol

A: ¿Puedes jugar al fútbol hoy?

B: Lo siento, pero no puedo. Tengo prisa. Son casi las nueve.

B: No puedo hoy, pero puedo jugar después de las clases mañana.

1. venir a comer con nosotros a las 6:30
2. jugar al tenis el domingo
3. ir al cine pasado mañana
4. leer la carta de tu amigo más tarde
5. hablar por teléfono con mi prima el sábado
6. ver mis fotos de Argentina y Chile ahora

¿Puedes ir al cine hoy?

Los pasatiempos

A. jugar al ajedrez

B. jugar a las damas

C. jugar al básquetbol

D. jugar a las cartas

E. jugar al fútbol americano

F. jugar al volibol

G. jugar a las maquinitas

H. dibujar

I. hacer aeróbicos

J. leer el periódico

6 ¿Quién juega?

Tell what the following people are doing, according to the letter that corresponds to the preceding illustrations.

Uds. (D)
Uds. juegan a las cartas.

1. ellos (B)
2. esas chicas (F)
3. ella (I)
4. Inés y David (A)
5. ella (C)
6. esos chicos (E)
7. tú (J)
8. ese chico (G)
9. Julio (H)

¿Te gusta jugar a las damas?

Conexión Cultural

Damas y caballeros

The games *ajedrez* (chess) and *damas* (checkers) are two of the world's oldest pastimes. Perhaps you have enjoyed playing one or both of these games yourself. Do not be confused, however, when you see the word *Damas* (Ladies) on the door of a public restroom not very far from another door labeled *Caballeros* (Gentlemen). Remember what you have learned: The meaning of any word may vary according to the context in which the word is used.

¿Damas o caballeros?

7 Los pasatiempos

Working in groups of four, prepare a brief summary of activities that members of your group do. First, pair up with one person in the group and find out which activities shown in the illustration *Los pasatiempos* your partner does. Next, find out another of your partner's pastimes that was not shown in the illustration. Then return to your group and report what you found out about your partner, taking notes as your classmates report their findings. Finally, one person from your group reports the information to the entire class.

A: ¿Juegas a las damas?
B: Sí, (No, no) juego a las damas. ¿Y tú?

8 ¿A qué hora vuelven?

Working with a partner, take turns asking and telling in Spanish when these people will be returning from various places (i.e., *el partido, el cine, la casa de un amigo o una amiga*). Use a different place and time for each sentence.

A: ¿A qué hora vuelve José del partido de fútbol americano?
B: José vuelve a las nueve y media.

José

1. Catalina

2. Ana y Pedro

3. Uds.

4. tú y yo

5. ellas

6. tú

9 Quiero comprar un televisor

Completa el siguiente párrafo con la forma apropiada de uno de los siguientes verbos: *poder, costar, jugar, preferir, recordar, ver.*

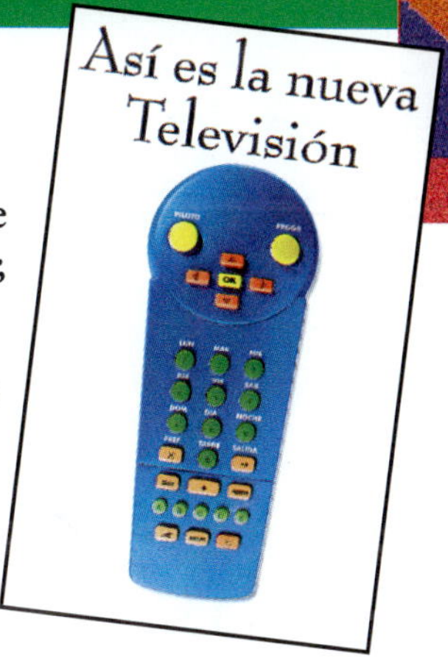

Me gustaría (1) comprar un televisor inmenso, uno de esos televisores que ocupan toda una pared. Yo no (2) tener ese televisor todavía porque (3) mucho dinero y porque mi casa no es grande. A mí me gusta (4) los programas de deportes. A mi padre le gustaría tener un televisor grande cuando (5) los Piratas de Pittsburgh, su equipo favorito. Pero también (6) que a mi hermana le gusta ver las telenovelas. A mí no me gustan las telenovelas y en ese momento (7) ir al cine o estar con mis amigos, especialmente si (8) al béisbol.

El tiempo libre

10 ¿Qué comprendiste?

1. ¿Cuántas horas hay en un día?
2. ¿Cuántos cuartos de hora hay en una hora?
3. ¿Cuántos segundos hay en un minuto?
4. ¿Cuántas semanas hay en un año?
5. ¿Cuántos años hay en un siglo?

11 Charlando

1. ¿Por cuánto tiempo hablas español en la clase de español? ¿Y en un día? ¿Y en una semana?
2. ¿Por cuánto tiempo ves televisión en una semana? ¿Qué programas ves?
3. ¿Por cuánto tiempo juegas a los deportes en una semana? ¿Cuáles? ¿Con quién?
4. ¿Cuánto tiempo libre tienes en una semana? ¿Qué haces?

Algo más

Expresiones con *hace*

To describe an action that began in the past and has continued into the present, use ***hace* + a time expression + *que* + the present tense of a verb.**

Hace cinco minutos que veo televisión.	I have been watching television for five minutes. (Five minutes ago I started watching television.)

Reverse the order of *hace* and the time expression if a form of *¿cuánto?* introduces the question.

¿Cuánto tiempo hace que ves televisión?	How long have you been watching television?

Look at the following:

¿Cuánto tiempo hace que no juegas al volibol?
Hace mucho tiempo que no juego.
¿Cuánto hace?
Hace un año, más o menos.

¿Cuánto tiempo hace que juegas al volibol?

12 ¿Hace mucho tiempo?

Tell how long the following activities have been taking place.

jugamos al volibol/un año
Hace un año que jugamos al volibol.

1. papá lee el periódico/media hora
2. jugamos al ajedrez/treinta segundos
3. mi sobrina dibuja una casa/un cuarto de hora
4. Uds. juegan a las maquinitas/veinte minutos
5. vivo aquí/quince años
6. haces aeróbicos/una hora
7. juegan al béisbol en los Estados Unidos/más de un siglo

13 ¿Cuánto tiempo hace?

With a partner, take turns asking and answering the following questions. Then summarize your partner's answers for each question.

A: ¿Juegas al básquetbol?
B: Sí, juego al básquetbol.
A: *(Write:* **B** juega al básquetbol.*)*

1. ¿Sabes jugar al ajedrez o a las damas?
2. ¿Cuánto tiempo hace que no juegas al ajedrez? ¿Y a las damas?
3. ¿Lees muchas revistas?
4. ¿Cuánto tiempo hace que no lees una revista?
5. ¿Sabes dibujar?
6. ¿Cuánto tiempo hace que no haces un dibujo? ¿Y un mapa?
7. ¿Te gusta ver televisión? ¿Te gustan las telenovelas?
8. ¿Cuánto tiempo hace que no ves una telenovela?
9. ¿Cuánto tiempo hace que no escribes una carta?
10. ¿Cuánto tiempo hace que estudias español?

14 Hacer una entrevista

Prepare five or six questions similar to the questions in the preceding activity. Then working with a partner, take turns interviewing one another about your pastimes.

¿Cuánto tiempo hace que no vas a un concierto?

Algo más

Para hablar del tiempo

¿Cuándo?
ayer, hoy y mañana
mañana (por la mañana/
por la tarde/por la noche)
a las siete de la noche (7:00 P.M.)
esta (mañana/tarde/noche)
la semana que viene
los lunes
en mayo
todavía no
ya fue

¿Cuánto?
a veces
muchas veces
dos veces (a la semana)
una vez (al día)
todos los días
(casi) nunca
(casi) siempre

15 ¿Qué haces tú?

Contesta las siguientes preguntas en español.

1. ¿Cuándo ves televisión?
2. ¿Cuándo juegas al béisbol?
3. ¿Cuántas veces a la semana tienes tarea?
4. ¿Cuántas veces al año juegas a las cartas?
5. ¿Cuántas veces al mes lees el periódico?
6. ¿Cuántas veces al año juegas a las damas?
7. ¿Cuándo dibujas?
8. ¿Cuándo recuerdas el cumpleaños de tu madre o tu padre?

16 ¿Y tú?

Working with a partner, take turns asking and answering five questions from the preceding activity. You may also create your own questions if you wish.

A: ¿Cuándo vas al cine?
B: Voy al cine esta noche.

B: ¿Cuántas veces al mes vas al cine?
A: Voy al cine dos veces al mes.

Alquilamos una película

PILAR: José, ¿estás **durmiendo?**°
JOSÉ: No, estoy **viendo** el partido de fútbol de mis equipos favoritos, Boca e Independiente. ¿Por qué?
PILAR: Porque quiero ir a **alquilar**° una película. ¿Quieres venir?
JOSÉ: **¿Ahora mismo?**° ¿Me **permites** unos minutos? Este partido termina pronto y podemos ir después.

PILAR: De acuerdo. **Antes de** salir, debes **apagar**° el televisor. El **control remoto** está sobre la mesa.
JOSÉ: Sí, claro.
PILAR: Aquí tengo una **lista** de las películas nuevas. La voy a **poner**° en mi mochila. No quiero ver las **mismas**° películas del mes pasado.
JOSÉ: Muy bien. ¡Qué **estupendo**° partido!

durmiendo *sleeping* **alquilar** *to rent* **Ahora mismo** *Right now* **apagar** *turn off* **poner** *to put* **mismas** *same* **estupendo** *wonderful*

17 ¿Qué comprendiste?

1. ¿Está José durmiendo?
2. ¿Qué quiere Pilar?
3. ¿Puede José ir ahora mismo? ¿Por qué?
4. ¿Qué debe hacer José antes de salir?
5. ¿Quién tiene una lista de las películas nuevas? ¿Por qué la tiene?
6. ¿Dónde la va a poner?

18 Charlando

1. ¿Ves televisión cuando vas a dormir?
2. ¿Tus padres te permiten alquilar películas de video?
3. ¿Dónde alquilas tú películas de video?
4. ¿Cuántas veces a la semana alquilas una película de video?
5. ¿Alquilas películas musicales? Explica.
6. ¿Alquilas la misma película más de una vez?

PELICULAS

IDIOMA

El presente progresivo

To describe something that is occurring right now it is helpful to know how to form the *presente progresivo,* which consists of the present tense of *estar* plus a present participle *(gerundio).* Review the present tense of *estar* and learn how to form present participles in order to use this verb tense.

*¿Qué **están haciendo** Uds.?*
*Pues, Laura **está dibujando,** Jaime **está viendo** televisión y yo **estoy saliendo.***

What **are** (all of) you **doing?**
Well, Laura **is drawing,** Jaime **is watching** television and I **am leaving.**

Form the present participle of most verbs in Spanish by changing the infinitive endings *(-ar, -er, -ir)* to *-ando* for an *-ar* verb or to *-iendo* for an *-er* or an *-ir* verb.

-ar	*-er*	*-ir*
alquilar → alquilando	*comer → comiendo*	*cumplir → cumpliendo*
apagar → apagando	*hacer → haciendo*	*salir → saliendo*
jugar → jugando	*poner → poniendo*	*vivir → viviendo*

¡Algo grande está pasando!

19 ¿Qué están haciendo ahora?

Tell what the following people are doing right now, using the *presente progresivo* and the provided cues.

nosotros/ver un partido
Nosotros estamos viendo un partido ahora.

1. Luis/alquilar una película estupenda de Argentina
2. mi padre y mi madre/salir de casa
3. Lucila/poner el televisor
4. Uds./apagar la luz de la cocina
5. mi hermano/buscar/el control remoto
6. tú/pensar en tus pasatiempos
7. yo/?

Estamos saliendo en moto.

20 Pasando el tiempo en un café

Imagine you are passing time at an outdoor café in Buenos Aires. Describe what you see from your table, using the *presente progresivo.*

el chico/mirar a sus padres
El chico está mirando a sus padres.

1. un señor/poner una mesa
2. los dos chicos/no/hablar
3. una chica/escribir una carta
4. la otra chica/dibujar
5. un muchacho/hablar por teléfono
6. unos hombres/jugar al ajedrez
7. un padre y una madre/comer con sus hijos
8. tú/salir

21 ¿Qué estás haciendo?

What would you most likely be doing right now if you were in the places mentioned in the sentences that follow?

Estoy comiendo en un restaurante.

1. Estoy (1) televisión con mi familia en la sala de mi casa.
2. Estoy (2) una pregunta en la clase de español.
3. Estoy en una fiesta en mi casa porque estoy (3) años.
4. Estoy en la tienda de videos porque estoy (4) una película estupenda.
5. Estoy (5) tango en Buenos Aires, Argentina.

Están bailando tango en Buenos Aires, Argentina.

IDIOMA

Los gerundios con irregularidades

Some verbs that have a stem change in the present tense require a different stem change in the present participle. This second change is shown in parentheses after infinitives in this book. Three verbs that follow this pattern are *dormir (ue, **u**)*, *preferir (ie, **i**)* and *sentir (ie, **i**)*.

verbo	*presente*	*gerundio*
dormir (**ue, u**)	d**ue**rmo	d**u**rmiendo
preferir (**ie, i**)	pref**ie**ren	pref**i**riendo
sentir (**ie, i**)	s**ie**nto	s**i**ntiendo
but:		
pensar (**ie**)	p**ie**nsas	pensando
volver (**ue**)	v**ue**lven	volviendo

Elisa está leyendo un libro.

Some verbs in Spanish have minor irregularities in their present participles. For example, the *i* in *-iendo* changes to *y* after most verb stems that end in a vowel and for the verb *ir*: *leer* (stem: *le*) ➔ *leyendo*; *oír* (stem: *o*) ➔ *oyendo*; *ir* ➔ *yendo*. The present participle for the irregular verb *venir* requires a change in the stem from *e* to *i*: *venir* ➔ *viniendo*. Finally, the present participle for *poder* involves a stem change from *o* to *u*: *pudiendo*.

¿Qué estás pensando?

22 Estoy....

Working with a partner, take turns asking and answering what you are doing right now, according to the illustrations.

A: ¿Qué estás haciendo?
B: Estoy jugando al fútbol.

1.

2.

3.

4.

5.

23 ¿Qué están haciendo?

Working with a partner, use the following cues and take turns trying to reach various people on the phone.

Javier/correr en el parque
A: Hola. ¿Puedo hablar con Javier, por favor?
B: Lo siento. Javier está corriendo en el parque ahora mismo.

1. Eva/oír la radio
2. Ud. o su hija/salir
3. María/dormir
4. tu padre y tu madre/ir de compras
5. tu hermano/jugar a las cartas en la casa de su abuela
6. Ud./hablar por el otro teléfono

Repaso *rápido*

El complemento directo

You have already learned to use direct objects in Spanish to show the person or thing in a sentence that receives the action of the verb. Do you remember the direct object pronouns?

me	*me*	**nos**	*us*
te	*you* (tú)	**os**	*you* (vosotros,-as)
lo	*him, it, you* (Ud.)	**los**	*them, you* (Uds.)
la	*her, it, you* (Ud.)	**las**	*them, you* (Uds.)

*No **la** veo.* — I do not see **her.** / I do not see **it.** *(la lista de las películas nuevas)*

*Nunca **lo** veo.* — I never see **him.** / I never see **it.** *(el programa)*

24 ¿Qué hacen ahora mismo?

Tell what the following people are doing right now, using direct object pronouns.

1. Pilar/buscar/el control remoto
2. nosotros/leer/un libro sobre Buenos Aires ahora
3. Uds./escribir/la lista de películas nuevas
4. la señora Fernández/empezar/un viaje a Venezuela
5. yo/oír/la radio ahora

Algo más

Más sobre los pronombres de complemento directo

As you have seen, direct object pronouns usually precede conjugated verbs. However, you have some freedom to choose where to place object pronouns. Sometimes direct object pronouns are attached to the end of an infinitive.

__La__ voy a terminar.
Voy a terminar__la__. — I am going to finish **it.** *(la tarea)*

Similarly, it is possible to attach an object pronoun to the end of a present participle. However, it is then necessary to add an accent mark to the present participle in order to maintain the original pronunciation of the present participle without the pronoun.

__Lo__ estamos leyendo.
Estamos leyéndo__lo__. — We are reading **it.** *(el periódico)*

Estamos leyéndolo.

25 ¿Están haciéndolo?

Imagine you and your friend are watching television and commenting on various characters and programs. Working in pairs, take turns asking and answering questions using the provided cues. Follow the model, attaching direct object pronouns to the verbs in each sentence.

mi equipo favorito/jugar un partido importante

A: ¿Está jugando mi equipo favorito un partido importante?

B: Sí, está jugándolo.

1. el cantante/cantar una canción de amor
2. Mónica/dibujar un mapa en la servilleta
3. los hermanos/leer el diario de la hermana
4. Julia/oír la radio
5. nosotros/ver esta telenovela
6. tú/buscar el programa

Ella está cantando una canción de amor.

Están viéndola.

26 Una vez más

Redo activity 25, attaching the direct object pronouns to the end of the present participle. Make any other appropriate changes.

PARA ti

Comparando el inglés con el español

You have learned to combine the present tense of *estar* with a present participle *(gerundio)* of a verb in Spanish to describe what is going on right now. This verb form is comparable to the *-ing* form of a verb in English. Notice, however, that words ending in *-ing* in English may require an infinitive in Spanish if the English word functions as a noun instead of a verb. Compare the following:

*Me gusta **jugar** al volibol.*	I like **playing** volleyball. *(noun)*
***Nadar** es divertido.*	**Swimming** is fun. *(noun)*

but:

*Estoy **jugando** al volibol.*	I am **playing** volleyball. *(verb)*
*¿Estás **nadando?***	Are you **swimming?** *(verb)*

¿A quién le gusta jugar al volibol?

¿Estás nadando?

27 Mis pasatiempos favoritos

Prepare a list of at least eight pastimes in Spanish *(jugar al ajedrez, jugar al básquetbol).* Then ask five people to rank the pastimes, with *1* being their favorite and *8* being their least favorite activity. Prepare a written summary of your findings. Follow the model.

¿Qué pasatiempos de mi lista son tus favoritos, en una escala de uno a ocho?

1. **Me gusta oír música.** 1 (2) 3 4 5 6 7 8
2. **Me gusta leer el periódico.** 1 2 3 4 5 6 (7) 8

A Miguel Indurain le gusta montar en bicicleta.

Mi pasatiempo favorito es jugar al béisbol.

28 ¿Qué están haciendo?

Mira a cuatro o cinco personas desde donde tú estás ahora. ¿Qué están haciendo?

Dos estudiantes están hablando con el profesor.

Autoevaluación. **As a review and self-check, respond to the following:**

1. Imagine that several friends have invited you to a soccer game. How would you tell your friends that you are unable to go tonight because you have to play volleyball with your team?
2. Name two of your favorite pastimes.
3. How long have you been studying Spanish?
4. Ask some friends how long they have done their favorite pastime.
5. Say five things people around you are doing right now.
6. A classmate asks if you have your Spanish book. Respond by saying that you are looking for it.
7. Name two or three interesting facts that you know about Argentina.

¡La práctica hace al maestro!

A Comunicación

Write the names in Spanish of at least five or six of your favorite pastimes. Next to the list, add columns telling where you participate in the activity, how long you have done the activity and with whom you do the activity. Then, working with a partner, take turns asking and answering questions about each other's pastimes.

A: ¿Cuál es tu pasatiempo favorito?
B: Mi pasatiempo favorito es jugar al volibol.
A: ¿Dónde juegas al volibol?
B: Juego en la playa.
A: ¿Cuánto tiempo hace que tienes este pasatiempo?
B: Hace dos años que tengo este pasatiempo.

B Conexión con la tecnología

Write an e-mail message in Spanish to a key pal describing what you are doing right now. Tell about some of your favorite pastimes (i.e., sports, extracurricular activities) and ask what activities are popular among teenagers in your key pal's school, community or country.

¿Cuál es tu pasatiempo favorito?

VOCABULARIO

Estrategia

Para aprender mejor: *learning vocabulary*

In Spanish, the gender (whether a word is masculine or feminine) of some words must be learned because you will not always know which article to use just by looking at the word. For example, some words are masculine and are used with a masculine article even though they end in *-a: el día, el mapa, el problema, el programa.* Other words may be used with the masculine article *el* although the words are actually feminine: *el agua.* In addition, some words that end in *-a* are used with a masculine article when they refer to a male, but they are used with a feminine article when they refer to a female: *el artista/la artista, el dentista/la dentista, el pianista/la pianista, el turista/la turista.*

Pasatiempos

los aeróbicos
el ajedrez
el básquetbol
las cartas
las damas
el equipo
el fútbol americano
hacer aeróbicos
la maquinita
el pasatiempo
el programa
la telenovela
el volibol

Expresiones de tiempo

ahora mismo
antes de
¿Cuánto *(+ time expression)* hace que *(+ present tense of verb)*...?
después de
esta noche
hace *(+ time expression)* que
el minuto
mismo
(number +) vez/veces al/a la *(time expression)*
por la (mañana, tarde, noche)
el segundo
el siglo
todavía

Verbos

alquilar
apagar
costar (ue)
dar
dibujar
dormir (ue, u)
jugar (ue)
permitir
poder (ue, u)
poner
recordar (ue)
volver (ue)

Expresiones y otras palabras

americano,-a
casi
el control remoto
estupendo,-a
la lista
mismo,-a
remoto,-a
el televisor
la vida

Mi pasatiempo favorito es nadar.

Lección 14

¿Cómo son las estaciones en Chile?

Contexto cultural
CHILE

Me gusta ir a Viña del Mar en la **primavera,** en octubre o noviembre, porque puedo salir a patinar o a **dar un paseo por** la playa. También me gusta mucho montar en bicicleta y casi siempre soy la primera de las muchachas cuando hay **competencias.** Es mi **estación**° favorita y hay muchas **flores por todos lados.**°

estación *season* **por todos lados** *everywhere*

En el verano, a mi familia le gusta ir a Arica para nadar porque allí casi nunca **llueve.** Siempre **hace sol.** Voy casi todos los años en febrero al Festival Internacional de la Canción en Viña del Mar. Si no puedo ir, **pongo** el televisor y lo veo en la sala de mi casa.

El **otoño** es mi estación favorita porque en mayo **no hace mucho calor. En cambio°** mis padres prefieren la primavera, cuando tampoco hace mucho calor. En el otoño mi hermano y yo podemos jugar al fútbol y al tenis, pero también tenemos otros pasatiempos.

En cambio *On the other hand*

Esquiar es mi deporte favorito. En el **invierno** siempre puedo ir a esquiar o a **patinar sobre hielo.** Bueno, casi siempre. A veces **hace frío** o **nieva** mucho. Mi familia y yo vivimos en Santiago, la **capital.** Los fines de semana nos gusta ir a Farellones. Este **lugar°** está a una hora más o menos de la capital. En agosto vamos a Portillo, que está más lejos. ¡Es un lugar **excelente** para esquiar!

lugar *place*

1 ¿Qué comprendiste?

1. ¿En qué estación están en octubre y noviembre en Chile?
2. ¿Por dónde le gusta a la chica dar un paseo en la primavera?
3. ¿En qué estación están en mayo en Chile?
4. ¿Cómo es Chile en mayo?
5. ¿En qué estación del año nieva?
6. ¿Qué le gusta hacer a la chica en el invierno?
7. ¿Qué lugar es excelente para esquiar?

Conexión cultural

¿Puedes esquiar en verano?

In the Southern Hemisphere the seasons are the reverse of the seasons in the Northern Hemisphere. For this reason, people snow ski in Chile from June to August because it is winter there. Similarly, the summer months in Chile are December, January and February.

Puedo esquiar en junio en Chile.

2 Charlando

1. ¿Cuál es tu estación favorita? ¿Por qué?
2. ¿Hace frío o calor en tu ciudad? Explica.
3. ¿Te gusta hacer un deporte? ¿Cuál? ¿Cuándo?
4. ¿Te gusta esquiar o patinar en el invierno? ¿Dónde?
5. ¿Te gustaría dar un paseo? ¿Adónde?

Nos gusta esquiar. (Chile)

Chile es...

... **D**esierto de cuyas entrañas surgen ricos depósitos de cobre y nitrato entremezclados con oasis de generoso verdor. En la zona norte del país, el Desierto de Atacama se extiende por más de 1.000 kilómetros, donde podrá explorar un mundo antiguo y misterioso que la arqueología moderna sólo comienza a descubrir.

... **N**ieve que invita a practicar el ski desde junio a diciembre en los numerosos centros invernales con que cuenta el país.

Conexión cultural

Chile

Chile is a long, narrow country located along the western coast of South America between the Andes Mountains (which serve as a border with Argentina) and the Pacific Ocean. It has an extensive seacoast that stretches from Peru all the way to Punta Arenas, the southernmost city in the world.

Many interesting islands also are part of Chile: the *Juan Fernández Islands,* where Robinson Crusoe lived for over four years; and Easter Island *(Isla de Pascua),* which is an island with a mysterious past and which is inhabited by people of Polynesian ancestry.

Chile is a Spanish-speaking country with approximately fourteen million people of mostly European descent. It is common to meet people with Italian, English or Irish ancestry, or to see names of streets or places that are obviously not of Spanish origin. For example, the southern city of Puerto Montt was for many years a German colony and the first liberator and ruler of Chile was named Bernardo O'Higgins.

The country has a prosperous economy and is a leading industrial nation in South America. Most of the citizens live in urban areas like the capital, Santiago, and are well educated. Chileans also have a strong literary tradition and are proud of their two Nobel prize-winning poets, Gabriela Mistral and Pablo Neruda.

Chile may seem to be a long distance from where you are reading this now. However, transportation today allows a traveler from the United States to reach most places in Chile in less than one day. Once there, you will discover a country of magnificent contrasts offering everything from snowy mountains to arid desert land and everything in between. In Chile visitors can experience a country lifestyle, or visit large, cosmopolitan cities like the capital, Santiago, which has skyscrapers *(rascacielos)* and the latest in modern-day conveniences, but which also faces many of the same problems as other urban areas throughout the world, such as air pollution *(contaminación ambiental).* Within short distances of Santiago, ski resorts like Portillo or Farellones in the Andes Mountains and resort beaches near Viña del Mar offer an escape from the pressures of modern life.

¿Te gustaría visitar la capital de Chile?

Isla de Pascua, Chile.

3 Chile

Answer the following questions about Chile. There may be some words that you do not know.

1. ¿Dónde está Chile?
2. ¿Cuál es la capital de Chile?
3. ¿Cuáles islas son de Chile?
4. ¿Cuál es la ciudad que está más al sur en Chile?
5. ¿Cómo se llaman los dos poetas chilenos que tienen premios Nobel?
6. ¿Qué tipo de edificios hay en la capital?
7. ¿Adónde puede ir uno a esquiar en Chile?
8. ¿Hace calor o frío ahora en Chile?

Los Andes están muy cerca de Santiago.

Chile Aventura

IDIOMA

El presente de los verbos *dar* y *poner*

You have already seen some verbs in Spanish that are regular in the present tense except for the *yo* form of the verbs: *hacer (yo hago), saber (yo sé), ver (yo veo), salir (yo salgo).* The verbs *dar* and *poner* also have irregular present-tense *yo* forms. In addition, the verb *dar* has an irregular *vosotros,-as* form.

dar	
doy	damos
das	**dais**
da	dan

poner	
pongo	ponemos
pones	ponéis
pone	ponen

4 ¿Qué haces en el invierno?

Contesta las siguientes preguntas con la forma apropiada de los verbos indicados.

1. ¿Sales a patinar sobre hielo en el invierno?
   Sí, (1) todos los fines de semana a patinar sobre hielo. (salir)
2. ¿Qué haces cuando hace frío o nieva?
   (2) el televisor. (poner)
3. ¿Qué programa pones?
   (3) mi telenovela favorita. (poner)
4. ¿Por qué no das un paseo con nosotros?
   No (4) un paseo con Uds. porque hace mucho frío. (dar)
5. ¿Sabes que hay lugares excelentes para esquiar cerca de aquí?
   Sí, ya lo (5). (saber)
6. ¿Qué más haces en el invierno?
   (6) la tarea por la noche. (hacer)
7. ¿Ves televisión después de hacer la tarea?
   Sí, a veces (7) televisión después de hacer la tarea. (ver)

5 En la primavera

Completa el párrafo con las siguientes palabras: *alquilar, apago, cuesta, ponemos, pongo, doy, salgo, ver.*

Es primavera. Estoy en casa con mi hermana y nosotros (1) el televisor. Hoy no está lloviendo y en media hora (2) un paseo con mi amiga, Paloma. Me gustaría (3) una película, pero (4) dinero. Quiero (5) una película cómica en la televisión, pero no hay. Ahora están las telenovelas. ¿Qué hago? ¿(6) el televisor y (7) la radio? Yo no sé qué hacer. (8) a caminar ahora con Paloma.

Una carta electrónica

ELENA: Carmen, ¿qué haces?
CARMEN: Escribo una carta por correo electrónico que quiero **enviar**° a Chile.
ELENA: **¿Todavía**° **continúas** con esa carta para Ricardo?
CARMEN: Voy a **copiar** su dirección en mi cuaderno y estoy **lista.**°
ELENA: De acuerdo. Vamos.
CARMEN: Estoy apagando la computadora ahora mismo.

enviar *to send* **Todavía** *Still* **lista** *ready*

6 Amigos por correspondencia

Contesta las siguientes preguntas en español.

1. ¿Qué va a hacer Ricardo?
2. ¿Por qué todavía no puede esquiar Carmen?
3. ¿Qué envía Carmen a Ricardo?
4. ¿Adónde va a enviar la carta?
5. ¿Qué tiene que hacer Carmen para estar lista y salir?
6. ¿Te gusta enviar cartas por correo electrónico? ¿A quiénes?
7. ¿Copias las direcciones de correo electrónico de tus amigos? ¿Y los números de teléfono?

Ellos esquían en Chile. ¿Y tú?

Algo más

¿Dónde pongo un acento?

Some verbs that end in *-uar* or *-iar* (*esquiar, enviar* and *continuar,* for example) require a written accent mark to indicate that a vowel should be stressed for all present-tense forms except for *nosotros.* You will have to learn which verbs follow this pattern since some verbs that end in *-uar* or *-iar* may not (such as the verb *copiar*).

esquiar: esqu**í**o, esqu**í**as, esqu**í**a, esquiamos, esquiáis, esqu**í**an
enviar: env**í**o, env**í**as, env**í**a, enviamos, enviáis, env**í**an
continuar: contin**ú**o, contin**ú**as, contin**ú**a, continuamos, continuáis, contin**ú**an

but:

copiar: copio, copias, copia, copiamos, copiáis, copian

7 ¿Qué hacen estas personas?

Working with a partner, take turns asking and answering what these people are doing. Follow the model.

Miguel/esquiar en Portillo
A: ¿Qué hace Miguel?
B: Esquía en Portillo.

1. Laura/patinar en el parque
2. las chicas/dar un paseo en la playa
3. nosotros/esquiar de noche
4. Diego y Gloria/continuar en la competencia
5. tú/esquiar en Farellones
6. Andrés/salir a jugar al fútbol
7. yo/continuar esta actividad
8. Ramón y Daniel/enviar cartas a la familia
9. Javier/poner el televisor
10. Claudia/copiar el número de teléfono

¿Qué tiempo hace?

8 ¿Qué comprendiste?

1. ¿En qué estación hace frío?
2. ¿En qué mes llueve mucho?
3. ¿Cuándo hace mucho calor?
4. Cuando va a llover, ¿cómo está?
5. ¿Qué tiempo hace en primavera? ¿Y en verano? ¿Y en otoño? ¿Y en invierno?
6. ¿En qué meses hace frío en Chile?
7. ¿Qué deportes juegan en la primavera donde tú vives? ¿Y en el verano? ¿Y en el otoño? ¿Y en el invierno?

Conexión cultural

¿Qué temperatura hace?

In the United States you may be accustomed to using degrees Fahrenheit *(grados Fahrenheit)* to talk about the weather, whereas in many places throughout the Spanish-speaking world the temperature is given in degrees centigrade *(grados centígrados)*. Therefore, learning to ask for and understand the temperature in Spanish implies you must learn to understand more than just the words that state the temperature. You must be able to use degrees centigrade. For example, the temperature at which water freezes is 0° in degrees centigrade and 32° in degrees Fahrenheit. You can make conversions using the following formula:

$$\frac{C^\circ}{5} \times 9 + 32 = F^\circ$$

¿Cuántos grados hace?

Tengo frío. Hace cinco grados centígrados.

Conexiones 9 Cruzando fronteras

Convert the temperatures from degrees centigrade to degrees Fahrenheit for the following cities in Chile. Then make up something about what the weather is like in the city.

Balmaceda 25°
Hace 77 grados. Llueve.

1.	Temuco	20°	5.	Santiago	32°
2.	La Serena	18°	6.	Punta Arenas	15°
3.	Arica	30°	7.	Iquique	25°
4.	Puerto Montt	20°	8.	Concepción	21°

10 Hace....

Look at the illustration and describe what you see to a classmate. Be sure to tell what the weather is like, what season it is and anything else you can say in Spanish.

11 ¿Qué tiempo hace en...?

In groups of three or four, take turns describing the weather during one of the seasons without naming the season. Others in the group have two opportunities to guess which season you have described.

12 Comparaciones: ¿primavera en octubre?

Imagine you are communicating with a key pal through e-mail in South America. How might the weather be different? Working with a partner, one person states what the weather is like where he or she is, according to the cues. The second student then says the weather is the opposite where he or she is.

hacer sol
A: Aquí hace sol.
B: En cambio, aquí llueve.

1. hacer frío
2. hacer buen tiempo
3. estar soleado
4. hacer calor
5. nevar
6. hacer fresco
7. hay flores en julio
8. la temperatura máxima en el invierno es ?

PARA ti

Proverbios y dichos

Even if things seem like they may not be going exactly how you planned, keep trying. Do not give up. Your Spanish skills will continue to improve if you keep studying and practicing, although some days may seem better than others. Remember, there is always a new day ahead. Sometimes the best medicine is to smile. *Al mal tiempo, buena cara* (A smile brightens a cloudy day).

Al mal tiempo, buena cara.

13 ¿Qué ves?

Indicate the letter of the illustration that matches each statement.

1. Ellos esquían.
2. Está soleado.
3. Él envía una carta.
4. Hace 32° F.
5. Está nublado.
6. Hace calor.
7. Está lista para esquiar.
8. Ella copia el número de teléfono.
9. Están en verano.
10. Todavía hay mucha nieve.

14 El tiempo de hoy

Imagine you are traveling in Chile with a friend. Working with a partner, take turns asking and answering the questions about the following weather forecast for various places you are planning to visit during your stay.

A: ¿Qué temperatura mínima hace en Arica hoy?

B: Hoy hace veinte grados centígrados.

1. ¿Qué temperatura mínima hace en Juan Fernández?
2. ¿Dónde hace mal tiempo hoy?
3. ¿Cómo está el día en Puerto Aysén?
4. ¿Hace sol en Balmaceda?
5. ¿Qué temperatura máxima hace en Valparaíso?
6. ¿Hace frío o calor en Arica?

15 ¿Qué deportes haces?

Name which sports you would prefer to do, according to the indicated weather conditions.

Hay mucha nieve.
Patino sobre hielo en el parque.

1. Hace mucho viento.
2. Está soleado/Hace mucho sol.
3. Está nublado.
4. Hace un poco de frío.
5. Hace buen tiempo.
6. Está lloviendo todo el día.
7. Hace fresco.
8. Hace un poco de calor.
9. No está nevando, pero va a nevar.

16 Las cuatro estaciones

Imagine each corner of the room represents one of the four seasons. (Your teacher will indicate which ones.) Choose the season you most prefer and go to that corner. Discuss with the other students there for five minutes in Spanish why each of you chose that season. All students in the group must write a list of the reasons of the other people in the group. In order to return to your seats, each student must state why a different student from the group prefers the season.

A: ¿Por qué prefieres la primavera?
B: Mi cumpleaños es en abril.
A: *B* prefiere la primavera porque su cumpleaños es en abril.

¿Cuál estación prefieres? ¿Primavera?

17 ¿Cómo está el tiempo?

Working in pairs, take turns guessing when and in what kind of weather the following events might be occurring. Be creative!

A: Estamos jugando al básquetbol en el parque.
B: Es sábado y no hace mucho calor.

1. Estoy jugando al tenis.
2. Nosotras esquiamos muy bien.
3. Alicia nada en la piscina.
4. Gerardo está listo para jugar al béisbol.
5. Eva está corriendo en el parque.
6. Tú estás jugando al fútbol.
7. Estoy patinando con Tara Lipinski.
8. Mis hermanas tienen práctica de básquetbol.

Está lloviendo.

Algo más

Para deportistas

To name the person who participates in a sport, add the endings *-ador, -adora* (***patinador*** or ***patinadora,*** for example). Some other names for athletes include ***esquiador(a), corredor(a), jugador(a).*** Another ending that sometimes is used to name someone who participates in a particular activity is the suffix *-ista: el/la* ***tenista,*** *el/la* ***basquetbolista,*** *el/la* ***futbolista.*** (Note that the accent mark is not used on the newly formed word when these endings are added.)

Los corredores están listos.

18 ¿Quiénes son?

Describe the people in the previous activity, using the following words: *basquetbolista, beisbolista, corredor(a), deportista, esquiador(a), futbolista, nadador(a), patinador(a), tenista.*

Estamos jugando al básquetbol.
Somos basquetbolistas.

Una profesión de altura

Se requiere de buena salud, agilidad, habilidad, resistencia, sentido de equipo y solidaridad.

El basquetbol es un deporte de equipo. El buen jugador debe tener un sentido nato del juego, pero también debe adaptarse a las reglas tácticas establecidas por el entrenador. El basquetbolista profesional recibe una cantidad extra de dinero al firmar un contrato y un salario fijo. Pero, al igual que otros deportistas profesionales, debe pensar en otro oficio para cuando se retire porque, aunque el prestigio de las grandes figuras atrae a muchos, hay pocos puestos.

DEPORTES

Oportunidades

El español y los deportes

You probably are familiar with a number of Spanish-speaking sports figures who learned English either before becoming famous or while traveling internationally as they participate in their sport. Knowing another language has helped them communicate with people they have met in their travels. What opportunities do you think might occur for you if you participate in sports and become really good? How might knowing Spanish help you if you are athletic? Can you think of ways Spanish might help if you were a member of a sports team that competes internationally?

Miguel Indurain es un ciclista famoso.

IDIOMA

Los números ordinales

The words *first, second, third* and so on are called ordinal numbers because they place things in order. Only the first ten ordinal numbers are used frequently in Spanish. They usually follow definite articles and precede nouns. Like other adjectives in Spanish you have learned, the ordinal numbers must agree in gender (masculine/feminine) and number (singular/plural) with the noun they modify.

*¿Cuáles son los **primeros** corredores en terminar?*

When *primero* and *tercero* appear before a masculine singular noun, they are shortened to *primer* and *tercer.*

*Pedro es el **primer** corredor en terminar.*
*Antonio es el **tercer** corredor en terminar.*

Ordinal numbers ending in *-o, -a, -os, -as* or *-er* are abbreviated by placing those letters at the upper right-hand side of the number: *primero* → 1°, *primera* → 1^{a}, *primeros* → 1os, *primeras* → 1as, *primer* → 1er, *tercer* → 3er.

19 La competencia

Indicate the final results of the boys' and girls' cross country track meet using the following information.

Pedro fue el <u>primer</u> corredor en terminar.

1. Elena fue la (1) corredora en terminar.
2. Antonio fue el (2) corredor en terminar.
3. Elena y Pedro fueron los (3) corredores en terminar.
4. Jaime fue el (4) corredor en terminar.
5. Elena y María fueron las (5) corredoras en terminar.
6. Catalina fue la (6) corredora en terminar.
7. Diego y Rosa fueron los (7) corredores en terminar.
8. Julio fue el (8) corredor en terminar.
9. Marta fue la (9) corredora en terminar.
10. Carlota fue la (10) corredora en terminar.
11. Luis fue el (11) corredor en terminar.
12. Andrés y Eva fueron los (12) corredores en terminar.

muchachos	muchachas
1° Pedro	1ª Flena
2° Jaime	2ª María
3° Antonio	3ª Inés
4° Carlos	4ª Catalina
5° Diego	5ª Rosa
6° Julio	6ª Julia
7° Roberto	7ª Marta
8° Andrés	8ª Eva
9° Luis	9ª Yolanda
10° Ramón	10ª Carlota

Conexión *cultural*

Los deportes olímpicos en el mundo hispano

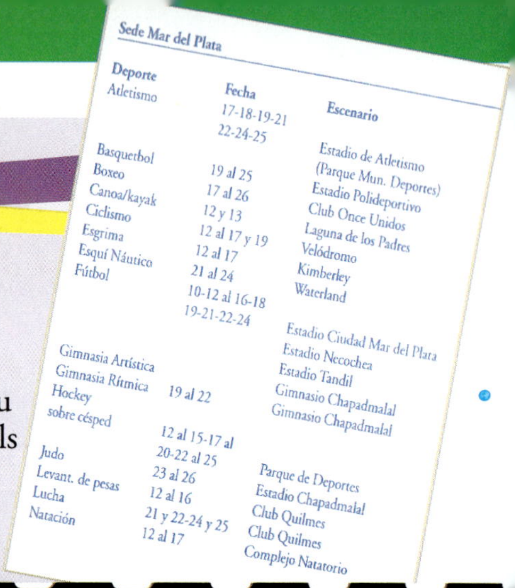

Sede Mar del Plata

Deporte
Atletismo
Basquetbol
Boxeo
Canoa/kayak
Ciclismo
Esgrima
Esquí Náutico
Fútbol
Gimnasia Artística
Gimnasia Rítmica
Hockey sobre césped
Judo
Levant. de pesas
Lucha
Natación

Fecha
17-18-19-21
22-24-25
19 al 25
17 al 26
12 y 13
12 al 17 y 19
12 al 17
21 al 24
10-12 al 16-18
19-21-22-24
19 al 22
12 al 15-17 al
20-22 al 25
23 al 26
12 al 16
21 y 22-24 y 25
12 al 17

Escenario
Estadio de Atletismo
(Parque Mun. Deportes)
Estadio Polideportivo
Club Once Unidos
Laguna de los Padres
Velódromo
Kimberley
Waterland
Estadio Ciudad Mar del Plata
Estadio Necochea
Estadio Tandil
Gimnasio Chapadmalal
Gimnasio Chapadmalal
Parque de Deportes
Estadio Chapadmalal
Club Quilmes
Club Quilmes
Complejo Natatorio

Sports play an important role in the Spanish-speaking world. In addition to soccer and bicycling, you have learned several other sports that are quite popular. As you might guess, Spanish-speaking countries have won medals in several popular sports in the Olympics, including swimming and diving *(natación y clavado),* boxing *(boxeo),* weight lifting *(levantamiento de pesas)* and equestrian sports *(equitación).* How much of the following did you know?

- First Spanish-speaking country to participate in the Olympics: Chile, 1896.
- First Hispanic Olympic medal winner: Ramón Fonst, Cuba, 1900.
- First Olympic Games to be held in a Spanish-speaking country: Mexico, 1968.
- Spanish-speaking country with most gold medal winners for one sport: Uruguay, eight athletes with two medals each in soccer.
- Country with the most gold medals: Cuba.
- Most recent Spanish-speaking nation to host the Olympics: Spain (Barcelona, 1992).

El estadio de los Juegos Olímpicos en Barcelona, España.

20 ¡Fútbol!

Diego's favorite sport in Chile is soccer. Unfortunately, this year at school he has been busy and has not been able to keep up on team standings. Tell him what position the teams are in, using the correct ordinal numbers.

1. La Serena es el (1) equipo.
2. La Católica es el (2) equipo.
3. El Everton es el (3) equipo.
4. El Palestino es el (4) equipo.
5. El Cobreloa es el (5) equipo.
6. La Española es el (6) equipo.
7. El Cobresal es el (7) equipo.
8. El O'Higgins es el (8) equipo.
9. El Concepción es el (9) equipo.
10. El Colo Colo todavía es el (10) equipo.

Tabla de posiciones

Equipos	PJ	PG	PE	PP	Pts.
1. Colo Colo	45	35	10	0	80
2. Católica	45	29	5	11	63
3. Española	45	28	5	12	61
4. O'Higgins	45	15	5	25	35
5. Concepción	45	15	1	29	31
6. Palestino	45	15	0	30	30
7. La Serena	45	13	2	30	28
8. Cobreloa	45	11	4	30	26
9. Cobresal	45	9	3	33	21
10. Everton	45	7	5	33	19

21 ¿Cuál es el primero?

Working in pairs, practice the ordinal numbers by asking and answering questions based upon the following cues. Remember that on Spanish calendars the week begins on Monday.

¿Qué es primero, el huevo o la gallina?

5° día de la semana
A: ¿Cuál es el quinto día de la semana?
B: El quinto día de la semana es el viernes.

1. 1er mes del año
2. 2° día de la semana
3. los dos 1os meses del otoño en Chile
4. 6° mes del año
5. 7° día de la semana
6. 3er mes del año
7. 8° día de la semana

22 Los deportes de dos hermanos

These illustrations depict two brothers who always participate in different sports. Describe the illustrations, saying what each brother is doing, what the season is, what the weather is like and anything else you can say in Spanish.

En el primer dibujo es primavera. Hace viento. Uno de los hermanos está jugando al béisbol. El otro hermano está corriendo.

Autoevaluación. As a review and self-check, respond to the following:

1. What activities do you enjoy doing during each of the seasons?
2. What is the weather like where you live in the summer? Fall? Winter? Spring?
3. How would you ask what the temperature is today in Santiago, Chile?
4. Imagine you wish to send a letter by e-mail. Ask a friend how you can send your letter and where to copy the address.
5. Imagine you are recording finishing times at a school track meet and it is your job to rank the runners as they finish. Using the ordinal numbers, count the first ten runners to cross the line in order to tell each runner where they are ranked.
6. What well-known islands are part of Chile?
7. What two writers from Chile have won Nobel prizes?

¡La práctica hace al maestro!

A Comunicación

Present a weather forecast to your class in Spanish using any props, charts and maps you wish or ones that you create. Pattern it after television weather reports, but personalize it. (You may wish to add some humor or mention how the weather will affect tomorrow's big sporting event, for example.)

B Conexión con la tecnología

Using the Internet, visit a Web site that gives weather information for different cities around the world. Find the current weather conditions for several Spanish-speaking countries. Then write several paragraphs in Spanish to summarize what you find. Be sure to include the following information: identify the different symbols used to represent weather conditions, describe today's weather in several cities, give the current temperature, tell what season it is and predict what people are doing now due to the weather.

¿Qué haces en el invierno?

Vamos a la playa en el verano. (Viña del Mar, Chile)

VOCABULARIO

Está nublado hoy.

¿Qué temperatura hace?

El tiempo

el cambio
está *(+ adjective)*
la estación
el fresco
el grado
hace *(+ weather expression)*
hay neblina/sol
el hielo
el invierno
la lluvia
máximo,-a
mínimo,-a
la neblina
la nieve
nublado,-a
el otoño
la primavera
¿Qué tiempo/temperatura hace?
el sol
soleado,-a
la temperatura
el tiempo
el viento

Para describir

buen
cuarto,-a
décimo,-a
excelente
listo,-a
mal
noveno,-a
octavo,-a
quinto,-a
segundo,-a
séptimo,-a
sexto,-a
tercero (tercer),-a
todavía

Deportistas

el basquetbolista, la basquetbolista
la competencia
el corredor, la corredora
el deportista, la deportista
el esquiador, la esquiadora
el futbolista, la futbolista
el jugador, la jugadora
el patinador, la patinadora
el tenista, la tenista

Verbos

continuar
copiar
enviar
esquiar
llover (ue)
nevar (ie)
patinar (sobre hielo)

Expresiones y otras palabras

la capital
dar un paseo
en cambio
la flor
el lugar
el paseo
por
por todos lados

Plaza de la Constitución, Santiago, Chile.

a leer

Estrategia

Preparación

Estrategia para leer: ***previewing***

Before beginning to read, try various activities to preview what a reading selection is about. For example, quickly looking over the reading that begins on this page will provide information that can make your efforts to read more productive.

Previewing Activities

- ✓ Read the title.
- ✓ Look for cognates.
- ✓ Skim the first paragraph.
- ✓ Skim the last paragraph.
- ✓ Ask yourself what the main points are.

Contesta las siguientes preguntas como preparación para la lectura.

1. ¿Cuál es el tema principal de esta lectura?
2. ¿Cuál es el deporte más popular en el mundo hispano?
3. ¿Cuántos cognados hay en la lectura *Los deportes más populares?* ¿Cuáles son?

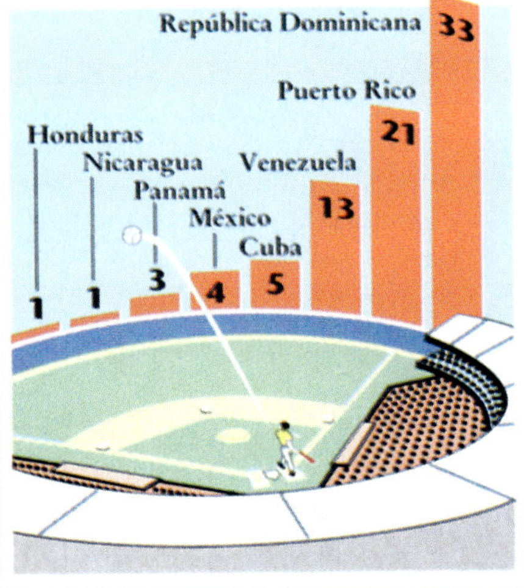

Los deportes más populares

En el **mundo hispano** los deportes son importantes y son muy populares. El deporte más popular para la **gente** hispana es el fútbol. Todas las semanas cientos de miles de personas van a los estadios de fútbol en España y en la América Latina para ver los partidos. La

Copa Mundial de fútbol es el evento más importante en este deporte y es comparable con el *Super Bowl* o la **Serie Mundial** de béisbol en los Estados Unidos. **Sin embargo,** la Copa Mundial **se realiza** una vez cada cuatro años y países de todo el mundo participan en este gran espectáculo del deporte.

Otro deporte muy popular en los países de la región del Caribe es el béisbol, **especialmente** en Cuba, la República Dominicana y Puerto Rico. También es muy popular en México. Muchos jugadores de estos países juegan también en los Estados Unidos. **Algunos** de los jugadores más famosos de todos los tiempos son hispanos, como Pedro Martínez y Sammy Sosa (de la República Dominicana) y Roberto Clemente (de Puerto Rico).

Otros deportes muy populares en el Caribe, México, la América Central y la América del Sur son el **boxeo, llamado** también el deporte de las **narices chatas**, el **frontón**, el jai-alai y el **ciclismo**. Estos dos **últimos** también son muy populares en España, **junto con** el básquetbol (también llamado baloncesto).

Estos son los deportes más populares del mundo hispano, pero muchos otros son **practicados** también. Para la gente hispana, como para el mundo **entero,** practicar deportes es un buen pasatiempo porque representa la buena **salud** y vida activa.

más *most* **mundo hispano** *Hispanic world* **gente** *people* **Copa Mundial** *World Cup* **Serie Mundial** *World Series* **Sin embargo** *However* **se realiza** *takes place* **especialmente** *especially* **Algunos** *Some* **boxeo** *boxing* **llamado** *called* **narices chatas** *flat noses* **frontón** *a sport that is similar to squash or handball* **ciclismo** *cycling* **últimos** *last* **junto con** *along with* **practicados** *practiced* **entero** *whole* **salud** *health*

A ¿Qué comprendiste?

1. ¿Cómo son los deportes en el mundo hispano?
2. ¿Qué deporte ven millones de personas cada semana en los estadios?
3. ¿Cuál es el evento más importante en el fútbol?
4. ¿Qué deporte es muy popular en la región del Caribe?
5. ¿Qué otros deportes son populares en el mundo hispano?

B Charlando

1. ¿Juegas a uno de estos deportes? ¿A cuál? ¿Dónde? ¿Con quién?
2. ¿Cuál es tu deporte favorito?
3. ¿Cuánto tiempo hace que juegas ese deporte?
4. ¿Sabes algo de los deportes en el mundo hispano? ¿Qué sabes?
5. ¿Ves muchos deportes en la televisión? ¿Cuáles?

a escribir

Estrategia

Estrategia para escribir: *questioning*

Writing a composition requires several steps before arriving at a finished product. These steps are sometimes referred to as the writing process. After selecting a topic, coming up with ideas you want to include in the composition can be challenging. You have already learned one technique to overcome this difficulty: brainstorming for ideas. Another way to get started involves answering questions that will guide you in considering your theme from different points of view.

Prepare to write on the theme *Mi tiempo libre* (My Free Time) by answering the questions shown below. Then select some of the ideas that you like and write a paragraph about your free time. Remember to incorporate some transition words *(en cambio, entonces, pero)* to tie your ideas together and make your composition flow smoothly.

1. ¿Cuáles de estas actividades te gustan?

practicar deportes
hacer ejercicios
montar en bicicleta
hacer un picnic
trabajar con la computadora
tocar un instrumento musical

ir a partidos de béisbol, fútbol, etc.
montar a caballo
ir de camping
leer novelas y revistas
ir a un concierto

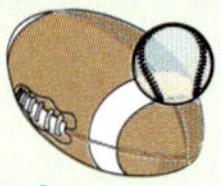

ir a fiestas con amigos
ir al cine
hablar por teléfono
ir de compras
ver la tele
escuchar música

2. ¿Qué otras actividades te gusta hacer?
3. Completa estas frases para considerar unos aspectos diferentes de tu tiempo libre.
   A. En el verano, me gusta....
   B. En el invierno, me gusta....
   C. Cuando hace mal tiempo, yo....
   D. Cuando estoy enfermo/a, prefiero....
   E. Si estoy aburrido/a, yo....
   F. Cuando estoy solo/a, me gusta....
   G. Cuando estoy con mi familia, prefiero....
   H. Cuando estoy con mis amigos,....
   I. Si tengo dinero, me gusta....
   J. Cuando no tengo dinero, prefiero....

repaso

Now that I have completed this chapter, I can...

- ✓ indicate a length of time.
- ✓ talk about everyday activities.
- ✓ offer an invitation.
- ✓ apologize and make excuses.
- ✓ discuss pastime activities.
- ✓ talk about how often something is done.
- ✓ state what is happening right now.
- ✓ describe the seasons and weather.
- ✓ use ordinal numbers.

Nuestro pasatiempo favorito es correr.

I can also...

- ✓ talk about life in Argentina and Chile.
- ✓ talk about pastimes and sports.
- ✓ talk about television and renting movies.
- ✓ write an e-mail message in Spanish.
- ✓ convert temperatures from degrees centigrade to degrees Fahrenheit.
- ✓ read a weather forecast in Spanish.

Hace mucho frío en Patagonia, Chile.

¿Qué haces en casa?

CAPÍTULO

8

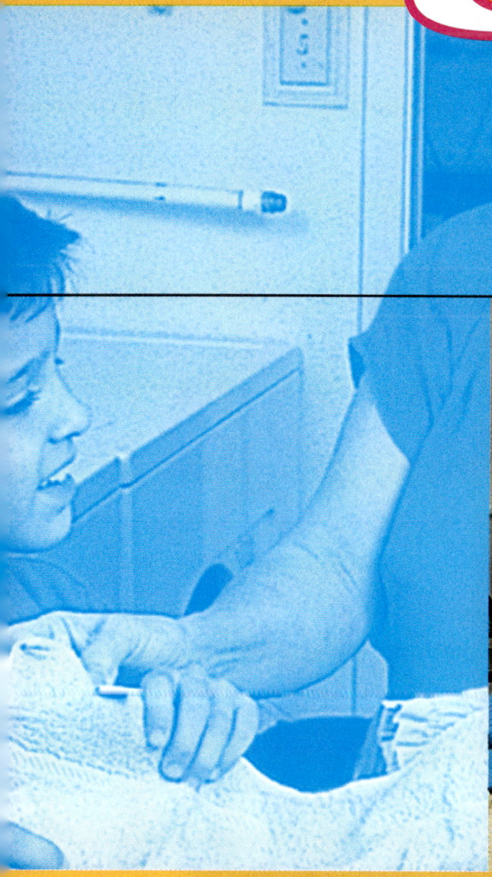

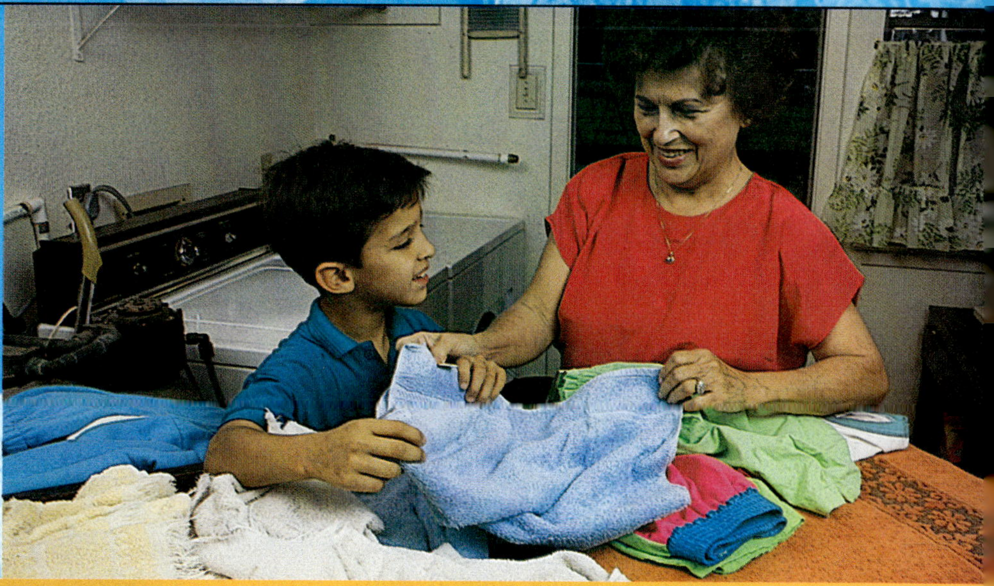

In this chapter you will be able to:

- talk about household chores
- talk about the recent past
- ask for and offer help
- discuss past actions and events
- write about everyday activities
- identify and describe foods
- discuss food preparation
- compare quantity, quality, age and size
- negotiate a price

Lección 15

Contexto cultural
ESPAÑA

Preparando una fiesta

*El club de ecología de un colegio en Madrid va a hacer **algo**° especial: va a dar una pequeña fiesta. Unas **personas** del club van a **preparar** una **paella.** Todos **llegan**° temprano a la casa de Paula para **adornar** y **arreglar**° la casa.*

PAULA: Para dar la fiesta en mi casa, primero tenemos que arreglar la casa. **Quizás**° debemos empezar **limpiando**° el piso de la cocina.

ANA: Bueno, entonces debemos hacer una lista de **quehaceres.**°

JAVIER: Está bien, pero vamos a **trabajar**° **juntos**° en cada **trabajo,** ¿no? Es más divertido.

PAULA: De acuerdo. Pero **sólo**° tenemos cuatro horas para terminar los quehaceres. ¡Vamos!

algo *something* **llegan** *arrives* **arreglar** *to arrange, to fix* **Quizás** *Perhaps* **limpiando** *cleaning* **quehaceres** *chores* **trabajar** *to work* **juntos** *together* **sólo** *only*

1 ¿Qué comprendiste?

1. ¿Qué va a hacer el club de ecología?
2. ¿En casa de quién va a ser la fiesta?
3. ¿Por qué llegan todos temprano a la casa de Paula?
4. ¿Qué van a preparar?
5. ¿Qué deben hacer primero? ¿Y después?
6. ¿Qué dice Javier del trabajo?
7. ¿Cuánto tiempo tienen para terminar?

¿Te gustaría comer una paella?

Conexión cultural

La paella

Have you ever tasted *paella?* The dish is considered one of Spain's best-known contributions to international cuisine. *Paella* contains rice *(el arroz)* as its primary ingredient, but do not confuse *paella* with the side dish referred to in the United States as Spanish rice. Authentic *paella* is much more.

Paella can be prepared many different ways and even varies from one region to another in Spain. In addition to rice that is flavored with saffron *(el azafrán),* the dish usually consists of some combination of meat *(la carne),* seafood *(los mariscos),* chicken *(el pollo)* and vegetables *(las verduras). Paella* originated in Valencia, a rice-growing region on the eastern coast of southern Spain. The style of *paella* that bears the name *paella valenciana* contains chicken and various types of beef. *Paella marinera* is made with various types of seafood such as lobster *(la langosta),* shrimp *(los camarones/las gambas),* clams *(las almejas)* or mussels *(los mejillones).*

Paella is one of the most popular foods in the Spanish diet. It is eaten at elaborate parties as well as for everyday meals, usually as a main course. At other times it is served as a *tapa* (an appetizer in Spain). If you have never tasted this wonderful treat, you have missed one of the most varied and enticing dishes to have originated in Spain.

2 La paella

Contesta en español las siguientes preguntas con oraciones completas.

1. ¿Cuál es el ingrediente principal de la paella?
2. ¿Dónde tiene su origen la paella?
3. ¿Qué otros ingredientes hay en la paella?
4. ¿Cuáles son dos ingredientes en la paella valenciana?
5. ¿Qué tiene la paella marinera?
6. ¿Es la paella una comida sólo para los domingos?

Arreglando la casa

PAULA: Mi cuarto es un **desastre.** Yo tengo que **subir** y **colgar** la **ropa** y hacer la **cama.** Toda la **gente**° puede **subir** sus **abrigos** a mi cuarto y **dejarlos**° allí.

ANA: **Traigo**° una **olla** grande de mi mamá para preparar la paella. Oye, yo **acabo de** leer la **receta.** ¿Quién va a **cocinar?**

JAVIER: ¡Yo! Bueno, si Paula me ayuda y tú me **prestas**° la receta.

ANA: ¡Claro! Puedes usarla.

ROSA: Y tú, Miguel, ¿qué vas a hacer?

MIGUEL: ¿Qué dices? No te **oigo.**

ROSA: Claro, con esa música no me puedes **oír.** Te pregunto ¿qué puedes hacer para ayudar?

MIGUEL: ¿Yo? Este..., por ejemplo puedo **sacar** la **basura.**

ROSA: ¡Qué **listo**° eres! Entonces tú y yo vamos al **supermercado.**

gente *people* **dejarlos** *leave them* **Traigo** *I bring* **prestas** *lend* **listo** *smart*

3 ¿Qué comprendiste?

1. ¿Qué dice Paula de su cuarto?
2. ¿Qué tiene que hacer ella?
3. ¿Qué puede hacer la gente con sus abrigos?
4. ¿Quién lee la receta para la paella?
5. ¿A quién le presta Ana la receta?
6. ¿Quién es muy listo pero perezoso? Explica.
7. ¿Quiénes van a ir al supermercado?

Tengo que sacar la basura.

4 Charlando

1. ¿Es tu cuarto un desastre? Explica.
2. ¿Cuántas personas ayudan con los quehaceres en tu casa? ¿Quiénes?
3. ¿Hacen Uds. muchos quehaceres juntos? ¿Cuáles?

Repaso rápido

Los pronombres de complemento directo

You have already learned to use direct object pronouns in Spanish to show the person or thing in a sentence that receives the action of the verb. Remember that direct object pronouns can precede conjugated verbs, attach to the end of an infinitive or attach to the end of a present participle.

me	**nos**
te	**os**
lo	**los**
la	**las**

5 ¿Qué están haciendo ahora?

¿Cuáles son las dos maneras de decir la misma oración, usando un pronombre como complemento directo? Sigue el modelo.

Estoy preparando *la comida.*
La estoy preparando./Estoy preparándola.

1. Estoy buscando *la receta.*
2. Estoy arreglando *las sillas de la sala.*
3. Estamos colgando *los abrigos.*
4. Miguel está sacando *la basura.*
5. Estamos adornando *el cuarto.*
6. Están cocinando *una paella marinera.*

PARA ti

El verbo *colgar*
The present tense of *colgar* (to hang) follows the pattern of other verbs that change from *o* → *ue*: *cuelgo, cuelgas, cuelga, colgamos, colgáis, cuelgan.*

6 Tus quehaceres

Trabajando en parejas, alterna con tu compañero/a preguntando y contestando las siguientes preguntas con los pronombres de complemento apropiados.

¿Arreglar la casa?
A: ¿Arreglas la casa?
B: Sí, (No, no) la arreglo.

1. ¿Hacer la cama?
2. ¿Poner la mesa?
3. ¿Preparar la comida?
4. ¿Limpiar la cocina los fines de semana?
5. ¿Colgar el abrigo?
6. ¿Sacar la basura?

Algo más

La expresión *acabar de*

Use a form of the verb *acabar* (to finish, to complete, to terminate) followed by *de* and an infinitive to indicate what has just occurred in the recent past.

acabar de	+	infinitive

***Acabo de preparar** la paella.*	I have just prepared the paella.
*Raúl **acaba de limpiar** el piso.*	Raúl has just cleaned the floor.

7 Todos hacen algo

A los amigos de Paula les gusta ayudar. Completa las siguientes oraciones, diciendo qué acaban de hacer para ayudarla.

¿La mesa?/Luisa/poner hace cinco minutos
Luisa acaba de ponerla hace cinco minutos.

1. ¿Los abrigos?/ Diego/colgar

2. ¿Las camas?/Paula y su hermana/ hacer ahora mismo

3. ¿El cuarto?/ Alejandro y yo/ arreglar juntos

4. ¿La sala?/ Rafael/adornar

5. ¿Los platos?/ yo/dejar en el comedor

6. ¿Las ventanas?/ Eduardo/limpiar hace media hora

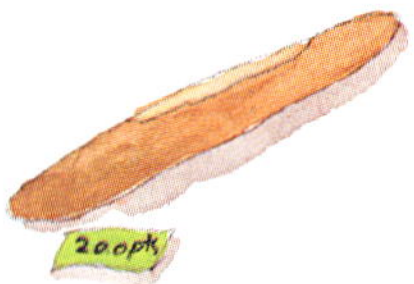

7. ¿El pan?/Paco y Silvia/ir a comprar

8 Preparando una fiesta

Imagine that you and a friend are organizing preparations for a party at your house and you would like to know if everyone is participating. Working with a partner, take turns asking and answering what the following people have just done, according to the cues.

Uds./preparar la comida
A: ¿Qué acaban de hacer Uds.?
B: Acabamos de preparar la comida.

1. Eva/llegar
2. José y Mónica/colgar la ropa
3. Blanca/limpiar las ventanas
4. tú/sacar la basura
5. Gloria/poner la mesa
6. Pablo/trabajar con Gloria
7. nosotros/arreglar la sala
8. yo/leer la lista de quehaceres

IDIOMA

El complemento indirecto

Just as the direct object in a sentence answers the question **who?** or **what?**, the indirect object is the person in a sentence **to whom** or **for whom** something is said or done.

Marta is talking **to whom?**
Marta is talking **to him.**

He is buying the book **for whom?**
He is buying the book **for her.**

Sometimes an indirect object pronoun *(pronombre de complemento indirecto)* is used in place of an indirect object. You have already learned to use indirect object pronouns with the verb *gustar.* They look the same as direct object pronouns except for *le* and *les.*

Mi abuela me hace el postre.

los pronombres de complemento indirecto

me	*to me, for me*	**nos**	*to us, for us*
te	*to you, for you* (tú)	**os**	*to you, for you* (vosotros,-as)
le	*to you, for you* (Ud.) *to him, for him* *to her, for her*	**les**	*to you, for you* (Uds.) *to them, for them*

Indirect object pronouns follow the same rules for placement in a sentence that you learned for the direct object pronouns:

- They usually precede the conjugated form of the verb, but may also follow and be attached to an infinitive or a present participle. (Add an accent mark to the present participle in order to maintain the original pronunciation of the present participle.)

*Ana **me** va a dar la receta.*
*Ana va a **darme** la receta.*
Ana is going to give **me** the recipe.

***Te** estoy hablando.*
*Estoy **hablándote.***
I am talking **to you.**

- Negative expressions (such as *nunca*) are placed before the indirect object pronouns.

***Nunca nos** recogen la mesa.* They **never** clear the table **for us.**

9 Ayudando en casa

Restate the following sentences by moving the italicized words and by making any other needed changes.

¿Te gustaría limpiar esta casa?

¿*Me* estás recogiendo la mesa?
¿Estás recogiéndo*me* la mesa?

1. ¿No *nos* puede Ud. adornar el cuarto?
2. Quizás *te* debo escribir una lista de quehaceres.
3. ¿Cuándo *me* puedes limpiar el piso?
4. *Les* estamos colgando la ropa.
5. Él nunca *le* puede arreglar la casa a ella.
6. ¿No *me* quieres comprar una olla grande para preparar paella?
7. Quizás Carlos *te* puede prestar la olla para la paella.

10 ¿Cuándo puedes...?

Imagine you must prepare the house for invited guests. Working with a partner, take turns asking one another when each of you will be able to help the other with various chores. The person responding should say he or she may be able to do the requested tasks at the indicated times.

arreglar el patio/por la tarde
A: ¿Cuándo me puedes arreglar el patio?
B: Quizás te puedo arreglar el patio por la tarde./Quizás puedo arreglarte el patio por la tarde.

1. sacar la basura/en un minuto
2. hacer la lista de quehaceres/en cinco minutos
3. preparar la paella/en una hora
4. poner la mesa/ahora mismo
5. adornar la sala/en media hora
6. tener todo listo/esta noche

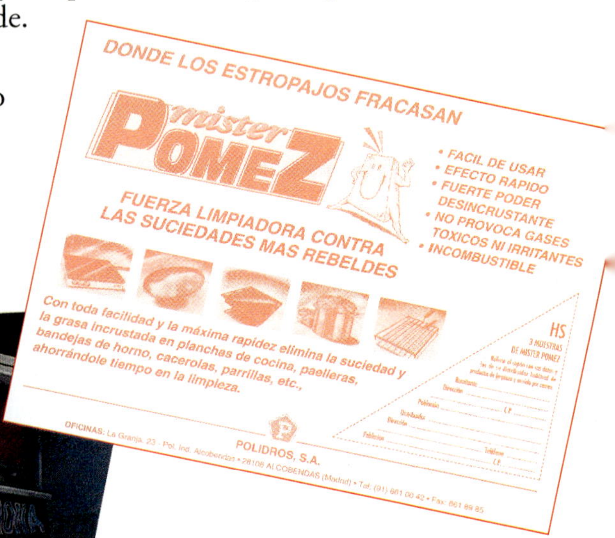

¿Me puedes comprar el pollo para la paella aquí?

11 Unos amigos quieren ayudarte

Varias *(several)* personas están ayudándote a preparar una fiesta en tu casa. Describe qué te están haciendo, según las ilustraciones.

María

María me está colgando la ropa./María está colgándome la ropa.

1. Isabel y Pedro

2. Carlos

3. Elisa

4. Juan y Ricardo

5. Antonio y Paloma

Los quehaceres

Algo más

El cambio de *g* → *j*

You have seen several verbs that are regular in the present tense except for a minor stem change *(poder, jugar)* or a spelling change. These changes do not affect the verb's present-tense endings. Additionally, for verbs that end in *-ger* (such as *recoger*) or *-gir* (such as *dirigir*), the letter *g* changes to *j* before the letters *a* and *o* to maintain pronunciation: *Yo recojo la mesa muchas veces; yo dirijo los quehaceres.*

12 Charlando

1. ¿Haces algo para ayudar con los quehaceres de tu casa? Explica.
2. ¿Haces la cama todos los días? Explica.
3. ¿Siempre cuelgas la ropa o la dejas en el piso?
4. ¿Quién lava tu ropa? ¿La lavas tú?
5. ¿Quién va al supermercado a buscar leche y pan en tu casa?
6. ¿Cuántas veces a la semana recoges la mesa en tu casa?
7. ¿Quién dirige los quehaceres en tu casa?

13 ¿Qué debo hacer?

Indica *(Indicate)* cuáles son los quehaceres que debes hacer, según los dibujos.

Debo lavar los platos.

¿Me puedes lavar la ropa?

1. 

2. 

3. 

4. 

5. 

6. 

7. 

8. 

Algo más

Para aclarar y para dar énfasis

It may be necessary to add *a Ud., a él, a ella* or *a* and a noun to a sentence in order to clarify the meaning of *le* or to add emphasis. It is likewise possible to add *a Uds., a ellos, a ellas* or *a* plus a plural noun or more than one noun to a sentence in order to clarify the meaning of *les* or to add emphasis.

Le escribo { *a Ud.* / *a él.* / *a ella.* / *a María.* / *a mi hermana.* }

Les escribo { *a Uds.* / *a ellos.* / *a ellas.* / *a María y a Mario.* / *a mis primos.* }

Le escribo a ella.

14 Toda la familia ayuda con los quehaceres

Nunca tenemos problemas en nuestra familia porque todos ayudan con los quehaceres. Completa las siguientes oraciones, siguiendo los modelos.

Tú me limpias mi cuarto a mí y yo te limpio la cocina a ti. (limpiar la cocina)

Nosotros les preparamos una fiesta a Uds. y Uds. nos preparan una paella a nosotros. (preparar una paella)

1. Tú me arreglas mi cuarto a mí y yo.... (colgar la ropa)
2. Nosotros les preparamos la comida a Uds. y Uds.... (limpiar el garage)
3. Tú me cuelgas la ropa a mí y yo.... (lavar la ropa)
4. Nosotros les compramos refrescos a Uds. y Uds.... (comprar el almuerzo)
5. Tú me recoges la mesa a mí y yo.... (sacar la basura)
6. Nosotros les damos una receta a Uds. y Uds.... (preparar la comida)

15 Mis quehaceres para esta semana

Imagine your parents have allowed you to invite some friends to your house next Saturday only if you do certain chores for the week between now and then. Make a list of what you must do, using the provided cues. Be sure to use the appropriate object pronouns in your sentences.

limpiar el baño/mi hermano
Le limpio el baño a mi hermano.

1. lavar las ollas/mi madre
2. colgar la ropa/mis hermanas menores
3. buscar la leche en la tienda/doña Esperanza
4. recoger la mesa/mi hermana mayor
5. barrer el piso de la cocina/mi madre

Le lavo los vasos a mi madre.

16 ¿Me ayudas, por favor?

Working with a partner, take turns asking one another for help with the chores indicated in the illustrations. The person responding may agree or refuse to help.

A: ¿Me haces la cama?
B: Sí, (No, no) te hago la cama.

hacer la cama

1. subir la ropa a mi cuarto

2. pasar la aspiradora por la sala

3. recoger la mesa

4. limpiar las ventanas de mi cuarto

5. lavar el mantel

6. barrer el patio

7. poner los cubiertos en la mesa

8. prestar la olla para la paella

IDIOMA

El presente de los verbos *oír* y *traer*

The verbs *oír* (to hear, to listen) and *traer* (to bring) are irregular.

No te oigo.

oír	
oigo	oímos
oyes	oís
oye	oyen
gerundio: oyendo	

traer	
traigo	traemos
traes	traéis
trae	traen
gerundio: trayendo	

Ellos traen la paella.

17 En mi casa

Completa el siguiente párrafo con las formas correctas del verbo *oír*.

En mi casa a todos nos gusta oír la radio. Mi abuelo (1) las noticias todas las noches. Mi abuela (2) un programa de música española por las tardes. Mis hermanos (3) los deportes, cuando no pueden verlos en la televisión, como cuando estamos en el parque o en la playa. Son muy listos. Si están trabajando en el garaje, (4) música popular. Mamá y yo siempre (5) el reporte del tiempo para saber si va a llover. Yo (6) la radio cuando escribo cartas a mis amigos y también siempre estoy (7) música cuando hago la tarea. Y tú, ¿cuándo (8) la radio en tu casa?

18 ¿Qué traen a la fiesta?

Trabajando en parejas, alterna con tu compañero/a preguntando y contestando qué trae todo el mundo a la fiesta del club de ecología.

A: ¿Qué trae Julio?
B: Julio trae los discos compactos.

Julio

1. Ana

2. Fernando y Tomás

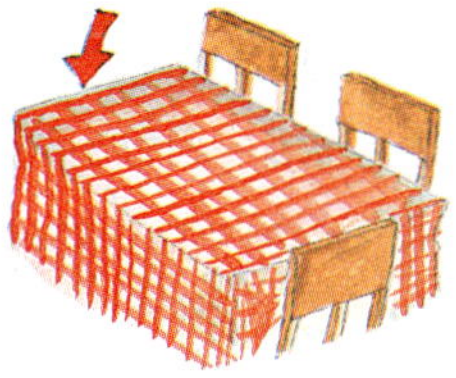
3. mi amiga y yo

4. Raúl

5. Carmen y Nora

6. Nicolás

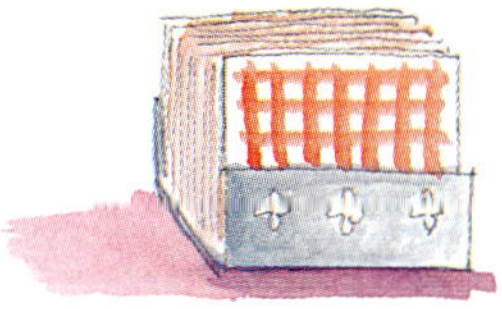
7. la profesora

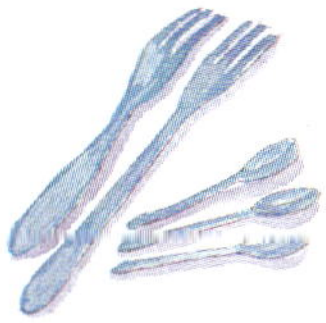
8. tú

Ellos traen la comida.

Después de la fiesta

PAULA: ¡Qué fiesta!
ANA: Sí. Fue una fiesta fantástica.
JAVIER: ¡Claro! **Trabajamos°** mucho preparándola.
ANA: Y a todos **les gustó°** mucho la paella que **preparasteis.°**

Trabajamos *we worked* **les gustó** *they liked* **preparasteis** *you prepared* (vosotros)

PARA ti

El uso de *vosotros*
In Spain, it is common to use the *vosotros* form of verbs when talking informally with two or more people.

IDIOMA

El pretérito de los verbos regulares *-ar*

Use the preterite tense to discuss actions or events that were completed in the past. To form the preterite tense of a regular *-ar* verb, remove the last two letters from the infinitive and add the indicated endings.

lavar					
yo	lav**é**	I washed	nosotros nosotras	lav**amos**	we washed
tú	lav**aste**	you washed	vosotros vosotras	lav**asteis**	you washed
Ud. él ella	lav**ó**	you washed he washed she washed	Uds. ellos ellas	lav**aron**	you washed they washed they washed

Regular verbs that end in *-car (buscar, explicar, sacar, tocar)*, *-gar (apagar, colgar, jugar, llegar, pagar)* and *-zar (empezar)* require a spelling change in the *yo* form of the preterite in order to maintain the original sound of the infinitive.

infinitivo			pretérito
busc**ar**	*c*	→	*qu* yo bus**qué**
apag**ar**	*g*	→	*gu* yo apa**gué**
empez**ar**	*z*	→	*c* yo empe**cé**

19 ¿Qué preparaste para la fiesta?

Completa las siguientes oraciones con la forma correcta del pretérito para decir lo que pasó ayer.

1. Ayer yo *(cocinar)* en mi casa.
2. Tú me *(prestar)* una receta.
3. Yo *(trabajar)* en la cocina todo el día.
4. Ana me *(ayudar)* a hacer una paella.
5. Yo *(sacar)* el arroz esta vez.
6. Todos *(llegar)* temprano.
7. Después de comer, Pepe *(lavar)* los platos.
8. Él también *(limpiar)* la cocina.
9. Todos *(hablar)* bien de la comida.

20 ¿Yo?

Working in pairs, take turns asking if your partner has completed various chores. Your classmate should say that he or she did not do the task because someone else already did it. Follow the model.

comprar la leche/Diego
A: ¿Compraste la leche?
B: No, yo no compré la leche porque Diego ya la compró.

1. colgar los abrigos/Felipe
2. preparar la comida/Javier y Paula
3. lavar la olla grande/Ana
4. buscar los platos/Alicia
5. limpiar el piso de la cocina/Rosa y Miguel
6. apagar la estufa/Julio
7. sacar la basura/Roberto

21 ¿Cocinaste ayer?

Completa el siguiente párrafo con la forma apropiada del pretérito de los verbos entre paréntesis.

Yo *(1. cocinar)* una paella ayer en mi casa para toda la familia. Mi hermana me *(2. ayudar)*. Yo *(3. empezar)* a preparar todo muy temprano. Primero yo *(4. buscar)* los ingredientes. Luego *(5. lavar)* la olla grande y *(6. sacar)* el arroz. Después *(7. preparar)* unos refrescos. Al terminar de cocinar, *(8. apagar)* la estufa y *(9. arreglar)* los cubiertos en la mesa. Entonces, *(10. llamar)* a todos a comer.

22 Mini-diálogos

Trabajando en parejas, escriban Uds. mini-diálogos según el modelo.

lavar/los platos sucios
A: ¿Lavaste los platos sucios?
B: Sí, (No, no) los lavé.

1. comprar/la leche
2. colgar/la ropa en tu cuarto
3. cocinar/el pollo para la paella
4. adornar/la casa
5. recordar traer/la olla grande

Nuestra PAELLA tiene 30 años ¡y cada día está mejor!

Conexión *cultural*

España

Cádiz, España.

Spain has a long and fascinating history. For example, in northern Spain (Altamira) cave paintings have been found that date from between 25,000 and 10,000 B.C. Spain also has had many different occupants throughout history and each group of inhabitants has made important contributions to the country's rich and varied past.

More than 4,000 years ago the Iberians *(íberos)* invaded the area that would later be named the Iberian Peninsula, and which is shared today by both Portugal and Spain. In 1100 B.C. the Phoenicians *(fenicios)*, from present-day Lebanon, founded cities where *Cádiz* and *Málaga* are located. Between 1000 and 500 B.C., the Celts *(celtas)* arrived from the north. They had blue eyes and blond hair, as do many of their Spanish descendants. The Greeks *(griegos)*, who arrived between 800 and 700 B.C., and the Phoenicians imported olive trees and grapevines. As a result, the production of both olives *(aceitunas)* and grapes *(uvas)* remains important in Spain's economy today.

Las naranjas españolas vienen de los moros.

Other people made their way to Spain later, including the Carthaginians *(cartagineses)*, from the area known today as Tunisia; the Romans *(romanos)*, who introduced Latin, which would eventually evolve into Spanish; the Visigoths *(visigodos)*, from the area known today as Germany; and the Arabs from northern Africa, also called Moors *(moros)*, who introduced the cultivation of rice and oranges *(naranjas)* and turned first *Córdoba* and later *Granada* into important and prestigious cities at the political center of the Muslim *(musulmán)* kingdom in Spain.

In 1492 the Moors were defeated in Granada and expelled from power by Catholic monarchs Ferdinand *(Fernando)* and Isabella *(Isabel)*. By this time, many elements in contemporary Spain had taken root and are still evident today.

Unas uvas españolas.

CONEXIONES

23 Cruzando fronteras

Conecta lógicamente la información sobre la historia de España de la columna I con la información de la columna II.

I	II
1. la Península Ibérica	A. rubios
2. los fenicios	B. Córdoba y Granada
3. los celtas	C. España y Portugal
4. los griegos y los fenicios	D. el latín
5. los romanos	E. Cádiz y Málaga
6. los moros	F. las aceitunas y las uvas

24 Surfeando la red

Visit your local library or search the Internet for a topic of Spain's history that interests you. Then give a report in Spanish to the entire class.

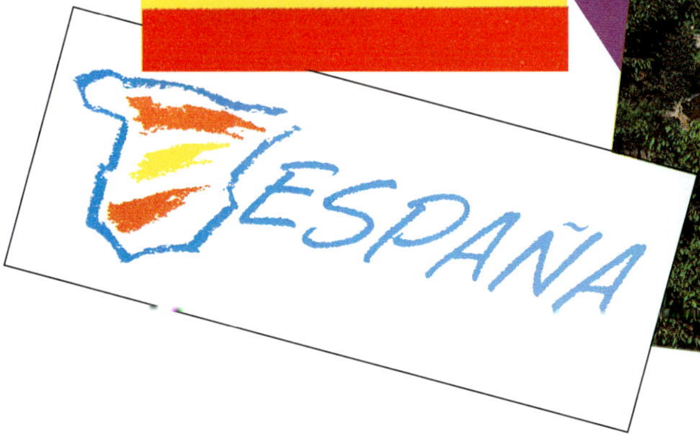

Granada, España.

Autoevaluación. As a review and self-check, respond to the following:

1. Name some chores you do to help around the house.
2. Name several ingredients in *paella.*
3. Imagine you are hosting a party for several friends at your house. Ask your sister or brother to do three or four things for you to help you get ready.
4. List five things you have just done or that you did already to prepare for the party.
5. Name some of the groups of people who have occupied Spain throughout its history.

¡La práctica hace al maestro!

A Comunicación

In groups of three, make a list of five chores that you all like to do and a second list of five chores that you do not like to do. Then each student pairs up with a student from another group to talk about each other's list.

Nos gusta.
preparar la comida

No nos gusta.
recoger la mesa

A: ¿Les gusta preparar la comida?
B: Sí, nos gusta prepararla.
A: A nosotros nos gusta también.

B Conexión con la tecnología

Search the Web for sites about Spanish cuisine using key words (cuisine, food, Spanish, paella, etc.). How many different recipes can you find? For example, how many ways can *paella* be prepared? How are the recipes different? List the ingredients. Can you locate any restaurants that serve *paella?* How much does it cost? Share your findings with the class.

VOCABULARIO

En casa

el abrigo
la aspiradora
la basura
la cama
la gente
la leche
la olla
la paella
pasar la aspiradora

la persona
el quehacer
la receta
recoger la mesa
la ropa

Verbos

acabar
adornar
arreglar
barrer
cocinar
colgar (ue)
dejar
dirigir
lavar
limpiar
llegar
preparar
prestar
recoger
sacar
subir
trabajar
traer

Expresiones y otras palabras

acabar de *(+ infinitive)*
algo
dar de comer
el desastre
junto,-a
listo,-a
quizás
sólo
el supermercado
el trabajo

Acabamos de preparar la comida.

Lavamos el perro.

¿Colgaste la ropa?

Lección 16

En el supermercado

JAIME: ¡Vamos a hacer una paella fantástica! Ya compré el **arroz,** que es **el ingrediente más importante de** la paella. ¿Qué más nos **hace falta?**

SILVIA: Vamos a ver. Aquí tengo la lista. Necesitamos **ajo fresco,°** un pollo y una **libra** de pescado.

JAIME: También vamos a necesitar unas **cebollas.**

SILVIA: Mira, aquí están los **tomates** para la ensalada. Hay que **escoger° los mejores,°** no muy **maduros.**

JAIME: ¿Qué tomates te **parecen** buenos?

SILVIA: Pues, aquellos tomates son **los peores de°** todos, y esos tomates son **mejores que°** estos tomates pero no están buenos todavía.

JAIME: Aquí están los **aguacates.** **¿Te importa** cuál escojo?

SILVIA: No. Me parece que todos están buenos.

JAIME: ¿Debemos **llevar**° **lechuga** o hacemos la ensalada **sin**° lechuga?

SILVIA: No, ya la tengo. Ahora nos hacen falta las comidas en **lata:** los **pimientos** y los **guisantes.** ¡Ay, caramba! ¿Sabes qué **olvidamos**° **añadir**° a la lista? ¡El **chorizo!**

JAIME: Vamos al **mercado** a buscarlo y, luego, a prepararlo.

fresco *fresh* **escoger** *to choose* **los mejores** *the best* **los peores de** *the worst of* **mejores que** *better than* **llevar** *take, carry* **sin** *without* **olvidamos** *we forgot* **añadir** *to add*

1 ¿Qué comprendiste?

1. ¿Qué están haciendo Silvia y Jaime?
2. ¿Es el aguacate el ingrediente más importante de la paella? Explica.
3. ¿Qué les hace falta para hacer la paella?
4. ¿Cuánto pescado compran?
5. ¿Cómo le gustan a Silvia los tomates?
6. ¿Qué piensan comprar para la ensalada?
7. ¿Llevan lechuga los chicos?
8. ¿Compran pimientos y guisantes frescos?
9. ¿Qué olvidaron añadir a la lista?

¿Te gustan los aguacates?

2 Charlando

1. ¿Sabes cocinar? ¿Cuándo cocinaste por última vez?
2. ¿Cuándo vas al mercado?
3. Si vas, ¿es porque quieres ayudar o porque tienes que ir?
4. ¿Qué compras? ¿Llevas las cosas que tú necesitas o llevas cosas para tu familia?
5. ¿Prefieres escoger comidas frescas o en latas? ¿Por qué?
6. ¿Sabes cómo hacer una paella?

¿Vas de compras al supermercado?

Conexión *Cultural*

Receta de la paella valenciana

LA PAELLA
(ingredientes para seis personas)

1 pollo en **pedazos**	2 zanahorias
1 libra de pescado	3 tomates
1/2 chorizo en pedazos	1 lata de pimientos
1/2 libra de jamón en pedazos	1 taza de guisantes
1 lata de almejas	5 **hilos** de **azafrán**
2 tazas de arroz	4 tazas de agua
1 cebolla	2 **cucharadas** de aceite de oliva
2 **dientes** de ajo	sal y pimienta

En una olla grande, poner un poco de aceite y añadir el pollo, el chorizo, el jamón, la cebolla, el tomate, la zanahoria, el ajo y cocinar por diez minutos. Luego, añadir el arroz y el agua y cocinar por otros diez minutos con la olla **cubierta.** Después, añadir media taza de guisantes, el pescado, los pimientos, las almejas, el azafrán y sal y pimienta **al gusto** y cocinar por otros diez minutos. Para terminar, adornar con la otra **mitad** de los guisantes, otra lata de pimientos (opcional) y un poco de **perejil.** Llevar a la mesa en la olla.

Está preparando una paella.

pedazos *pieces* **dientes** *cloves* **hilos** *threads* **azafrán** *saffron* **cucharadas** *tablespoonfuls* **cubierta** *covered* **al gusto** *to taste* **mitad** *half* **perejil** *parsley*

Contesta las siguientes preguntas.

1. ¿Cuánto pescado tiene esta paella?
2. ¿Cuáles de los ingredientes en esta receta no son frescos?
3. ¿Qué verduras tiene la paella? ¿Qué carnes tiene?
4. Después de añadir el arroz, ¿cuánto tiempo hay que cocinar la paella?
5. ¿Con qué puedes adornar la paella?
6. ¿Te gustaría preparar una paella? ¿Por qué?
7. ¿Hay un restaurante en tu ciudad con paella en el menú? ¿Cuál?

UNA HISTORIA

El arroz

Este grano es el principal alimento de aproximadamente el 50% de la población mundial y es originario de la India. El 80% proviene de los países afectados por los monzones. Alejandro Magno lo llevó a Francia de su campaña en la India en el siglo III a. C., y los moros lo introdujeron en España en el siglo VIII. En este momento, Italia es el más grande productor de arroz en Europa. La primera plantación en América se hizo en el año 1685, exactamente en Carolina del Sur, en Estados Unidos.
En la actualidad existen más o menos 2.500 especies de arroz, algunas rojas, azules o púrpuras y hay cultivos en todo el mundo.

Una paella deliciosa.

Conexiones 3 — Cruzando fronteras

Based upon what you have read about *la paella,* prepare a list of ingredients you would need to make a *paella.* Then write how much of each item you would need to make enough *paella* for three people. Finally, gather the ingredients and prepare your *paella.* How does it taste?

Algo más

Hacer falta, parecer e *importar*

The expressions *hacer falta* (to need), *parecer* (to seem) and *importar* (to matter) all use indirect object pronouns and follow a pattern like the one you learned for the verb *gustar.*

Me gusta la paella.	I like *paella.* (*Paella* is pleasing to me.)
Me hace falta un tomate.	I need a tomato.
Me parece buena la receta.	The recipe seems good to me.
No me importa si el ajo no es fresco.	It does not matter to me if the garlic is not fresh.

¿Qué te parecen estos tomates?

4 ¿Qué opinan?

Di lo que *le(s) gusta, le(s) hace falta, le(s) parece* o *le(s) importa* a cada una de las siguientes personas, según el modelo.

a mí/parecer bien/ir/el mercado
(A mí) Me parece bien ir al mercado.

1. a Silvia/no importar/ir/el supermercado
2. a Uds./hacer falta/la comida en lata
3. a Jaime/gustar más/ir/el mercado
4. a la señora Sánchez/gustar/cocinar/para su familia
5. a Diego y a Jorge/importar/comprar/los mejores aguacates
6. a Tomás/hacer falta/comprar/los tomates y el maíz
7. a los dos chicos/hacer falta/llevar el queso, las habichuelas y el café
8. a mí/importar/el precio

¿Te gusta el queso?

PARA ti

Proverbios y dichos

In Spanish-speaking countries, family and home life are very important. Being invited to a person's home is a special occasion. For this reason, consider yourself honored if your host invites you to return and says: *Mi casa es su casa* (My house is yours).

Mi casa es su casa.

IDIOMA

Para comparar

Comparatives are used to compare people or things. Use the following patterns to make comparisons in Spanish:

más/menos	+	noun/adjective/adverb	+	*que*

*Hay **más/menos tomates que** uvas.*	There are **more/less (fewer) tomatoes than** grapes.

tanto-a, -os, -as	+	noun	+	*como*

*Hay **tanto chorizo como** pollo en esa paella.*	There is **as much sausage as** chicken in that *paella.*

tan	+	adjective/adverb	+	*como*

*Estos tomates no están **tan maduros como** esos tomates.*	These tomatoes are not **as ripe as** those tomatoes.

verb	+	*tanto como*

*Jaime **cocina tanto como** Ana.*	Jaime **cooks as much as** Ana.

Another way to make comparisons is to single out a person, group, object or attribute as the best, most or least by using the following patterns:

definite article (+ noun)	+	*más/menos*	+	adjective

*El arroz es **el ingrediente más importante.***	Rice is **the most important ingredient.**

verb	+	*lo*	+	*más/menos*	+	adverb	+	*posible*

*Debes prepararla **lo más temprano posible.***	You should prepare it **as early as possible.**

Los mejores jamones están en este supermercado.

Some adjectives and adverbs may use these irregular comparative forms:

bueno,-a	→	mejor
bien	→	mejor
malo,-a	→	peor
mal	→	peor
grande	→	mayor/más grande
pequeño,-a	→	menor/más pequeño,-a
joven	→	menor/más joven
viejo,-a	→	mayor/más viejo,-a

*Ese supermercado es **bueno,** pero aquel supermercado es **mejor** y este supermercado es **el mejor de la ciudad.***	That supermarket is **good,** but that supermarket over there is **better** and this supermarket is **the best in the city.**

- When referring to size, the comparative forms of *pequeño* and *grande* are *más pequeño* (smaller) and *más grande* (bigger). When referring to quantity, the comparative forms of *pequeño* and *grande* are *menor* (lesser, smaller, fewer) and *mayor* (greater, larger).

*Hay un **menor (mayor)** número de comidas en lata que de comidas frescas.*	There is a **smaller (greater)** number of canned foods than fresh foods.

- Use *más* or *menos* with forms of *grande, pequeño, joven* and *viejo* when referring to animals or objects.

*Es **el** supermercado **más grande** de mi ciudad.*	It is **the biggest** supermarket in my city.

- The words *mayor* (older) and *menor* (younger) are used to compare people's ages.

*Don Diego es **mayor que** doña Juana.*	Don Diego is **older than** doña Juana.

- Use *más de* or *menos de* and a number for stating there are "more than" or "fewer than" the number of items or people indicated.

*Veo **más de/menos de** diez estudiantes.*	I see **more than/fewer than** ten students.

5 ¿Cómo se comparan?

Imagine you are shopping for food items. Compare the following items, following the model and the cues given.

esta lechuga/estar más fresco/esa lechuga
Esta lechuga está más fresca que esa lechuga.

1. los guisantes/ser más pequeño/las cebollas
2. este pescado/ser más grande/ese pescado
3. estos tomates/estar menos maduro/aquellos tomates
4. este aguacate/estar más maduro/ese aguacate
5. las comidas frescas/ser mejor/las comidas en lata
6. el mercado/estar más lejos/el supermercado
7. el ajo en lata/ser peor/el ajo fresco
8. esta papa/ser más grande/la otra

¿Los guisantes en lata son mejores que los frescos?

Este pescado es más grande que el otro.

6 Haciendo comparaciones

Make as many comparisons from the following information as you can.

Información: Los aguacates del supermercado son pequeños pero los aguacates del mercado son grandes.
Comparación 1: Los aguacates del supermercado no son tan grandes como los aguacates del mercado.
Comparación 2: Los aguacates del mercado son más grandes que los aguacates del supermercado.
Comparación 3: Los aguacates del supermercado son menos grandes que los aguacates del mercado.

1. Julia cocina todos los días y Marta cocina una vez a la semana.
2. Compran dos latas de guisantes y dos latas de pimientos.
3. Hay mucho arroz en una paella valenciana pero no hay mucho ajo.
4. Silvia puede preparar una paella valenciana en dos horas pero yo necesito tres horas para prepararla.
5. Jaime va al mercado dos veces al mes y Silvia va al mercado dos veces al mes.
6. Jaime tiene quince años, Silvia tiene dieciséis años y Mario tiene dieciocho años.
7. María tiene tres libras de pescado y Carlos tiene tres libras de pescado.

7 El más....

Working with a partner, take turns asking and answering questions based upon the cues. Follow the model.

el supermercado más grande
A: ¿Cuál es el supermercado más grande de la ciudad donde vives?
B: El supermercado más grande de la ciudad donde vivo es....

1. el supermercado más nuevo
2. el supermercado más viejo
3. el mejor restaurante
4. el peor restaurante

8 El mejor restaurante

Imagine you are the owner of a restaurant. What instructions might you give your employees during the week, according to the following cues?

llegar al restaurante/temprano
Debes llegar al restaurante lo más temprano posible.

1. sacar la basura/tarde
2. recoger las mesas/rápidamente
3. leer la receta/bien
4. preparar una paella valenciana/pronto
5. barrer el suelo/bien

EL MENU DUCAL

Conexión *cultural*

Imágenes de España

When you hear the word **Spain**, what images come to mind? Can you taste the *churro* pastry and hot chocolate in a *café* in Madrid? Do you feel the blistering hot sand of a Mediterranean beach beneath your feet? Can you smell the aroma of *paella* being cooked in the kitchen of a restaurant in Valencia? Do you see dancers and hear the sound of guitars and castanets in Granada? Spain incorporates all these images and much more.

¿Quieres comer churros con chocolate?

El flamenco es un baile muy popular en España.

Una playa bonita en San Sebastian, España.

9 Imágenes de España

When you think about Spain, what do you associate with the country? Prepare a list of at least ten Spanish words that you associate with Spain. Try to include words that relate to Spain's history as well as to modern Spain.

En el mercado

SUPERMERCADOS
A L D I
BDEZ. DE CASTRO, 39 SUP:039
C.I.F.: A33006214 C:0039
20:47 220 003 399
FRUTAS Y VERDURAS 89
PESCADERIA 493
MARIA FONTANED.200 78
FRUTAS Y VERDURAS 110
YOPLAIT CON PINA *
4 X 53 212
HUEVO CORRAL S-2CL 222
CHARCUTERIA-CARNICO 309
FLAN NINO 6 SOBRES 140
Y.YOPLAIT NATURAL
3 X 39 117
REGALO Y.YOPLAIT NA -19
15 T O T A L...: 1751
ENTREGADO....: 1751
P.V.P. I.V.A. INCLUIDO
ADEMAS DE NUESTRAS OFERTAS,
SI EN EL ERES MAMA, ALDI
TE REGALA UNA CANASTILLA

10 Charlando

1. ¿Llevas frutas y verduras cuando vas al mercado?
2. ¿Cuál es tu verdura preferida?
3. ¿Comes muchas frutas? ¿Cuáles prefieres? ¿Por qué?
4. ¿Qué verduras prefieres en una ensalada?
5. Para el Día de Acción de Gracias, ¿comes pollo, carne, pescado, jamón u otra comida?
6. ¿Qué helados te gustan?

¿Vas al mercado para comprar las frutas o las verduras? (Mallorca, España)

11 ¿Qué es?

Match the items in column I with the items in column II.

I	II
1. la fresa	A. una verdura
2. la manzana	B. un sándwich
3. la habichuela	C. una ensalada
4. la lechuga con tomates, aceite y vinagre	D. una fruta más grande que una uva
5. el helado	E. una fruta tan grande como una uva
6. el pan con jamón y queso	F. un postre

12 ¿Cuál no está en su lugar?

Imagine you work in a supermarket and you are responsible for reorganizing the food shelves and produce sections after customers have moved the foods from their proper locations. Say which food item does not belong in each of the following groups.

1. leche	chorizo	queso	mantequilla
2. papa	aguacate	chocolate	cebolla
3. uva	manzana	plátano	habichuela
4. pollo	maíz	pescado	carne
5. naranja	fresa	uva	huevo
6. café	lechuga	tomate	zanahoria

13 ¿Qué comida te gusta?

Trabajando en parejas, hagan preguntas para comparar siete comidas o bebidas *(drinks)* diferentes para saber cuál les gusta más.

A: ¿Te gusta la leche tanto como el agua mineral?
B: Sí, (No, no) me gusta la leche tanto como el agua mineral.

14 ¿Qué comes?

Working with a partner, take turns asking and answering at least seven questions about what you eat and drink. Follow the model.

A: ¿Qué comes más, carne o verduras?
B: Como más carne (verduras) que verduras (carne)./Como tanta carne como verduras.

¿Te gustan las frutas?

15 El menú del día

Trabajando en parejas, escriban un menú balanceado *(balanced)* con todas las comidas básicas para uno de los días del fin de semana. El menú debe incluir el desayuno *(breakfast)*, el almuerzo y la cena *(dinner)*.

16 Comparaciones en el mercado

Imagine you are at an open market standing in front of two vendors. Look at the illustration and make the following comparisons, according to the cues.

plátanos/estar maduro
Los plátanos de doña Eva están más maduros que los plátanos de don Diego.

1. manzanas/ser grande
2. naranjas/ser pequeño
3. fresas/ser pequeño
4. naranjas/ser mejor
5. doña Eva/ser joven
6. don Diego/estar cansado
7. uvas/ser mejor

¿Cuántos pimientos quieres comprar?

Compramos las frutas en el mercado. (Barcelona, España)

Buscando el mejor precio

SILVIA: Señora, ¿cuánto pide por esos huevos?
SEÑORA: Ciento noventa y cinco pesetas.
SILVIA: ¡Uy! Yo hablé con aquel señor y él los tiene por ciento cincuenta. Le doy ciento cuarenta y me los llevo.
SEÑORA: Señorita, le **di**° el mejor **precio.** No puedo.
SILVIA: Entonces, no los llevo, gracias.
SEÑORA: Bueno, está bien. Puede llevarlos por ciento cuarenta.

di *gave*

17 ¿Qué comprendiste?

1. ¿Cuánto pide la señora por los huevos?
2 ¿Por qué precio los tiene el señor?
3. ¿Cuánto dice Silvia que le da por los huevos?
4. ¿Los da la señora por ciento cincuenta?

¿Cuánto pide la señora por los pimientos?

Oportunidades

Ellas pueden regatear en el mercado.

Regatear

It is a common and accepted practice in the markets of many Spanish-speaking countries to negotiate *(regatear)* the price for an item. These negotiations can be a lengthy but worthwhile way for both parties to mutually benefit. Away from the marketplace, however, most shops and stores have a fixed price *(precio fijo),* and trying to negotiate a lower price is not appropriate. How might knowing Spanish help you negotiate a price while visiting a Spanish-speaking country? Do you feel confident enough with your Spanish skills to be able to negotiate a price? The more you study the language, the better your skills will become and you might be surprised at how well you can converse and function in a Spanish-speaking environment.

18 Charlando

1. ¿Por qué crees que a la gente de otros países le gusta regatear?
2. ¿Te gusta la idea de regatear? Explica.
3. ¿Puedes regatear en las tiendas de la ciudad donde vives? Explica.
4. ¿Buscas siempre el mejor precio cuando compras algo? ¿El precio te importa?

Estrategia

Para aprender mejor: *survival skills*

Is there a flea market where you live? Go there and practice bargaining for items. Learning how to bargain will be beneficial if you travel to a Spanish-speaking country where you can combine your ability to bargain with your ability to speak Spanish.

19 Regateando

Imagine you are at an outdoor market shopping for ingredients to make a *paella*. Working with a partner, take turns playing the roles of the vendor and the client. Remember to bargain for items and agree on prices and quantities.

Repaso *rápido*

El pretérito de los verbos regulares *-ar*

Do you remember how to form the preterite tense of a regular *-ar* verb? Remove the last two letters from the infinitive and add the indicated endings.

lavar			
yo	lav**é**	nosotros nosotras	lav**amos**
tú	lav**aste**	vosotros vosotras	lav**asteis**
Ud. él ella	lav**ó**	Uds. ellos ellas	lav**aron**

Note: Regular verbs that end in *-car (buscar, explicar, sacar, tocar), -gar (apagar, colgar, jugar, llegar, pagar)* and *-zar (empezar)* require a spelling change in the *yo* form of the preterite.

¿Lavaste el coche?

20 La fiesta fue ayer

A Ana le gusta escribir en su diario. ¿Qué cosas puede ella escribir después de la fiesta del club de ecología? Usa el pretérito como en el modelo.

nosotros/no olvidar nada
Nosotros no olvidamos nada.

1. yo/empezar a preparar todo muy temprano
2. nosotros/comprar verduras frescas
3. yo/buscar los ingredientes de la receta
4. Javier/preparar la paella
5. Paula/ayudar a Javier a preparar la paella
6. yo/trabajar con Jaime todo el día
7. las muchachas/limpiar la casa
8. Jaime/buscar los tomates buenos

IDIOMA

El pretérito de *dar* y *estar*

The verbs *dar* and *estar* are irregular in the preterite tense.

Nos dieron tortilla española en la cafetería.

dar	
di	dimos
diste	disteis
dio	dieron

estar	
estuve	estuvimos
estuviste	estuvisteis
estuvo	estuvieron

21 Todos dieron comida

Last week your school prepared a dinner for disadvantaged families. Working with a partner, take turns reporting what food items people donated for the dinner. Follow the model.

tú/unos huevos
A: ¿Qué diste tú?
B: Yo di unos huevos.

1. Antonio/dos libras de tomates y cinco aguacates
2. los hermanos García/tres libras de arroz
3. María/tres latas de guisantes
4. Dolores y Rafael/los ingredientes para hacer cien ensaladas
5. la profesora/cuatro libras de café
6. tú y yo/tres latas de guisantes y tres latas de pimientos
7. el señor y la señora Ramiro/cinco pollos
8. yo/tres libras de papas y una lata de maíz

22 ¿Cuándo estuvieron?

Di cuándo estuvieron las siguientes personas en el supermercado.

Alfonso/el lunes pasado
Alfonso estuvo el lunes pasado.

1. Alejandro y Mario/el jueves
2. Jaime y Ana/anteayer
3. Ud./el sábado
4. las señoritas Peralta/esta mañana
5. mi madre/la semana pasada
6. tú/el fin de semana pasado
7. yo/ayer
8. Uds./el miércoles

La semana pasada estuvimos en Barcelona.

23 Una fiesta en casa

Completa el siguiente párrafo con la forma apropiada del pretérito de los verbos entre paréntesis.

El viernes pasado yo *(1. dar)* una fiesta en mi casa para el cumpleaños de mi padre. Casi toda mi familia y mis amigos *(2. estar)* allí. Mi tía Ana no *(3. estar)* y mis primos Orlando y Antonio tampoco *(4. estar)*. Todos nosotros *(5. estar)* muy contentos. Mi madre *(6. dar)* una comida excelente que a todos nos *(7. gustar)*. Luego, mis amigos Alberto y Esperanza *(8. dar)* un concierto fantástico. Ella *(9. cantar)* cinco canciones y él las *(10. tocar)* en el piano. Yo *(11. estar)* contento porque mi padre *(12. estar)* muy contento. Todos le *(13. dar)* muchos regalos *(gifts)* a él y él les *(14. dar)* las gracias a todos. La fiesta *(15. estar)* muy bien.

Autoevaluación. **As a review and self-check, respond to the following:**

1. Name several foods you might buy at a supermarket. Which ones could you also find at an outdoor market *(mercado al aire libre)*?
2. Name some of the ingredients and how much of each is needed in a recipe to make *paella* for six people.
3. Make several comparisons in Spanish to talk about foods you like and dislike.
4. Name two or three things that are the most, the best or the worst possible.
5. Imagine you keep a journal and every day you write where you went, where you were and other interesting information about what you did during the day. Make a brief list of five things that you would write about today in your journal.
6. After reading about Spain, what are three things you associate with the country?

¡La práctica hace al maestro!

A Comunicación

Working with three or four classmates, create six to eight questions comparing different foods. You may ask about whether your classmates eat in restaurants as often as they eat at home, whether they pay more or less often than the people with whom they eat, what the best foods are and why, what price they pay for foods from different places and so forth. Take notes and report your findings to the class.

A: ¿Cuál es la comida más popular en tu casa?
B: La comida más popular en mi casa es la paella.

B Conexión con la tecnología

Search the Web for a recipe *(receta)* that appeals to you for a main dish or dessert from one of the Spanish-speaking countries. Try the recipe at home. Finally, tell the class about your recipe: ingredients, preparation, how it tasted.

El flan es un postre muy popular en España.

FLAN DE QUESO

INGREDIENTES
Para 6 personas
Un bote pequeño de leche condensada,
2 vasos de leche,
1 tarrina de queso Philadelphia,
4 cucharadas de azúcar,
1 limón

PREPARACION
1 hora

DIFICULTAD
Para principiantes

PRESENTACION
Adornado con nata

CONSERVACION
2 días

MODO DE HACERLO

■ Mezclar la leche condensada con la leche, añadir el queso con el zumo y ralladura de medio limón. Remover hasta que todo esté bien unido. Agregar los huevos batidos.

■ Con el azúcar y el zumo del otro medio limón hacer un caramelo clarito. Bañar un molde de rosca de 20 cm. Llenar con la crema.

■ Tapar con papel de aluminio y cocer en el horno al baño María unos 45 minutos.

■ Desmoldarlo templado

VOCABULARIO

En el mercado

el aguacate
el ajo
el arroz
el café
la carne
la cebolla
el chocolate
el chorizo
la fresa
la fruta
el guisante
la habichuela
el helado
el huevo
el ingrediente
el jamón
la lata
la lechuga
la libra
el maíz
la manzana
el mercado
la papa
el pimiento
el plátano
el precio
el queso
el tomate
la uva
la verdura
el vinagre
la zanahoria

Para describir

fresco,-a
maduro,-a
mayor
mejor
menor
peor

Verbos

añadir
escoger
importar
llevar
olvidar
parecer

Expresiones y otras palabras

el/la/los/las *(+ noun)* más/menos *(+ adjective)*
el/la/los/las mejor/mejores/peor/peores *(+ noun)*
hacer falta
lo más/menos *(+ adverb)* posible
más/menos *(+ noun/adjective/adverb)* que
sin
tan *(+ adjective/adverb)* como
tanto como
tanto,-a *(+ noun)* como

Este restaurante es el mejor.

María ayuda con los ingredientes de la comida.

¿Quieres un helado?

a leer

Estrategia

Preparación

Estrategia para leer: ***gathering meaning from context***

When reading in another language, you will often encounter words you do not know. Before looking in a dictionary, look for clues that tell you what a word means. For example, you have already learned to recognize some unknown words because they are cognates *(e.g., familia)* or because they are related to words you have already learned *(e.g., baile/bailar)*. At other times it may be necessary to look at the words before and after an unknown word (the context) in order to guess its meaning. Looking for these contextual clues will help improve your reading skills and will also make reading more enjoyable because you spend less time looking up words in a dictionary.

¿Qué quieren decir las palabras *reunirse* y *aperitivos* en las siguientes oraciones?

1. Una vieja tradición española es **reunirse** con unos amigos en un café o un restaurante para hablar.
   - A. tener prisa
   - B. recordar hacer una cosa
   - C. tener una reunión con amigos
   - D. recoger la mesa
2. Muchas veces los españoles comen **aperitivos** con sus amigos antes de ir a casa para comer.
   - A. agua mineral
   - B. comida pequeña antes de una comida principal
   - C. plato grande de naranjas
   - D. mucha comida

Las tapas: una tradición española

A los españoles les gusta mucho pasar tiempo con sus amigos. Una vieja tradición española es la de reunirse con los amigos en un café o un restaurante para hablar y comer tapas (o aperitivos) antes de ir a casa para comer o **cenar** con la familia. Hay una razón muy práctica para comer tapas en España, ésta es que los españoles comen muy tarde (a las 2:00 o a las 3:00 de la tarde) y también cenan muy tarde (a las 9:00 o a las 10:00 de la noche).

Comer tapas es un pasatiempo divertido y social que no cuesta mucho dinero. Los precios son razonables porque los clientes pueden comprar una **ración** o media ración de las tapas que quieren comer.

Las tapas pueden ser fáciles de preparar. Pueden consistir en nada más que pan con jamón. Otras tapas son más complicadas y necesitan más preparación, como la **tortilla española.** Hoy día hay restaurantes en los Estados Unidos que sirven tapas.

Aquí está el menú del Restaurante Andalucía que te ofrece una buena variedad de tapas. ¿Cuál de estas tapas te gustaría comer?

atún *tuna*
empanadas *meat-filled pastry*

cenar *to eat supper* **ración** *serving* **tortilla española** *potato omelette*

A ¿Qué comprendiste?

1. ¿Qué son las tapas?
2. ¿Cuál es la tradición de comer tapas en España?
3. ¿Por qué es muy práctica esta tradición?
4. ¿Por qué no cuesta mucho dinero comer tapas?

B Charlando

1. ¿Te gustan los aperitivos? ¿Los comes mucho? ¿Dónde? ¿Cuándo?
2. ¿Cuáles son las tapas del Restaurante Andalucía que te gustaría comer?
3. ¿Cuáles son las tapas del restaurante que no te gustaría comer?

¿Cuáles son las tapas?

a escribir

Estrategia

Estrategia para escribir: *using graphic organizers*

Before beginning the writing process, it can be useful to brainstorm ideas about your topic. If you are writing about subjects that are related in some way, a graphic organizer such as a Venn diagram will help you visualize different aspects of your theme. A Venn diagram, consisting of two intersecting circles, is especially good when your writing includes a comparison of what two subjects (such as people, places or events) have in common.

A. Imagine you and a friend want to have a party to celebrate a special event. At the top of a piece of paper write the name of the type of party you want *(cumpleaños, fiesta sorpresa, etc.)*, and the date and the time the event will begin. Next, draw two intersecting circles (a Venn diagram). In one circle, list in Spanish the things you plan to do. In the second circle, list the things your friend plans to do. In the shared space, list the activities that the two of you plan to do together. Place each activity you think of in the appropriate area of the graphic. Be sure to include the *quehaceres* that must be completed both before and after the fiesta and list which *tapas* each person will bring and which ones you will make together.

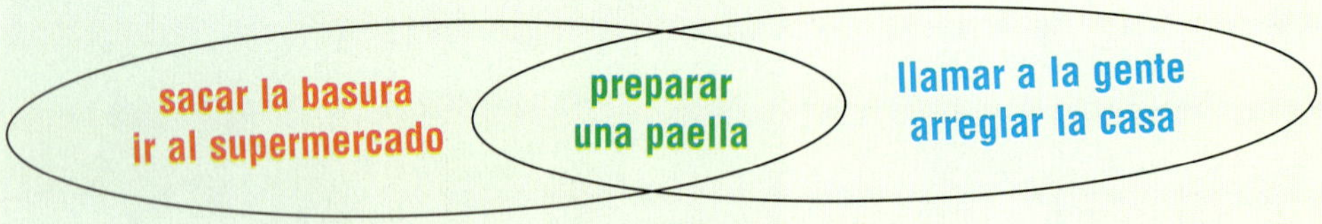

B. Underneath the circles of the Venn diagram you prepared, write a paragraph in Spanish describing the party you are planning, who is invited and who is responsible for carrying out the preparations. Finally, add decorative graphics or artwork to make the paper visually interesting.

repaso

Now that I have completed this chapter, I can...

- ✓ talk about household chores.
- ✓ talk about the recent past.
- ✓ ask for and offer help.
- ✓ discuss past actions and events.
- ✓ write about everyday activities.
- ✓ identify and describe foods.
- ✓ discuss food preparation.
- ✓ compare quantity, quality, age and size.
- ✓ negotiate a price.

I can also...

- ✓ read about *paella* and its preparation.
- ✓ read about the history of Spain.
- ✓ talk about life in Spain.
- ✓ use survival skills.

Vamos de compras al mercado.

El señor Cárdenas es más viejo que nosotros.

ESPIRAL
CENTRO COMERCIAL
SHOPPING
CENTER
CENTRO COMERCIAL
ESPIRAL

En la tienda

CAPÍTULO 9

In this chapter you will be able to:

- identify articles of clothing
- identify parts of the body
- describe clothing
- discuss size
- express past actions and events
- express negation or disagreement
- discuss price and payment
- write a summary

Lección 17

La ropa

Ropa para mujeres
el zapato de tacón
la ropa interior
el zapato bajo
la bota
las pantimedias
el vestido
Para todos
la blusa de seda
la falda
el traje de baño
la chaqueta
el sombrero
el guante
el anillo
el abrigo de lana
el impermeable

Algo más

¿Uso un artículo?

Use a definite article when naming colors in Spanish. A definite article is not usually required when a color describes an object because the color is an adjective.

Me gusta **el** (color) *anaranjado.*	I like orange.
but:	
Compré una camisa azul ayer.	I bought a blue shirt yesterday.

Sometimes, a word being described is omitted in order to avoid repeating a noun. In such cases the article remains and the adjective must agree with the noun that was omitted.

¿Prefieres el suéter verde o ***el** (suéter)* ***rojo?***	Do you prefer the green sweater or **the red one?**
Compré la chaqueta azul, no ***la amarilla.***	I bought the blue jacket, not **the yellow one.**

PARA ti

Los colores

Do you remember learning the following colors?

azul amarillo blanco gris negro rojo verde

1 ¿Qué comprendiste?

Describe la ropa del dibujo anterior usando los colores.

1. la blusa
2. los zapatos
3. los calcetines
4. la camisa
5. la corbata
6. la falda
7. los pantalones

Pienso que debes comprar el rojo.

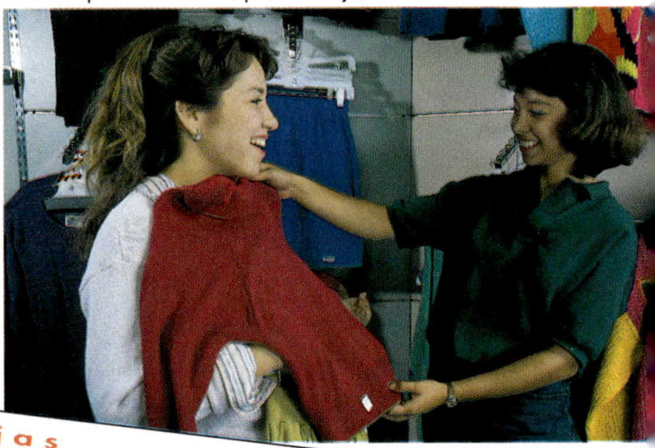

2 Charlando

1. ¿Tienes un color favorito para la ropa?
2. ¿Es de seda o de algodón tu camisa/blusa?
3. ¿Cuándo van tus amigas al colegio con zapatos de tacón?
4. ¿Quién va al colegio con corbata?
5. Describe la ropa de un chico o de una chica de tu colegio.

Conexión cultural

Panamá

El Canal de Panamá.

You probably associate Panama with the canal *(el Canal de Panamá)* that divides the country in two. This small Spanish-speaking country not only connects the Atlantic and Pacific oceans, but Panama may also be considered the link between Central and South America, making the country an important crossroads for the world.

Panama's people *(los panameños)* have a varied background. When Rodrigo de Bastidas, Juan de la Cosa and Vasco Núñez de Balboa arrived in 1501, and when Columbus landed in Panama in 1502, the land was inhabited primarily by natives of two indigenous groups, the *cuna* and the *chocó*. Today Panama's citizens are descendants of these and other indigenous groups, Spanish conquistadors, African slaves and workers from China (who were involved in constructing the railroad in the mid-1800s), among others. Direct descendants of the *cuna* and *chocó* people still inhabit the San Blas archipelago.

Somos parientes de los cunas.

Ciudad de Panamá, Panamá.

For the most part, Panama's geography consists of either mountains or lowland jungle. Most people live in cities of varying sizes along the canal. For example, Panama City *(Ciudad de Panamá),* the capital and largest city, with approximately 500,000 inhabitants, is located along the canal. Although Panama City is not as large as many other capitals, it has become one of the most important financial centers in Latin America, with more than ninety banks from around the world registered to do business.

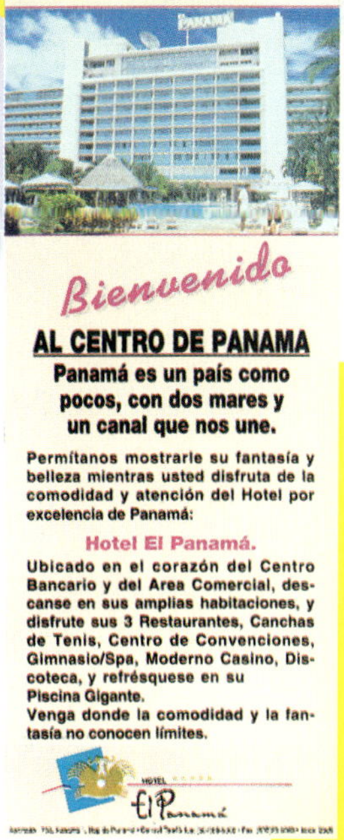

Conexiones 3: Cruzando fronteras

Completa lógicamente las oraciones con una de las siguientes respuestas: ***más de; español; 500.000; más grande; Canal de Panamá; los cunas y los chocós; Ciudad de Panamá; Bastidas, la Cosa y Balboa.***

1. El (1) divide el país en dos.
2. Hablan (2) en Panamá.
3. La (3) es la capital de Panamá.
4. Unas (4) personas viven en la capital.
5. La capital es la ciudad (5) del país.
6. (6) llegaron en 1501.
7. Los descendientes de (7) viven todavía en el archipiélago de San Blas.
8. La capital tiene (8) noventa bancos internacionales.

4 ¿Te gusta la ropa?

Trabajando en parejas, habla con tu compañero/a de la ropa del dibujo de la tienda de ropa en la Plaza Paitilla en Panamá. Señalen Uds. *(Point out)* con el dedo los artículos de ropa.

A: ¿Qué ropa del dibujo te gustaría comprar?
B: Me gustaría comprar un sombrero como este sombrero.

5 ¿Dónde lo pones?

Conecta lógicamente las palabras de la columna I con las palabras en la columna II.

I	II
1. la pierna	A. el sombrero
2. el brazo	B. el guante
3. la cabeza	C. el anillo
4. el dedo	D. la camisa
5. la mano	E. las pantimedias

¿Soy castaño o rubio?

Conexión Cultural

Palabras diferentes para decir lo mismo

In Spanish, you have seen that words used to name items can vary greatly from one country or region to the next. Even common articles of clothing are referred to in many different ways. The item you know as a *falda,* for instance, may be called a *saya* in the Caribbean or a *pollera* in parts of South America. In the Caribbean, *zapatos de tacón* are sometimes called simply *tacones.* In addition, an *abrigo* may be called a *sobretodo* in Chile, and many people use *almacén* instead of *tienda de ropa* to refer to the place where they shop for clothing.

Also notice that there are many different words to refer to the color brown. In countries that have been influenced by the French many people favor the word *marrón* for **brown.** Spaniards use *pardo.* In the Caribbean, *carmelita* and the expressions *color café* or *color tabaco* are used. In some countries the word for **brown** may vary according to what is being described. For example, the word *castaño* describes brown hair or brown eyes.

¿Te gusta esta pollera?

Estrategia

Para comunicar mejor: *asking questions*

If you hear a new word in a conversation but do not understand what it means, do not be afraid to ask someone to fill you in. Many words in Spanish have different uses depending on the region or country where they are used. So the next time you hear a word or expression you are unsure of, do not be embarrassed; ask someone to explain it to you.

6 Una variedad de ropa

Working in pairs, talk about the types of clothing you see around you. Begin by saying who owns the article of clothing. Your partner then must describe the material or color. Each student must name and describe at least five articles of clothing.

A: Estoy mirando el suéter de Julia.
B: Su suéter es rosado y es de lana.

7 En mi vida

Complete the following sentences with an appropriate adjective to describe some items in your life.

Mi casa es <u>blanca</u>.

1. Tengo un abrigo <u>(1)</u>.
2. Mis zapatos son <u>(2)</u>.
3. Me gustan los pantalones <u>(3)</u>.
4. Quiero comprar dos camisas <u>(4)</u>.
5. Tengo mucha ropa <u>(5)</u>.

8 ¿Qué vas a comprar?

Imagina que tienes $300. Haz una lista de la ropa que te gustaría comprar este sábado, añadiendo los colores que te gustan y los materiales (seda, algodón, lana).

Julia compró ropa

Panamá, 15 de abril

Querida Elena,

Como te prometí,° te escribo para contarte° lo que compré en el centro comercial para mis vacaciones en la isla Contadora en Panamá. Primero, estuve en la Vía España donde no compré nada.° (¡Todo lo que venden° cuesta mucho!) Después, estuve por las tiendas del centro comercial, la Plaza Paitilla. Estuve allí por dos horas y media y compré tantas cosas que casi no me quedó° dinero. Compré un vestido azul de algodón para llevar° por la noche y, para tener algo° cómodo, compré un pantalón rosado. Como sabes, el rosado es mi color favorito porque me queda° bien. Luego, compré dos blusas de seda para combinar con el pantalón y un traje de baño. Pronto vas a verlo todo. ¿Qué compraste tú?

Debes escribirme pronto, antes de mi viaje a Contadora. Adiós.

Tu prima que te quiere,

Julia

prometí *I promised* **contarte** *to tell you* **nada** *nothing* **venden** *they sell* **quedó** *remained* **llevar** *to wear* **algo** *something* **me queda** *it suits me*

¿Te gustan los zapatos que compré?

9 ¿Qué comprendiste?

1. ¿Adónde va Julia durante sus vacaciones?
2. ¿Qué ropa venden en la Vía España?
3. ¿Dónde compró muchas cosas?
4. ¿Cómo es el vestido que compró?
5. ¿Qué más compró?
6. ¿Cuál es el color favorito de Julia? ¿Por qué?

10 Charlando

1. ¿Hablas de ropa con tus amigos/as? ¿Con tu familia? ¿De qué hablan?
2. ¿Qué ropa compras antes de ir de vacaciones?
3. ¿Te importa si la ropa cuesta mucho dinero?
4. ¿Qué colores te quedan bien?
5. ¿Qué ropa llevas cuando hace calor? ¿Cuando hace frío?

Pilar aconseja tel. 2873908

Querida Lectora:

Ya se que Usted es una mujer moderna que tiene decidido estar siempre a la moda, o "in" que llaman ahora. Entonces, lo que tiene que hacer es visitar el almacén **Juana Teresa** y actualizar su guardarropa con los más hermosos conjuntos, vestidos y suéteres en lana; conjuntos y blusas en challis con diseños exclusivos; chaquetas, pantalones en paño, y sensacionales minifaldas en todos los materiales. En accesorios, ni hablar! Cinturones divinos, blusas, fantasías, vestidos de baño... Todo finísimo y de actualidad. **Juana Teresa** está esperándola en la Cl. 95 No. 13-82, tel 218 10 04.

11 ¿Qué debo llevar?

Imagínate en estas situaciones. ¿Qué vas a llevar? Escoge la palabra apropiada para completar lógicamente las siguientes oraciones.

Si no hace frío no llevo un (falda, <u>suéter</u>, camisa).

1. Quiero llevar una (chaqueta, corbata, camisa) porque hace frío.
2. Hace mucho viento y no debo llevar el (sombrero, café, suéter).
3. El pantalón del (rosado, traje, falda) está sucio.
4. Ay, está nevando y no tengo (corbata, amarillo, botas).
5. Hace sol y calor. Debo llevar mi (suéter, traje de baño, falda) a la playa.
6. Me gusta caminar por la playa sin (zapatos, seda, gris).

12 Muy de moda

Working in pairs, talk about this fashion advertisement. Discuss what the people are wearing, the colors of each article of clothing and whether you like the item or not. Finally, take turns asking one another to identify the parts of the body shown in the illustration that you have learned in this lesson.

PARA ti

Proverbios y dichos

The degree to which clothes and fashion are important in our everyday lives varies from one person to another. A Spanish proverb says that it is not the clothes you wear that are important, but rather who you are. As the saying goes: *Aunque la mona se vista de seda, mona se queda* (Even though it may be wearing silk, the monkey is still a monkey).

Aunque la mona se vista de seda, mona se queda.

13 ¿Qué ropa necesitas?

Haz una lista de la ropa que necesitas para esquiar en la nieve y otra lista para pasar un día en la playa.

¿Qué necesitas para ir a la playa?

¿Qué ropa llevas cuando vas a esquiar?

14 ¿Cómo es la ropa?

In groups of three to five students, take turns asking one another about the color of a particular piece of clothing worn by someone in the group. The person asking then selects a student in the group to answer. The selected student must answer and then ask a different question of someone else in the group.

¿De qué color es el pantalón de Sara?
Es azul.

Repaso *rápido*

El pretérito de los verbos regulares *-ar*

You have already learned how to form the preterite tense of a regular *-ar* verb to express simple past actions. Remove the last two letters from the infinitive and add the indicated endings.

El chico me vendió la fruta.

comprar			
yo	compr**é**	nosotros nosotras	compr**amos**
tú	compr**aste**	vosotros vosotras	compr**asteis**
Ud. él ella	compr**ó**	Uds. ellos ellas	compr**aron**

IDIOMA

El pretérito de los verbos regulares *-er* e *-ir*

To form the preterite tense of regular *-er* and *-ir* verbs, remove the last two letters from the infinitive. Then add the same set of endings for either type of verb.

vender	
vend**í**	vend**imos**
vend**iste**	vend**isteis**
vend**ió**	vend**ieron**

escribir	
escrib**í**	escrib**imos**
escrib**iste**	escrib**isteis**
escrib**ió**	escrib**ieron**

¿Qué le ***vendieron*** *a Julia en la Plaza Paitilla?*

What **did they sell** Julia at Plaza Paitilla?

*¿Le **escribió** Julia una carta a su prima?*

Did Julia **write** a letter to her cousin?

Stem changes that occur in the present tense for *-ar* and *-er* verbs do not occur in the preterite tense. However, *-ir* verbs that have a stem change in the present tense require a different stem change in the preterite tense for *Ud., él, ella, Uds., ellos* and *ellas.* This second change is shown in parentheses after infinitives in this book. Some verbs that follow this pattern include *dormir (ue, **u**), mentir (ie, **i**), pedir (i, **i**), preferir (ie, **i**), repetir (i, **i**)* and *sentir (ie, **i**).* The stem changes do not interfere with the verb endings.

dormir	
dormí	dormimos
dormiste	dormisteis
durmió	durmieron

pedir	
pedí	pedimos
pediste	pedisteis
pidió	pidieron

preferir	
preferí	preferimos
preferiste	preferisteis
prefirió	prefirieron

15 ¿Qué hiciste ayer?

State ten things you did or did not do yesterday, using each of the indicated verbs one time: *abrir, aprender, barrer, comer, correr, dormir, escribir, mentir, recoger, repetir, salir.*

abrir
Abrí mi libro de español./No abrí la ventana de mi cuarto.

16 Trabajando en el centro comercial

Imagine you work in a clothing store at the mall and your boss has just returned from vacation. What questions might you have to answer? Working with a partner, play the part of the employee or the boss, based upon the provided cues. Follow the model.

pedir más guantes de lana
A: ¿Pediste más guantes de lana?
B: Sí, (No, no) los pedí.

1. recoger las camisas
2. escoger las corbatas para los clientes
3. vender los nuevos suéteres cafés
4. aprender a arreglar los pantalones
5. barrer siempre la tienda por la mañana
6. añadir los sombreros nuevos a la ventana

¿Vendiste algunos zapatos de mujer hoy?

17 ¿Qué pasó ayer?

Haz ocho oraciones completas para decir qué pasó ayer, usando elementos de cada columna.

Yo estuve en el centro comercial.

I	II	III
Mario y ella	prometer	en el centro comercial
tú	vender	el precio dos veces
Uds.	estar	comprarte un anillo nuevo
yo	preferir	los abrigos de lana
Pilar	repetir	ayuda
tú y yo	pedir	a la tienda de ropa
Ud.	correr	ropa interior blanca
el señor Vega	dormir	toda la tarde

18 ¿Qué pasó en el centro comercial?

Working with a partner, take turns asking and answering what happened at the shopping center yesterday, according to the cues and the following illustrations.

A: ¿Qué pidió ver Paloma?
B: Paloma pidió ver unos zapatos de tacón rojos.

Paloma/pedir ver

1. Paula y su hermana/escoger

2. Carlos/preferir comprar

3. sus primos/ pedir ver

4. David/escoger

5. Juan y su hermano/volver para comprar

6. la prima de José/correr a comprar

IDIOMA

El pretérito de los verbo *ir* y *ser*

You have already seen forms of the preterite tense of *ser.* The irregular preterite-tense forms of *ir* (to go) and *ser* (to be) are identical.

ir/ser	
fui	fuimos
fuiste	fuisteis
fue	fueron

*¿Quién **fue** a la tienda ayer?*	Who **went** to the store yesterday?
*¿**Fueron** Uds. a la tienda?*	**Did** you **go** to the store?

but:

*¿Qué día **fue** ayer?*	What day **was** yesterday?
*Esos días **fueron** fantásticos.*	Those days **were** fantastic.

Fue una vacación fantástica. (San Blas, Panamá)

Fuimos de compras a una tienda del centro comercial.

Ellos fueron al centro de Panamá.

19 Fueron a comprar....

Imagina que tus amigos y tú fueron de compras al centro comercial el sábado pasado. Di lo que las siguientes personas fueron a comprar. Sigue el modelo.

Felipe fue a comprar un pantalón café.

Felipe

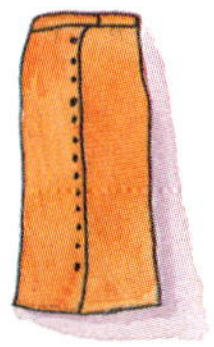

1. Isabel

2. Cristina y Laura

3. tú

4. nosotros

5. yo

20 ¿Quién fue?

Working with a partner, take turns asking and answering who did the following, according to the cues.

prometer/llevarte al centro comercial/tu padre (mi abuela)
A: ¿Quién prometió llevarte al centro comercial? ¿Tu padre?
B: No, fue mi abuela.

1. prestarte/el dinero/Inés (Marta)
2. preguntarles/el precio de las botas/Isabel (yo)
3. vender/las corbatas de seda/la señora de la tienda (el señor)
4. comprarle/un anillo/Roberto (sus tíos)
5. pagar/la chaqueta/Mamá (tú)
6. pedir ayuda/ellos (nosotros)

21 De compras en la isla Contadora

Completa el siguiente párrafo con el pretérito de los verbos indicados para decir qué ropa compraron Julia y sus dos hermanas en la isla Contadora.

Primero yo *(1. escoger)* un traje de baño porque el que tengo no me queda bien. Lo *(2. comprar)* por poco dinero. Mis hermanas también *(3. comprar)* en la misma tienda unos vestidos de algodón muy bonitos. Cuando nosotras *(4. volver)* al centro comercial, yo *(5. ir)* a buscar otro traje de baño para mí. Ese día en la tienda, *(6. vender)* todos los trajes de baño rápidamente. Nosotras *(7. comprar)* el último. Me gustaría tener dos. Luego, mi tía Julia *(8. ir)* con nosotras de compras. Ella *(9. prometer)* comprarme ropa para mi cumpleaños y yo le *(10. pedir)* unos zapatos bajos, de color café. ¡Qué bonitos son! Nosotras *(11. estar)* comprando todo el día y *(12. llegar)* tarde al hotel, ¡cansadas pero contentas!

IDIOMA

Las expresiones afirmativas y negativas

You have learned to make a sentence negative by placing *no* before a verb.

No veo la corbata. — I do **not** see the tie.

Unlike English, in Spanish it is sometimes possible to use two negative expressions in the same sentence. The following chart contains a list of common negative expressions along with their affirmative counterparts.

Expresiones afirmativas	Expresiones negativas
sí *(yes)* **Sí,** ella quiere ir. Ella dice que **sí.**	**no** *(no)* **No,** él **no** quiere ir. Él dice que **no.**
algo *(something, anything)* ¿Quieres comprar **algo?** ¿Compraste **algo** para tu viaje?	**nada** *(nothing, anything)* **No** quiero comprar **nada.** **Nada** me gusta.
alguien *(somebody, anybody)* ¿Lo sabe **alguien?** **Alguien** debe saberlo.	**nadie** *(nobody, anybody)* **No** lo sabe **nadie.** **Nadie** lo sabe.
algún, alguna,-os,-as *(some, any)* ¿Le gusta **algún** pantalón? ¿Le gusta **alguna** falda? ¿Compras **algunos** calcetines? ¿Buscas **algunas** camisas?	**ningún, ninguna,-os,-as** *(none, not any)* No, **ningún** pantalón me gusta. No, **ninguna** me gusta. No, **no** compro **ningunos** calcetines. No, **no** busco **ningunas** camisas.
o... o *(either...or)* Puedes comprar **o** un abrigo **o** un sombrero.	**ni... ni** *(neither... nor)* **No** voy a comprar **ni** un abrigo **ni** un sombrero.
siempre *(always)* Él **siempre** lleva botas.	**nunca** *(never)* Ella **no** lleva botas **nunca.** Ella **nunca** lleva botas.
también *(also, too)* Ella viene hoy **también.** Ella **también** viene hoy.	**tampoco** *(neither, either)* Él **no** viene mañana **tampoco.** Él **tampoco** viene mañana.

¿Te gusta algún sombrero?

Note: The words *alguno,-a* (some, any) and *ninguno,-a* (none, not any) sometimes are used as pronouns.

*¿Va **alguno** o **alguna** de Uds. al centro comercial ahora?* — *No, **ninguno*** de nosotros va al *centro comercial ahora.*

When combining negative expressions in one sentence in Spanish, it is often possible to use one of the negative expressions before the verb and another negative expression (and sometimes even more than one) after the verb. However, *no, nada, nadie, nunca, tampoco* and forms of *ninguno* may be used alone, before the verb, without the word *no.*

***No** voy **nunca** al centro.* ***Nunca** voy al centro.*	I **never** go downtown.
No** estoy comprando* ***nada tampoco. ***Tampoco** estoy comprando **nada.***	I am **not** buying **anything either.**

When *nadie* or a form of *ninguno* are direct objects referring to people they require the personal *a.*

***No** veo **a nadie** aquí.*	I don't see anyone here.
***No** veo **a ningún** amigo aquí.*	I don't see any friends here.

22 Afirmativo o negativo

Completa lógicamente las siguientes oraciones, usando *algo, alguien, nada* o *nadie.*

1. ¿Va (1) con Uds.?
2. Sí, Paula va con nosotras porque quiere comprar (2).
3. ¿Ves a (3) en esa tienda de ropa?
4. No, no veo a (4).
5. ¿Hay (5) que te gustaría comprar?
6. No, no hay (6) que me gustaría comprar.
7. (7) debe ir con Uds.
8. No quiero ir con (8).
9. (9) te llama por teléfono.
10. Juana te quiere decir (10).

No hay ningunos zapatos amarillos en esta tienda.

23 ¡Digo que no!

Contesta las siguientes preguntas en forma negativa.

¿Qué quieres comprar?
No quiero comprar nada.

1. ¿Con quién fuiste de compras ayer?
2. Yo no voy al centro. ¿Y tú?
3. ¿Siempre vas de compras al centro de la ciudad?
4. ¿Te gustaría vender ropa interior o carros?
5. ¿Tus padres siempre te dan dinero para ir de compras?
6. ¿Compraste un suéter anaranjado o un suéter verde?
7. ¿Ves a algún amigo de Panamá?
8. ¿Viste alguna blusa de algodón?
9. ¿Quiénes de Uds. son de Panamá?

¿Ves algún suéter bonito?

24 Nadie lo hace

Trabaja con tu compañero/a para hacer una lista de siete cosas que nadie hace nunca. Luego, deben leer la lista a la clase.

Nadie va de compras sin zapatos.

Autoevaluación. **As a review and self-check, respond to the following:**

1. Describe at least two of your favorite clothing items. What color are they? What material are they made of?
2. Imagine you are going on a winter ski trip. What kind of clothing will you need to bring? What will you need for a trip to the beach?
3. Name three things you did yesterday.
4. Name two places you went yesterday.
5. Make two affirmative and two negative statements about something that occurred yesterday.
6. Name three things you learned about Panama.

Este vestido rojo es mi favorito. ¡Siempre lo llevo!

¡En esta tienda hay blusas, pantalones y chaquetas muy bonitas!

¡La práctica hace al maestro!

A Comunicación

Working with a partner, talk about the role that clothing plays in your life. Discuss such topics as the kind of clothing you like to wear and when, the colors you prefer and why, when and where you purchased some of your favorite clothing, which articles of clothing each of you purchased last week/month/year (naming a specific time) and so forth. Use the dictionary to look up any terms you do not know.

A: ¿Qué ropa llevas mucho?
B: Llevo esta camisa verde casi todas las semanas.
A: ¿La compraste en el centro comercial?
B: No. Nunca compro nada en el centro comercial. Prefiero las tiendas pequeñas.

B Conexión con la tecnología

Search the Internet to find information about weather conditions throughout the world. Find out what the weather is like in Panama or a neighboring country. What is the temperature? Is it sunny or cloudy? Then consider what effect the weather has on our lives. For example, does the weather affect our clothing choices? How does the weather affect what we do? Summarize your findings about the weather in the place you researched, and try to guess what people there are wearing and what they may be doing.

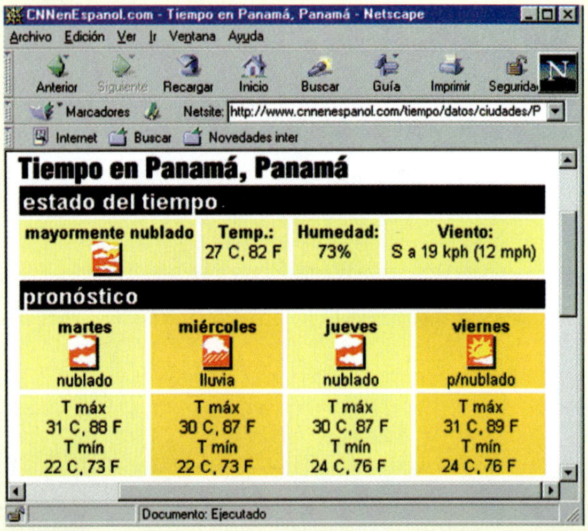

VOCABULARIO

Para describir
- algún, alguna
- anaranjado,-a
- café
- ningún, ninguna
- rosado,-a

Pronombres
- algo
- alguien
- alguno,-a
- nada
- nadie
- ninguno,-a

La ropa
- el anillo
- la blusa
- la bota
- el calcetín
- la camisa
- la chaqueta
- la corbata
- la falda
- el guante
- el impermeable
- el pantalón
- las pantimedias
- la ropa interior
- el sombrero
- el suéter
- el traje (de baño)
- el vestido
- el zapato (bajo/de tacón)

Partes del cuerpo
- el brazo
- la cabeza
- el cuerpo
- el dedo
- la mano
- el pie
- la pierna

Verbos
- combinar
- contar (ue)
- llevar
- prometer
- quedar
- vender

Expresiones y otras palabras
- el algodón
- el centro comercial
- el hombre
- la lana
- la mujer
- ni... ni
- o... o
- quedarle bien a uno
- la seda
- las vacaciones

¿Prefieres los amarillos o los anaranjados?

El señor Ramos siempre compra camisas de algodón.

¿Me queda bien?

Lección 18

Un regalo para Carmencita

DIEGO: ¿Le gustaría a Carmencita el suéter rojo que vimos ayer?
PEDRO: Ese suéter es **demasiado**° **corto.**
DIEGO: ¿Y este suéter blanco?
PEDRO: Pues, no. Me parece **bastante**° **largo.**
DIEGO: ¡Qué **lindo**° es aquel **paraguas**! Es **perfecto** para ella.
PEDRO: Ella me dijo que le gustaría **recibir**° algo **personal.**
DIEGO: Sí, claro, un anillo o aquel **collarcito**° de **perlas.**°
PEDRO: ¡Qué cómico! Bueno, vamos al **departamento** donde venden **regalos.** ¿Quieres **usar** la **escalera automática?**
DIEGO: No, podemos ir más rápidamente en el **ascensor.** Allí está.

demasiado *too* **bastante** *rather, fairly* **lindo** bonito **recibir** *to receive* **collarcito** *little necklace* **perlas** *pearls*

Algo más

Los diminutivos

In Spanish, it is often possible to indicate affection or to convey the idea that something is small simply by replacing the final vowel of a noun with the endings *-ito, -ita, -itos* and *-itas: Teresa (Teresita).* For nouns that end in a consonant, add the endings *-cito, -cita, -citos* or *-citas* to the complete word: *suéter (suétercito).*

Additional diminutive endings you may encounter include *-illo, -illa, -uelo, -uela, -ico* and *-ica.* Other words may require a spelling change: *poquito (poco).*

Although many exceptions exist for the diminutive forms, most are easily recognized: *papelito (papel), Miguelito (Miguel).* It is best to learn the variations as you encounter them since they can vary from country to country and even from one person to another within countries.

Anita y Teresita.

1 ¿Qué comprendiste?

1. ¿Qué están buscando los dos chicos?
2. ¿Cómo es el suéter rojo? ¿Y el blanco?
3. Según Diego, ¿qué regalo es perfecto para Carmencita?
4. ¿Qué dijo Carmencita que le gustaría recibir?
5. ¿Qué dice Diego que Pedro puede comprarle a ella?
6. ¿A qué departamento quiere ir Pedro?
7. ¿Quiere Pedro tomar el ascensor?
8. ¿Qué prefiere usar Diego?

Vamos al centro comercial a comprar regalos.

2 Charlando

1. ¿Es fácil o difícil para ti escoger un regalo para alguien?
2. Cuando compras un regalo, ¿vas con alguien a escogerlo? ¿Con quién vas?
3. ¿Te importa qué le parece el regalo a otra persona?
4. ¿Qué tipo de regalo prefieres recibir? ¿Algo personal?
5. En el centro comercial, ¿cómo vas de un piso a otro?

Voy a comprar esta blusa de seda. Es un regalo para mi mejor amiga.

Conexión cultural

Quito, Ecuador.

Ecuador

Ecuador is located along the Pacific Ocean on the western coast of South America, southwest of Colombia and north of Peru. The equator *(ecuador)* cuts through the northern half of the country only a few miles north of the nation's capital, Quito, which is located high in the Andes Mountains. A monument here marks the dividing point between the Northern and the Southern Hemisphere. The location is just one of many interesting features this small, Spanish-speaking country offers its own citizens and visitors alike.

Ecuador's most famous point of interest is probably the *Archipiélago de Colón,* which is located off the coast of Ecuador in the Pacific Ocean. You may know the archipelago by its more common name, the Galapagos Islands *(Islas Galápagos).* The islands were formed by volcanic eruptions. Today they have become a national park *(parque nacional)* consisting of more than 600 miles of coastline where an interesting mix of tropical and cold-climate animals *(animales)* and plants *(plantas)* live that cannot be found in any other part of the world.

Un animal que vive en las Islas Galápagos.

Ecuador once formed a part of the Incan Empire. When the Incan emperor Huayna Cápac died in the sixteenth century, he divided the empire between two sons: Atahualpa ruled the portion that was based in Quito, and Huáscar ruled the portion that was based in Cuzco, Peru. Huayna Cápac did not know, however, that the division would drastically weaken the empire and lead to its rapid conquest by the Spanish conquistadors. Ecuador remained Spanish until becoming the first South American nation to declare its independence in 1809. Not all remnants of Ecuador's indigenous past were destroyed, however. Remains of Ecuador's colorful past are still evident throughout the nation today.

Conexiones 3 Cruzando fronteras

Estos pájaros viven en las Islas Galápagos.

Contesta las siguientes preguntas sobre Ecuador.

1. ¿Qué divide el mundo en norte y sur?
2. ¿Cuál es la capital del Ecuador?
3. ¿En qué océano están las Islas Galápagos?
4. ¿Qué hay en las Galápagos ahora?
5. ¿Por qué son especiales los animales de las Islas Galápagos?
6. ¿De qué imperio famoso formó parte el Ecuador?
7. ¿En qué año declaró el Ecuador su independencia?

IDIOMA

¿Oíste la banda de mis amigos?

El pretérito de *leer, oír, ver, decir, hacer* y *tener*

The preterite tenses of the verbs *leer, oír, ver, decir, hacer* and *tener* all have irregularities. For example, for *leer* and *oír,* an *i* between two vowels changes to a *y.* In addition, both *leer* and *oír* require additional accent marks to separate vowel sounds and to indicate how these words are pronounced. The preterite tense of the verb *ver* uses the regular *-er* verb endings, but without any accent marks.

leer	
leí	leímos
leíste	leísteis
leyó	leyeron

oír	
oí	oímos
oíste	oísteis
oyó	oyeron

ver	
vi	vimos
viste	visteis
vio	vieron

Learning the irregular preterite-tense stem of *decir (dij), hacer (hic)* and *tener (tuv)* and the endings *-e, -iste, -o, -imos, -isteis* and *-ieron* will help you when you wish to use the preterite tense of these three irregular verbs. **Note:** The *c* in the preterite-tense stem for *hacer* changes to *z* in *hizo*; *dijeron* is an exception to the above because no *i* is required for the preterite ending.

decir	
dije	dijimos
dijiste	dijisteis
dijo	dijeron

hacer	
hice	hicimos
hiciste	hicisteis
hizo	hicieron

tener	
tuve	tuvimos
tuviste	tuvisteis
tuvo	tuvieron

4 ¿Qué hiciste ayer?

Di seis cosas que hiciste o que no hiciste ayer, según las actividades indicadas.

ver una película
Vi una película ayer./No vi una película ayer.

1. hacer una pregunta en español
2. leer el periódico
3. oír un disco compacto nuevo
4. tener que ir al dentista
5. decir la verdad todo el día
6. comprar un regalo perfecto para mi abuela

Compré un regalo perfecto. (Mercado de Otavalo, Ecuador)

5 Yo hice....

Trabajando en parejas, alterna con tu compañero/a para preguntar y contestar lo que hicieron o ayer o la semana pasada.

A: ¿Qué hiciste el jueves?
B: Vi una película fantástica.

6 ¿Qué dijiste?

Imagina que no oíste un comentario. Por ejemplo, ¿qué debes decir si estás oyendo varias conversaciones pero no puedes oír muy bien? Sigue el modelo.

tu amiga
¿Qué dijo tu amiga? No la oí.

1. los muchachos
2. ese señor
3. ellas
4. tú
5. la mesera

7 ¿Qué hicieron?

Haz oraciones completas en el pretérito usando la siguiente información y diciendo qué hicieron las personas indicadas.

mi mamá/leer una revista/y/oír un programa en la radio
Mi mamá leyó una revista y oyó un programa en la radio.

1. mi padre/tener que ir a la oficina/y/volver a casa muy cansado
2. nosotros/hacer una lista de regalos/pero/nunca comprar ningún regalo de la lista
3. mi hermanita/ver televisión/y/hacer su tarea
4. Uds./tener que estudiar para un examen/pero/hablar mucho de los deportes también
5. Elena/hacer aeróbicos/pero/ir a comer después a un restaurante con sus amigas
6. mi abuela/tener que ir de compras/pero/no comprar nada
7. nosotros/oír discos compactos nuevos/y/hablar de nuestras canciones favoritas

8 Un domingo por la tarde

¿Qué hicieron algunas personas el domingo por la tarde, según las ilustraciones?

Algunas personas jugaron al básquetbol.

1. 

2. 

3. 

4. 

5. 

6. 

En el departamento de regalos

9 ¿Qué comprendiste?

1. ¿De qué materiales puede ser un bolso? ¿Un abrigo?
2. ¿Para qué es una billetera?
3. ¿Cuándo llevas bufanda y guantes?
4. ¿De qué puede ser un vestido?
5. ¿Qué puede ser de oro?
6. ¿Qué puede ser de perlas?
7. ¿De qué puede ser un anillo?
8. ¿Qué puede ser de seda?

10 Charlando

1. ¿Qué regalos te gusta comprar para tus amigos? ¿Y para tus amigas?
2. ¿Te gusta usar perfume o prefieres regalarlo a alguien?
3. ¿Es tu cinturón de material sintético?
4. ¿Llevas guantes al colegio? ¿Cuándo?
5. ¿Quién lleva aretes? ¿Cómo son?
6. ¿Tienes algo de oro, de plata o de perlas? ¿Qué es/son?
7. ¿Es tu paraguas un regalo, o lo compraste tú?

PARA ti

Diciéndolo de otra manera

Many of the items you just learned may be said in other ways. For example, you may hear *cartera* or *bolsa* in place of *bolso.* Instead of *el pijama,* some people use *el/la payama* or *el piyama.* A *pulsera* may be called a *brazalete,* although technically a *brazalete* is usually worn on the arm *(el brazo).* Sometimes a gold or silver necklace is a *cadena* (chain). Synthetic materials are often made of *plástico, rayón* or *acrílico.* Earrings are *aretes,* but they may also be *zarcillos,* or specifically they may be *aros* or *aritos* (hoops), *pendientes* (if they are large) or *dormilonas* (if they are small, have no hoops and you can leave them in while you sleep).

11 ¿Qué les gustaría recibir?

Haz oraciones completas diciéndole a alguien qué dijeron las siguientes personas que les gustaría recibir para su cumpleaños.

Rosita

Rosita dijo que le gustaría recibir un collar de perlas

1. Uds.

2. tú

3. mis hermanitas

4. mis tíos

5. mis abuelas

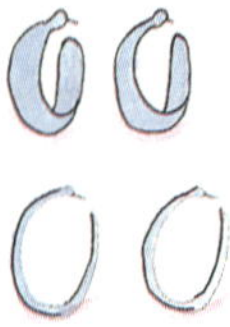
6. nosotras

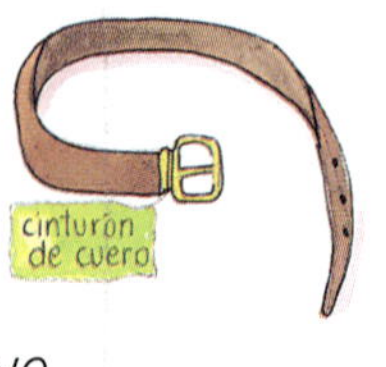

7. yo

8. mi abuelo

9. mi mamá

12 Regalos para hombres o para mujeres

Con tu compañero/a, prepara tres listas de regalos, indicando si cada uno es para hombres, para mujeres o para hombres y mujeres. Uds. deben tener tres o cuatro regalos en cada columna.

Para hombres	Para mujeres	Para hombres y mujeres
?	?	?

¿En efectivo o a crédito?

Antonio y Dolores están en el centro comercial Unicentro, en Guayaquil, Ecuador. Dolores está ayudando a Antonio a escoger un lindo regalo.

DOLORES: Está bastante **barato.**
ANTONIO: De acuerdo. No está **caro,** porque **está en oferta** especial.
DOLORES: Vas a **ahorrar** dinero porque puedes comprar dos por el precio de uno.
ANTONIO: ¿Te parece que el **tamaño°** está bien? ¿Es buena la **calidad?°** ¿Piensas que puede ser más barato en otra tienda?
DOLORES: Ay, Antonio, ¡es difícil ir de compras **contigo!°** Vamos a la **caja** a **pagar.°** ¿Vas a pagar **en efectivo?°**
ANTONIO: No, voy a pagar **a crédito** porque no tengo **bastante°** dinero aquí.

tamaño *size* **calidad** *quality* **contigo** *with you* **pagar** *to pay* **en efectivo** *in cash* **bastante** *enough*

13 ¿Qué comprendiste?

1. ¿Dónde está el centro comercial Unicentro?
2. ¿Le parece a Antonio que la calidad del regalo es buena?
3. ¿Dónde pagan el regalo?
4. ¿Cómo pueden pagar?
5. ¿Por qué va a pagar a crédito Antonio?

14 Charlando

1. ¿Necesitas mucho tiempo para comprar algo?
2. ¿Sabes cuándo algo está en oferta especial? ¿Cómo lo sabes?
3. ¿En qué mes del año es más barata la ropa de verano?
4. ¿Qué es más importante para ti, la buena calidad o el buen precio?
5. ¿Cómo te gusta pagar?

15 ¿Qué puede ser el regalo?

En el diálogo anterior, Dolores y Antonio hablan de comprar un regalo, pero no dicen qué es. Trabajando en grupos de tres estudiantes, deben tratar de resolver *(to solve)* el misterio. Hagan una lista de regalos posibles de acuerdo con el diálogo anterior.

Oportunidades

En el mercado internacional

When you buy a product in a store, it may have come from just about anywhere in the world. People throughout the United States deal internationally with other countries and must use language skills to arrange for importing and exporting a wide variety of goods. Have you ever considered using your Spanish skills in international trade?

16 ¿Qué hiciste?

Imagina que fuiste a comprar algunos regalos en un centro comercial. ¿Cómo puedes completar las siguientes oraciones para decir que hiciste lo opuesto de las palabras indicadas?

No compré el pijama *caro,* preferí el pijama barato.

1. No lo *vendí,* lo (1).
2. No fui a comprar una bufanda *fea,* fui a comprar una bufanda (2).
3. No me gustó *el bolso de cuero,* me gustó (3).
4. No pagué *a crédito* con mi tarjeta, pagué (4) en una de las cajas.
5. No compré ningún pañuelo *de mala calidad,* compré un pañuelo (5).
6. No vi ningún cinturón de cuero demasiado *largo,* vi un cinturón de cuero demasiado (6).
7. No *recibí* un regalo de mis papás, les (7) un regalo a mis papás.
8. No vi el collar *caro*, vi el collar (8).

Repaso rápido

Las preposiciones

You have learned to use several prepositions in Spanish. Look at the following list and see how many you remember:

preposiciones	
a	hasta
con	para
de	por
desde	sin
en	sobre

Hay una iglesia en la Plaza de la Independencia. (Quito, Ecuador)

IDIOMA

¿Puedes ir al cine conmigo?

Usando las preposiciones

You have already seen prepositions used with prepositional pronouns. For example, the prepositional pronouns are used in combination with the preposition *a* to add emphasis or to clarify the meaning of a sentence: *A mí me gusta ahorrar dinero cuando voy de compras.* The following prepositional pronouns also may be used with the other prepositions you have learned.

los pronombres después de las preposiciones			
sin **mí**	*without me*	sin **nosotros,-as**	*without us*
sin **ti**	*without you*	sin **vosotros,-as**	*without you*
sin **Ud.**	*without you*	sin **Uds.**	*without you*
sin **él**	*without him*	sin **ellos**	*without them*
sin **ella**	*without her*	sin **ellas**	*without them*

Two exceptions to the above are the words *conmigo* (with me), which is used instead of *con* followed by *mí,* and *contigo* (with you), which is used instead of *con* followed by *ti.*

¿Puedes ir ***conmigo*** *ahora?*	Can you go **with me** now?
No, no puedo ir ***contigo*** *ahora.*	No, I cannot go **with you** now.

17 ¿Puedes buscar un regalo conmigo?

Completa lógicamente el siguiente párrafo, escogiendo palabras de la siguiente lista: *conmigo, contigo, ella, mí, nosotros, ti.* Puedes usar las palabras más de una vez.

Querida Silvia,

El domingo es el cumpleaños de la abuela y tengo que comprar un lindo regalo para (1). Necesito tu ayuda otra vez. Ella no vive con (2) y quiero ir (3) porque tú sabes más sobre (4) que yo. Si voy (5) todo va a ser más fácil para (6). Por favor, ¿puedes venir (7)? De veras, sin (8) no voy a poder comprarle un buen regalo. Por favor, dime que sí.

Tu primo desesperado,
Pedro

18 ¡Te invito!

Trabajando en parejas, alterna con tu compañero/a para invitar y dar excusas diferentes para cada invitación.

el centro comercial
A: ¿Puedes venir conmigo al centro comercial?
B: No, no puedo ir contigo porque no tengo tiempo.

1. la tienda de música
2. el departamento de regalos
3. el cine
4. la cafetería
5. a comprar un lindo paraguas

¿Puedes ir conmigo a comprar unos aretes en esta tienda?

19 Un día en el centro comercial

Escribe una conclusión lógica para la siguiente información. Usa las preposiciones y pronombres apropiados, siguiendo las indicaciones.

Yo llegué al centro comercial a las seis y diez, tu amigo llegó a las seis menos diez y tú llegaste allí a las cinco y media. (yo/después de)
Conclusión: (Yo) Llegué después de Uds.

1. Mi amigo y yo compramos regalos el uno para el otro. Yo compré un regalo para mi amigo. (él/para)
2. Son las siete y mi amigo y yo estamos mirando anillos en el departamento de regalos y tú y tu amigo están mirando anillos en el mismo departamento. (Uds./al lado de)
3. Tú llegaste primero porque vives más cerca del centro comercial que yo. (yo/lejos de)
4. Tu amigo me dijo que vive en la Calle 6a, N° 248, y mi familia y yo vivimos en la Calle 6a, N° 241. (él/cerca de)
5. Yo voy a recibir un anillo de mi amigo y tú también vas a recibir un anillo de tu amigo. (nosotras/de)

¿Qué piensan de este sombrero?

Podemos comer en el centro comercial. ¡Ir de compras me da hambre!

20 ¿Quién fue contigo?

Tus amigos siempre quieren saber qué pasó. Trabajando en parejas, hagan Uds. mini-diálogos, tomando elementos de cada columna.

A: ¿Adónde fuiste ayer por la noche?
B: Fui al centro comercial.
A: ¿Quién fue contigo?
B: Mi amigo Luis.

I	II	III
después de la fiesta	la tienda	mi hermano
el viernes	la biblioteca	mi prima
el sábado por la mañana	el centro comercial	mis tíos
la semana pasada	la playa	mi amigo/a
ayer por la noche	de compras	nadie
antes de venir aquí	el supermercado	mis padres
el domingo por la tarde	el cine	mi novio/a

Hay miles de ofertas en esta tienda de ropa.

Algo más

Para hablar de dinero

¿Cuánto cuesta(n)?
Es demasiado caro.
Está en oferta especial.
El precio es muy alto.
Por ese dinero, la calidad no es mala.
Quiero ahorrar dinero.
Tengo bastante dinero.
Quiero pagar en efectivo.
Quiero comprarlo a crédito.
No tengo tarjeta de crédito.
Quiero usar mi tarjeta (de crédito).

21 En una tienda

Trabajando en parejas, deben preparar un diálogo de cinco o seis oraciones cada uno usando las expresiones de la sección Algo más de la página anterior. Uds. pueden hablar de lo que quieren comprar, el precio, la calidad, el tamaño y cómo lo van a pagar.

A: ¿Cuánto cuesta esta chaqueta?
B: Cuesta quinientos dólares.
A: Es demasiado cara.

22 ¿Cuándo fuiste de compras?

Trabajando en parejas, alterna con tu compañero/a para preguntar y contestar cuándo fue la última vez que fueron de compras, qué compraron y para quién lo compraron.

A: ¿Cuándo fue la última vez que fuiste de compras?
B: Fui el sábado pasado.

Autoevaluación. **As a review and self-check, respond to the following:**

1. Name at least three things you read, heard or saw yesterday.
2. Imagine you are buying a gift for your best friend. Describe the item you purchased.
3. What gift would you like to receive for your birthday?
4. Name three items that can be made of gold, silver or pearl.
5. Do you pay cash for most items or do you use credit?
6. Imagine you are shopping in a Spanish-speaking country. How would you ask how much an item costs and if it is on sale?
7. Name three things you learned about Ecuador.

¡La práctica hace al maestro!

A Comunicación

Form groups of eight to ten. Each group then forms two circles, with four or five students in an inside circle facing the same number of students in an outside circle. Then take turns asking and answering what each of you bought the last time you went to a *centro comercial* and what each of you would like to buy when you return there. Take notes as your partner speaks. Then students in the outer circle move one to the right and begin a similar conversation with the new partner. Continue until you have spoken with everyone in the other circle. One person from each circle should report the findings to the class.

A: ¿Qué compraste la última vez que fuiste al centro comercial?

B: No compré nada.

B Conexión con la tecnología

You learned about creating a dialog journal in the section *A escribir* at the end of *Capítulo 2.* Create an electronic dialog journal entry to send to your teacher. Write about your last trip shopping for something that was important (clothing for yourself, a gift). Tell where you went, with whom you went, what you purchased, how much you paid and whom the gift was for. Include any other information you wish and e-mail the journal entry to your teacher.

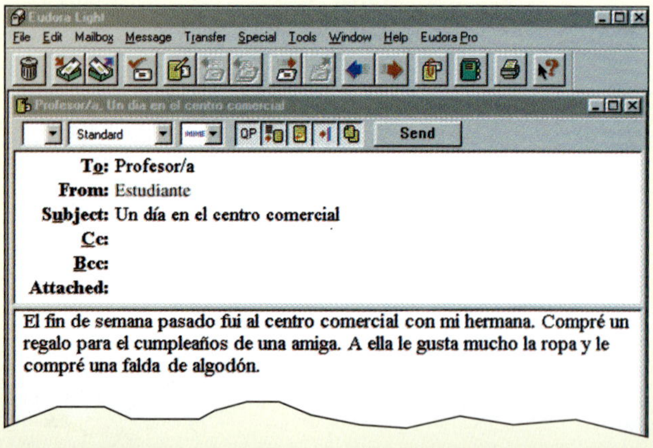

VOCABULARIO

Para describir

automático,-a
barato,-a
bastante
caro,-a
corto,-a
demasiado
largo,-a
lindo,-a
perfecto,-a
personal
sintético,-a

En la tienda

el arete
el ascensor
la billetera
el bolso
la bufanda
la caja
la calidad
el cinturón
el collar
el crédito
el cuero
el departamento
el efectivo
la escalera automática
el material
la oferta
el oro
el pañuelo
el paraguas
el perfume
la perla
el pijama
la plata
la pulsera
el regalo
el tamaño
la tarjeta (de crédito)

Verbos

ahorrar
pagar
recibir
usar

Expresiones y otras palabras

a crédito
conmigo
contigo
en efectivo
estar en oferta

¡Mira! Este collar es muy barato.

¿Te gustan mis aretes?

Mi padre me dio este anillo para mi cumpleaños.

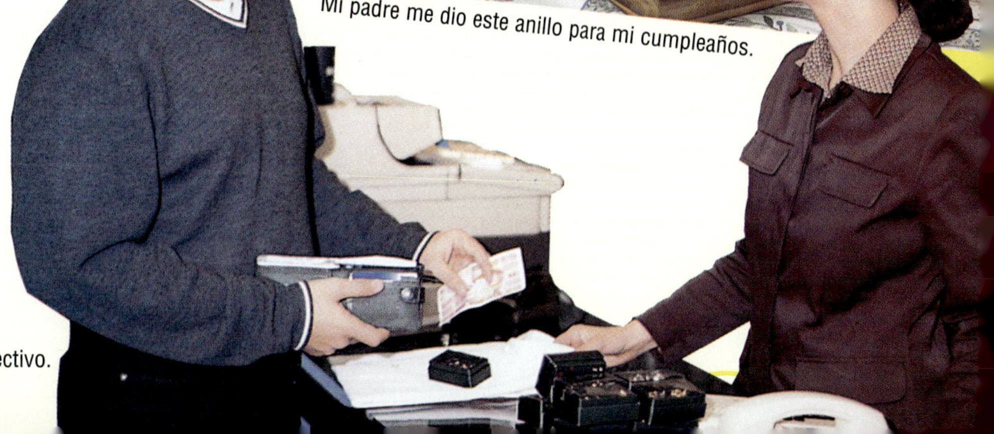

¿Cuánto cuesta? Prefiero pagar en efectivo.

a leer

Estrategia

Preparación

Estrategia para leer: ***using visual format to predict meaning***

The style, format and other visual details of a reading can tell you a lot about its probable content. For instance, the format of a letter indicates if it is for business or if it is personal. Similarly, cartoons are easily recognized by the style of illustration and the content. Before actually reading a passage, look at the layout, artwork, pictures, titles and format of the writing for hints about its content and meaning.

Como preparación para la lectura, observa la forma, el arte y el título de esta lectura y contesta las siguientes preguntas.

1. En una encuesta, uno tiene que...
   A. escribir una carta.
   B. contestar unas preguntas.
2. La Plaza Paitilla es...
   A. un centro comercial de Panamá.
   B. un deporte de Panamá.

Encuesta de la Plaza Paitilla

ENCUESTA

Nombre y apellidos: ______________________________
Dirección: ______________________________
Ciudad: ______________ País: ______________
Sexo: ❑ M ❑ F Edad: ______________

1. ¿Cuánto dinero tiene al mes para ir de compras? ______________
2. ¿Cuántas veces a la semana viene a la Plaza Paitilla? ______________
3. ¿Cuántas veces al mes viene a la Plaza Paitilla? ______________
4. ¿Compra para Ud. o para su familia? ______________
5. ¿A qué piso va primero? ______________
6. ¿Qué compró hoy? ______________
7. ¿A qué tipo de tienda va Ud. de compras con frecuencia?
   ❑ de ropa ❑ de deportes ❑ de revistas y libros
   ❑ de zapatos y botas ❑ de música ❑ de comida
8. ¿Compra Ud. ropa para personas de su familia? ______________
9. ¿A quiénes les compra? ______________
10. ¿Qué les compra? ______________
11. Cuando un amigo o amiga cumple años, ¿qué le compra Ud.?
    ❑ ropa ❑ discos ❑ libros ❑ chocolates ❑ flores
12. ¿Qué ropa compra Ud. con más frecuencia? ______________
13. ¿Qué ropa compra Ud. con menos frecuencia? ______________
14. ¿En qué otros centros comerciales compra Ud.? ______________

A ¿Qué comprendiste?

1. ¿Cuántas preguntas tiene la encuesta?
2. ¿Qué información personal te preguntan en la encuesta?
3. ¿Te preguntan tu número de teléfono?
4. ¿Pregunta la encuesta qué persona de tu familia compra más?
5. ¿En cuál de las preguntas tienes que decir si compraste algo ese día?
6. ¿Cuántos pisos tiene este centro comercial?

B Charlando

1. ¿Qué piensas de las encuestas?
2. ¿Preparaste alguna encuesta este año?
3. ¿Adónde vas de compras con más frecuencia?
4. ¿Cuáles son algunos de los regalos que prefieres dar a tus amigos/as?
5. ¿Qué centro comercial tiene encuestas donde vives?
6. ¿Dices la verdad cuando contestas una encuesta?

a escribir

Estrategia

Estrategia para escribir: *indicating sequence*

You have already learned to use transition words to make your writing flow smoothly. When you write about activities or events that have already taken place, transition words can indicate the sequence in which actions occurred. Some sequence words you may want to use in your writing include the following: *primero* (first), *luego* (later, then), *antes de* (before), *después de* (after), *finalmente* (finally).

A mall is more than just a convenient place to shop. Going to a *centro comercial* often can become a social event that offers shoppers an opportunity to spend time with friends and to meet new people. What does shopping at the mall mean to you? Write a short composition telling about your last visit to the mall *(Mi última visita al centro comercial)*. Include when you went, with whom you went, what places you visited, what you did, whom you met, what you bought and any other information you wish. Be sure to use connecting words for making smooth transitions and for telling the sequence of the events.

Un centro comercial en Argentina.

repaso

Now that I have completed this chapter, I can...

- ✓ identify articles of clothing.
- ✓ identify parts of the body.
- ✓ describe clothing.
- ✓ discuss size.
- ✓ express past actions and events.
- ✓ express negation or disagreement.
- ✓ discuss price and payment.
- ✓ write a summary.

Vendemos muchas camisas en la tienda donde trabajo.

I can also...

- ✓ talk about life in Panama and Ecuador.
- ✓ ask questions when I do not understand something.
- ✓ use affirmative and negative expressions in conversations.
- ✓ talk about personal taste in clothing.
- ✓ use diminutives to express affection or that something is small.

¿Necesitas algún cinturón o billetera?

De vacaciones

CAPÍTULO 10

In this chapter you will be able to:

- express past actions and events
- discuss everyday activities
- talk about the future
- express emotion
- indicate wishes and preferences
- talk about the recent past
- make polite requests
- describe personal characteristics
- describe interpersonal relationships

Lección 19

Contexto cultural PERÚ

¿Qué hiciste el fin de semana pasado?

JULIO: ¿Qué hiciste el fin de semana pasado, Ana?

ANA: ¡Ay, hombre! Trabajé en mi proyecto de historia. Tengo que presentarlo en dos días y todavía tengo mucho que hacer.

JULIO: Ah, ¿sí? ¿Cuál es el tema?

ANA: Bueno, sabes que me gustaría ser arqueóloga, ¿no? Entonces, mi proyecto es sobre el imperio inca y las culturas indígenas del Perú. Y tú, ¿qué hiciste el fin de semana pasado?

JULIO: Pues, el sábado, fui de compras. Compré unas cosas para las vacaciones con mi familia. Vamos a las playas de Cancún.

ANA: ¡Chévere, hombre! Y, ¿vas a visitar las ruinas de los mayas cerca de Cancún?

JULIO: No es mala idea si tenemos tiempo. Pero, durante mis vacaciones sólo quiero dormir hasta muy tarde, ir a la playa y bailar en los clubes por la noche. Pero, antes de mi viaje, ¿te gustaría hacer algo juntos?

ANA: Bueno, ¿qué te parece si vamos al cine este sábado?

PARA ti

Expresiones de emoción

¡Chévere!	*Great!*
¡Fantástico!	*Fantastic!*
¡Caramba!	*Darn!*

1 ¿Qué comprendiste?

1. ¿Qué hizo Ana el fin de semana pasado?
2. ¿Cuándo tiene que presentar su proyecto de historia?
3. ¿Cuál es el tema de su proyecto?
4. ¿Adónde fue Julio el sábado?
5. ¿Adónde van Julio y su familia de vacaciones?
6. ¿Qué le gustaría a Julio hacer en sus vacaciones?

2 Charlando

1. ¿Qué hiciste el fin de semana pasado?
2. ¿Tienes que hacer proyectos? ¿En qué clases haces proyectos?
3. ¿Cuánto tiempo estudias los fines de semana?
4. Cuando haces planes para el fin de semana, ¿piensas primero en si tienes algo que estudiar? Explica.
5. ¿Adónde te gustaría ir de vacaciones?

3 ¿Qué hiciste el fin de semana pasado?

En parejas, pregúntale a tu compañero/a si participó en las siguientes actividades el fin de semana pasado.

hablar con tus amigos/as por teléfono

A: ¿Hablaste con tus amigos/as por teléfono el fin de semana pasado?

B: Sí, (No, no) hablé con mis amigos/as por teléfono.

1. estudiar para un examen
2. comer en un restaurante elegante
3. ir al cine con tus amigos
4. ver televisión
5. limpiar tu cuarto
6. dormir hasta muy tarde
7. leer el periódico
8. montar en bicicleta
9. pasar tiempo con tu familia
10. trabajar mucho

4 La encuesta

Trabajando en grupos, pregunten a sus compañeros de clase qué hicieron durante el fin de semana pasado. Una persona debe reportar los resultados de la encuesta a la clase.

¿Hablaste por teléfono el fin de semana pasado?

Conexión *cultural*

El Perú

Una máscara de oro en el museo de Oro, Lima, Perú.

Peru is located on the Pacific Ocean along the western shores of South America. Situated between Ecuador and Chile, the region that became modern-day Peru formed the center point of the Incan Empire *(el imperio inca)*. Its rich gold and silver deposits quickly attracted the Spanish explorers in the sixteenth century. Although the Spanish introduced their language and religion, the influence of the Inca civilization is evident throughout the culture of Peru. Descendants of the indigenous peoples still populate the Andean highlands and the jungles of eastern Peru. Many of them do not speak Spanish and they continue to live as their ancestors did centuries ago.

In direct contrast to Peru's indigenous past is the country's contemporary capital, Lima. Thirty percent of Peru's population lives and works in this cosmopolitan city, making it the most important area of development in the country. However, remnants of the past can be found even in this modern city. One example is the University of San Marcos, which is one of the oldest universities in the world. Elsewhere, charming hand-carved wooden balconies *(balcones)* give a stately and historic atmosphere to many parts of Lima.

Una familia indígena en Cuzco, Perú.

Peru has experienced a long and varied past, including natural disasters and political turmoil. Three earthquakes in 1630, 1746 and 1970 devastated the population. The political and economic situation in the country continued to be turbulent until the 1990s when Alberto Fujimori was elected. He began programs to reduce Peru's tremendous inflation and privatize its economy. Although Fujimori's efforts brought about more stability, the economic hardships they imposed led to an escalation of violence from leftist guerrilla groups. In spite of this, however, the Peruvian people continue to handle the challenges of their economic and political problems. Today, stability and peace are evident to visitors and Peruvians alike.

5 Cruzando fronteras

Para aprender sobre la cultura del Perú, debes ir a la biblioteca y buscar la siguiente información usando libros de referencia, mapas, la Internet, etc.

1. El lago más grande y alto en Sudamérica está entre Bolivia y el Perú y se llama (1).
2. Hiram Bingham, un arqueólogo de Yale, descubrió las ruinas de (2) en 1911.
3. Las dos lenguas oficiales del Perú son el español y (3).
4. El nombre oficial del dinero es (4).
5. Hoy la capital es Lima, pero antes, la capital de los incas fue (5).
6. Los animales que los incas montaron y usaron para trabajar fueron (6).
7. Los caballos famosos del Perú son (7).

Un barco en el Lago Titicaca.

Oportunidades

En otro país

Have you ever visited another country? What did you see? What did you do there? After studying Spanish for a year, you probably realize the many opportunities that are available to you to use your language skills. Have you ever considered attending school in a different country for a year? Studying and living in a Spanish-speaking country could increase the Spanish skills you have already begun to acquire this year.

Alejandra y Norma son estudiantes de Costa Rica.

¡Vamos a viajar a Perú!

Repaso *rápido*

Tener que

You are already familiar with the phrase *tener que* to indicate a need to do something. Remember to use the expression *tener que* (+ infinitive) when you want to express what someone has to do.

Julio ***tiene que comprar*** *unas cosas para sus vacaciones en Cancún.*	Julio **has to buy** some things for his vacation in Cancún.

Estrategia

Para aprender mejor: *the importance of reviewing*

It is important to review what you have learned. No one remembers everything they have studied. You have made progress this year with Spanish, and reviewing will help keep everything fresh in your mind.

6 ¿Qué tienen que comprar para las vacaciones?

Trabajando en parejas, alterna con tu compañero/a en decir lo que Julio y su familia tienen que comprar para sus vacaciones.

A: ¿Qué tiene que comprar Rosa?
B: Rosa tiene que comprar un sombrero amarillo.

Rosa

1. su hermano

2. Julio

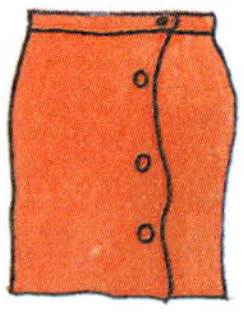

3. su hermana

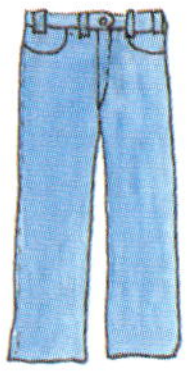

4. Julio y su hermano

5. su papá

6. todos

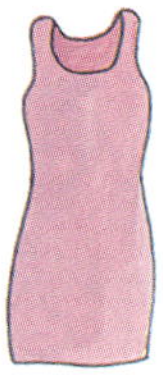

7. su mamá

7 De compras

Trabajando en parejas, organiza las siguientes oraciones en orden lógico.

A. Me queda bien.
B. Entro en la tienda.
C. Lo llevo a la caja.
D. Tomo el ascensor.
E. Busco un suéter de mi tamaño.
F. ¿Cómo voy a pagar?
G. Veo unos suéteres en oferta especial.
H. Me gustaría comprar este suéter.
I. Voy a pagar en efectivo.

8 Nuestras clases favoritas

Usa esta encuesta para descubrir las clases favoritas de tus compañeros. Primero, completa la siguiente encuesta de las clases que hay en tu colegio. Escribe el número que representa tu opinión de las clases. Después, deben formar grupos de 4 o 5 para hablar de los resultados. Finalmente, deben contestar las siguientes preguntas y reportar los resultados a la clase.

1. ¿Cuáles son las clases favoritas de tu grupo?
2. ¿Por qué son muy populares?
3. ¿Cuáles son las clases menos favoritas de tu grupo?
4. ¿Por qué no son muy populares estas clases?

0 = No sé. No tengo una opinión.
1 = Es horrible. No me gusta para nada.
2 = Es aburrida. No me gusta mucho.
3 = Es regular. Me gusta un poco.
4 = Es excelente. Me gusta mucho

UNA ENCUESTA - LAS CLASES FAVORITAS

1.	el español	0	1	2	3	4
2.	el inglés	0	1	2	3	4
3.	las matemáticas (álgebra, geometría, etc.)	0	1	2	3	4
4.	la historia	0	1	2	3	4
5.	las ciencias (biología, química, etc.)	0	1	2	3	4
6.	los estudios sociales	0	1	2	3	4
7.	la computación (las computadoras)	0	1	2	3	4
8.	la educación física	0	1	2	3	4
9.	la educación doméstica (cocinar, etc.)	0	1	2	3	4
10.	la música (banda, orquesta, coro, etc.)	0	1	2	3	4
11.	el arte	0	1	2	3	4
12.	(¿otras?) ________________	0	1	2	3	4

9 A escribir

Escribe uno o dos párrafos en español sobre tu vida escolar este año. En tu composición, debes describir tu rutina diaria, hablar de tus clases favoritas y las actividades que más te gustan. Luego, escribe una oración en el pasado describiendo un evento especial que ocurrió durante el año.

Conexión cultural

La arqueología de las civilizaciones indígenas

The Incas, the Mayans and the Aztecs all built upon the accumulated knowledge of many outstanding civilizations that preceded them. For instance, take the Moche (*moche,* in Spanish) of the coastal valleys of northern Peru. By the first century they were able to feed large numbers of people by collecting food and handmade goods for redistribution by the state, a practice that was used later by the Incas. The concept was important because it allowed skilled artisans freedom to create remarkable artwork instead of having to labor in the fields.

By the ninth century the Moche Empire had mysteriously disappeared. In the twelfth century the powerful Incas arrived from the Andes Mountains and established an empire centered in Cuzco, Peru. The Incas were warriors seeking to conquer other people. They incorporated the ideas of the cultures they conquered and gradually imposed the Quechua language to unite their extensive empire. Incan rulers claimed to be direct descendants of the sun, so they had their artisans construct temples to the sun and moon. The Incan Empire flourished due to heavy taxation.

However, when Francisco Pizarro and the Spanish conquistadors arrived in *Birú (Perú)* in 1524, the Incan Empire had been weakened by two warring heirs, thus beginning the decline of their empire. Once more, as has occurred so many times throughout history, the conquerors themselves were doomed to be conquered.

TIPS PARA VISITAR SITIOS ARQUEOLÓGICOS

1. No extraer nada del sitio arqueológico.
2. No caminar sobre las piedras, pueden estar resbalosas.
3. Al fotografiar pinturas, murales o esculturas, no utlilizar flash.
4. No alimentar a los pájaros o a los animales, ya que –por ejemplo, las iguanas– dañan las estructuras de los sitios.
5. Respetar las restricciones en el uso de tripiés.
6. Procurar visitar los sitios muy temprano o en las tardes, cuando el sol no es tan fuerte.
7. Llevar agua para beber; el calor y la caminata pueden ser difíciles.
8. Utlilizar cremas protectoras para que los rayos solares no dañen su piel.
9. Llevar zapatos cómodos.
10. Respetar las restricciones sobre el ascenso a los edificios.
11. No escribir en las piedras.
12. No arrojar monedas a los monumentos o pozos.
13. No tirar basura.
14. No vender o adquirir piezas arqueológicas; en México, hacerlo es un delito federal.

Machu Picchu es una gran ciudad de los incas.

Unos arqueólogos están trabajando.

10 Los moches y los incas

Contesta las siguientes preguntas.

1. ¿Quiénes usaron originalmente el sistema inca de coleccionar y distribuir la comida?
2. ¿Cómo se llamó la capital del imperio inca en el siglo XII?
3. ¿Qué lengua hablaron todos los indígenas del imperio inca?
4. ¿En honor de qué construyeron los incas unos templos?

PARA ti

Proverbios y dichos

Every day you are faced with decisions. Just as Julio had an opportunity to visit Mayan ruins while his family was on vacation, you also are faced with decisions about when to take advantage of an opportunity and when to let the opportunity pass. However, when a really good opportunity presents itself, do not be slow to act. As the Spanish proverb says *Ocasión perdida, no vuelve más en la vida* (Opportunity seldom knocks twice).

Ocasión perdida, no vuelve más en la vida.

11 ¿Eres artista?

Crea un collage que represente una conexión cultural con alguno de los países de habla hispana que estudiaste durante el año.

Autoevaluación. As a review and self-check, respond to the following:

1. Use the preterite tense to state in Spanish eight things you did this year.
2. State three things you learned about Peru.
3. Name five opportunities you have because you know Spanish.
4. What three things do you have to do this week? During the summer?
5. Why is it important to review what you have learned?
6. Summarize the results of the survey you did about favorite classes for Activity 8.
7. What do you want to do this summer?
8. Name a cultural group that is native to Central, North or South America. State two things you know about the group.

Lima, Perú.

¡La práctica hace al maestro!

A Comunicación

Working in pairs, take turns interviewing one another about your lives at school. You may use some of the questions below combined with at least four original questions. They may be about classes this year, classes for next year, school-related activities, daily schedules, etc. Be imaginative! Take notes about what is being said and prepare a written report about your interview.

1. ¿Qué clases son fáciles para ti? ¿Cuáles son difíciles?
2. ¿Qué clases pueden ser importantes en tu vida?
3. ¿En qué clases tienes que hacer proyectos?
4. ¿Prefieres trabajar sólo o en grupo en la clase?
5. ¿Qué te gusta de la escuela? ¿Qué no te gusta?
6. ¿Participas en los clubes de la escuela? ¿En cuáles?
7. ¿Participas en los programas de deportes de la escuela? ¿En cuáles?
8. ¿Es importante aprender algo sobre otras culturas y otras personas? ¿Por qué sí o por qué no?

B Conexión con la tecnología

Prepare an electronic survey like the survey you completed in this lesson about *clases favoritas.* Send the survey to another classroom (in your school or in another school), asking the students to answer via the Internet. Share the results with your classmates, comparing and contrasting those with the results of your class survey.

¿Qué te gusta de la escuela?

¿Qué recuerdas?

1.

2.

3.

4.

5.

Lección 20

Contexto cultural
GUATEMALA

El correo electrónico

ANA: Oye, Julio. ¿Sabes qué? Acabo de recibir unas cartas por correo electrónico de una chica de Guatemala. Ella es mi amiga por correspondencia.

JULIO: ¡Chévere, Ana! Y, ¿qué te dice? ¿Algo interesante de Guatemala?

ANA: Bueno, sí. Le escribí a ella de mi proyecto del imperio inca del Perú. Entonces, me escribió sobre todas las ruinas del imperio maya que están por muchas partes de México y Guatemala. Me gustaría mucho ver las ruinas de Tikal en Guatemala. Son increíbles, ¿no es verdad?

JULIO: ¡Claro, Ana! ¿Sabes algo? Ahora, a mí también me gustaría visitar unas ruinas mayas.

ANA: Bueno, hombre. No hay problema. Puedes visitar las ruinas de Chichén Itzá durante tu viaje a México. Las pirámides allí son fantásticas y no están muy lejos de Cancún.

JULIO: Muy buena idea, Ana. Y, especialmente para ti, vas a poder ver mis fotos de las ruinas mayas después del viaje. ¿Quién sabe? Quizás vas a ser una arqueóloga famosa algún día.

La vieja ciudad de Tikal está en Guatemala.

Chichén Itzá, México.

1 ¿Qué comprendiste?

1. ¿Qué acaba de recibir Ana?
2. ¿Quién es la chica de Guatemala?
3. ¿Cuál es el tema de las cartas de correo electrónico?
4. ¿Dónde están las ruinas mayas de Tikal?
5. ¿Qué le gustaría visitar a Julio?
6. ¿Qué puede ver Ana después del viaje de Julio a Chichén Itzá?

PARA ti

Me gustaría

Remember to use *gustaría* combined with *me, te, le, nos* and *les* in order to make a request, to politely express a wish or to ask about another person's wishes.

***Me gustaría** ver las ruinas.*
*¿**Te gustaría** sacar unas fotos para mí?*

2 Charlando

1. ¿Piensas hacer un viaje durante tus vacaciones? ¿Adónde te gustaría ir?
2. ¿Te gustaría visitar unas ruinas indígenas? ¿Dónde?
3. Cuando estás de vacaciones, ¿sacas muchas fotos? ¿De qué?

¡Hay muchas escaleras en el Castillo de Chichén Itzá!

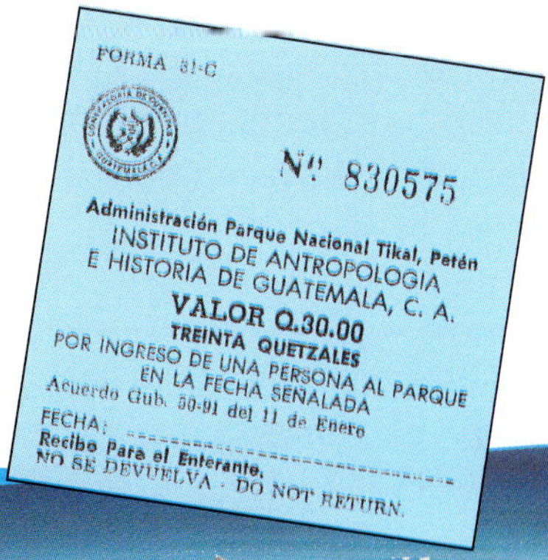

¿Te gustaría ir a Cancún?

Conexión *Cultural*

MUNDO MAYA®
Encuentro con la Naturaleza, el Hombre y el Tiempo
GUATEMALA
MUNDO MAYA®

Guatemala

Picturesque natural sites, such as *el lago Atitlán,* abound in the Central American country of Guatemala. Its capital, Guatemala City *(Ciudad de Guatemala),* offers all the conveniences of modern-day life. However, one aspect of Guatemala that fascinates anyone who visits the country is that Guatemala is the land of the Maya Indian civilization.

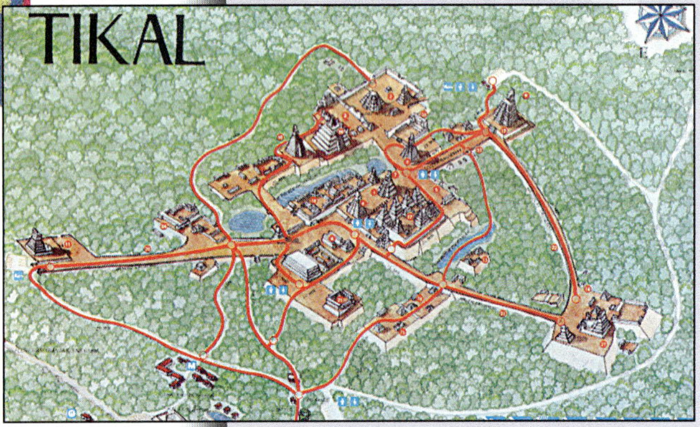

¡Qué colores!

Although the ancient Mayan civilization disappeared mysteriously, traces of the advanced Mayan culture remain today. The Mayans had an extensive knowledge of astronomy, mathematics and architecture. Tikal, the greatest of the Mayan cities, was founded around 700 B.C. The Mayan languages (mainly *quiché*) and traditions are still very much alive among the Mayans in today's Guatemala. The colors and patterns of the traditional ceremonial costumes that Mayan descendants wear are visible evidence of one tradition that has been passed on for many years from one generation to the next.

In 1524, Pedro de Alvarado conquered for Spain the area that has become present-day Guatemala, thus beginning Guatemala's colonial period. The cities of *Antigua, Chichicastenango, Huehuetenango* and *Quetzaltenango* still contain remnants of this period of time. Guatemala City was founded in 1776, and in 1821 the region declared its independence from Spain.

El lago Atitlán.

Today Guatemala offers a mix of old and new, rustic and urban. The modern capital is the commercial, industrial, educational and governmental center of the country. However, Guatemala's rich farmland serves as the main source of income for the country's 9.2 million inhabitants, just as it has for centuries.

La Catedral, Ciudad de Guatemala.

3 Guatemala

Di si las siguientes oraciones sobre Guatemala son verdaderas (V) o falsas (F).

1. La capital de Guatemala, la Ciudad de Guatemala, es muy moderna.
2. Guatemala es un centro de la civilización Atitlán.
3. Los mayas estudiaron la astronomía, las matemáticas y la arquitectura.
4. La ciudad más famosa del imperio maya es Chichicastenango.
5. Pedro de Alvarado fue el conquistador de la zona que hoy es Guatemala.
6. Antigua es una ciudad colonial.

4 Conexión con la tecnología: ¿te gustaría hacer un viaje?

Piensa en algún lugar en el mundo hispano que te gustaría visitar. ¿Qué te gustaría ver o hacer allí? Busca información sobre el lugar en la Internet. Luego, debes planear un itinerario con fechas, hoteles, restaurantes, lugares interesantes para visitar, precios, etc. Prepara un póster de viaje para el lugar y presenta la información a la clase.

¿Adónde te gustaría viajar?

5 Una entrevista: los planes para el verano

Trabajando en parejas, pregúntale a tu compañero/a la siguiente información en combinación con unas preguntas originales sobre sus planes para el verano. Después de la entrevista, escribe un párrafo sobre los planes de tu compañero/a este verano.

1. ¿Qué trabajo te gustaría hacer este verano?

cuidar a niños	*trabajar en una oficina*
trabajar en un supermercado	*trabajar en una tienda*
enseñar tenis	*reparar autos*
trabajar en un banco	*trabajar en un campamento para niños*
trabajar en un restaurante	*ser salvavidas de una piscina o de una playa*
trabajar en un hotel	*pintar casas*

2. ¿Qué otro trabajo te gustaría hacer?
3. ¿En cuáles de los trabajos tienes experiencia? ¿Cuánta experiencia tienes?
4. ¿Cuáles de los trabajos no te gustaría hacer? ¿Por qué no?
5. ¿Vas a hacer un viaje durante las vacaciones? ¿Adónde?

6-10. ¿...?

Yo cuido a mi hermanita.

Laura trabaja en una oficina durante el verano.

Yo soy un salvavidas en la playa.

Oportunidades

Carreras en las que se puede usar el español

You are already aware that knowing how to communicate in a foreign language can enhance your career *(carrera)* opportunities. The following are some interesting careers requiring foreign language expertise that you may want to consider investigating:

Yo hablo español en mi trabajo. Soy agente de viajes.

Domestic Market

- bilingual administrative assistant
- border patrol agent
- court interpreter
- language teacher
- hotel sales manager
- imported clothing merchandiser
- customer service representative

Foreign Market

- international financial manager
- international marketing manager
- lawyer
- foreign diplomat
- foreign broadcaster
- journalist
- travel agent

6 Tu carrera ideal

Numera del 1 al 12 las siguientes carreras en el orden de tu preferencia. La número 1 debe ser la más interesante para ti y la número 12 la menos interesante. Luego, en grupos de tres, compara el orden de las carreras de cada persona. Explica por qué ciertas carreras son más populares que otras. Considera el salario, los beneficios, las condiciones de trabajo, las horas de trabajo, la demanda, etc. Reporta los resultados del grupo a la clase.

agricultor(a)	artista	arquitecto/a
banquero/a	cocinero/a	veterinario/a
programador(a)	enfermero/a	maestro/a
hombre/mujer de negocios	ingeniero/a	médico/a

No soy banquero, soy médico.

Pilar es una artista.

CONEXIONES 7

Cruzando fronteras

Lee el siguiente párrafo sobre la combinación de la ecología con la cultura en un centro para turistas. Después, contesta las preguntas.

El proyecto del Mundo Maya

El Mundo Maya es un proyecto regional en la América Central que busca integrar en un área de unas 1.500 **millas** todos los elementos arqueológicos y las **riquezas** naturales del territorio maya, para crear un centro ecológico y cultural para el turismo internacional. Esta región pasa por cinco países: empieza en México, en la península de Yucatán, pasa por los estados de Chiapas, Tabasco, Campeche, Yucatán y Quintana Roo y continúa hasta Belice, Guatemala, Honduras y El Salvador.

La región maya fue muy importante en su tiempo. Hoy sigue siendo muy importante para el mundo moderno por sus grandes riquezas naturales, **arqueológicas**, culturales y coloniales, que son únicas en el mundo. En la ruta de esta región hay mucho para preservar, las pirámides y los templos mayas, las **selvas tropicales**, los **pájaros** (hay más de 20.000 flamencos de color rosa en la región), el **arrecife** de coral más grande del continente americano (en Belice), los observatorios mayas de astronomía, la acrópolis de Tikal, la ciudad de Antigua en Guatemala y **pueblos** donde todavía hay tradiciones mayas de hace 3.000 años.

¿Te gustaría visitar el Mundo Maya algún día?

millas *miles* **riquezas** *riches* **arqueológicas** *archeological* **selvas tropicales** *tropical jungles* **pájaros** *birds* **arrecife** *reef* **pueblos** *towns*

Este mono vive en la selva tropical.

¿Te gustaría viajar al Mundo Maya?

Unos flamencos de color rosa.

1. ¿Qué es el Mundo Maya?
2. ¿Qué puede ver uno allí?
3. ¿Qué países forman parte del Mundo Maya?
4. ¿Por qué es importante la región?
5. ¿Qué hay para preservar en la ruta de esta región?

Unas mujeres y unas niñas en las montañas de Guatemala.

Los mayas usaron este observatorio para ver las estrellas. (Chichén Itzá, México)

Una calle en Antigua, Guatemala.

8 Amigos por correspondencia

Lee la información de esta revista sobre diferentes personas hispanas y contesta las siguientes preguntas.

Marcela Granados
16 años, Retorno Platino #179, Fracc. Valle Dorado, Ensenada, B.C., México C.P. 22890

pasatiempos: tener amigos por correspondencia, jugar softbol, oír música, estar con mis amigos, ver juegos de beisbol.

Adriana Rivero Vargas
14 años, José María Olloqui 184-202, Col. del Valle, México, D.F. C.P. 03100

pasatiempos: pintar cerámica, coleccionar postales, libros, ir al cine o al boliche y hacer chocolates.

Juan Carlos Mejía
16 años, Apartado Postal 326, Tuxla Gutiérrez, Chiapas, México, C.P. 29000

pasatiempos: intercambiar postales, estampillas, escuchar música, jugar fútbol y patinar.

Luz Gutiérrez
14 años, Jr. España #503, La Perla Alta, Callao 04, Lima, Perú

pasatiempos: oír música, hacer amigos, practicar deportes, escribir poemas, leer *Tú* y contestar mi correspondencia.

Mónica Moncada
16 años, Urb. Pirineos 1 Calle 02, #63, Lote E, San Cristóbal, Edo. Tachira, Venezuela

pasatiempos: patinar, nadar, coleccionar todo lo referente a Michael Jackson, comer pizza, salir con mis amigos y conocer otras culturas.

Ciber@migos

Luisa Guzmán V.
13 años
lguzman@mv.net.gt

pasatiempos: leer, patinar, oír música, conocer gente y lugares, bailar.

Gloria María Castañón
14 años
gloria@avan.net

pasatiempos: modelar, patinar, ver televisión, leer la revista *Tú*, comer, ir al cine y hacer muchos amigos.

Lisa Guerra Torres
16 años
lguerra@coqui.net

pasatiempos: salir con mis amigos, ir al cine, hablar por teléfono, conocer nuevos amigos, ver televisión, leer *Tú*.

Kasuko Nomura
14 años
infa@lacochinita.com.mx

pasatiempos: jugar solitario, meterme al Internet y escuchar música.

Me llamo Luisa Guzmán. Busco una amiga por correo electrónico.

1. ¿De dónde son ellos?
2. ¿Qué información personal dan?
3. ¿Cuáles de los pasatiempos son más populares para ellos?
4. ¿Quiénes buscan amigos por correo electrónico?

9 ¿Te gustaría tener un amigo por correspondencia?

Contesta las siguientes preguntas que podrías preguntarle a un nuevo amigo o amiga de otro país.

1. ¿Cómo te llamas?
2. ¿Cuántos años tienes?
3. ¿Cuál es tu dirección?
4. ¿Cuáles son tus pasatiempos favoritos? ¿Qué te gusta hacer?

10 ¿Qué buscas en tu amigo/a ideal?

¿Cuáles de estas características son importantes para ti en tu amigo/a ideal? Incluye otras características originales también.

honesto/a	aventurero/a	ambicioso/a
inteligente	independiente	romántico/a
cómico/a	organizado/a	CREATIVO/A
generoso/a	sentimental	popular
divertido/a	responsable	tranquilo/a
guapo/a	sincero/a	extrovertido/a
rico/a	tímido/a	

Mis amigos son muy cómicos.

11 Relaciones personales

En parejas, cada persona debe describir a su amigo/a ideal. Explica por qué sus características son importantes para ti.

Mi amigo/a ideal tiene que ser puntual porque no me gusta esperar mucho.

12 En resumen

Escribe una composición sobre tu mejor amigo/a. Describe los aspectos de su personalidad, su apariencia física y las actividades que Uds. hacen juntos. Puedes incluir una foto de él o ella para añadir interés a la composición.

13 ¿Eres poeta?

Escribe un poema o una canción en español sobre algún tema que aprendiste este año. Después, puedes leer tu poema o cantar tu canción para la clase.

Autoevaluación. As a review and self-check, respond to the following:

1. How would you say you have just received an e-mail letter from a friend in Guatemala?
2. Where is *Tikal?*
3. What two things would you like to see in Guatemala?
4. Name a Spanish-speaking part of the world you would like to visit. Why would you like to go there?
5. Name three careers that may be open to you because you know Spanish.
6. What do you know about the *Mundo Maya*?
7. Describe your ideal friend.
8. Tell what you are going to do this summer. Say where you are going to go, whom you are going to be with and what you are going to do there.

¡La práctica hace al maestro!

A Comunicación

Working in groups of three, discuss in Spanish a report that the three of you are going to prepare for a presentation to the class. Begin by deciding upon a theme that deals with something from this lesson *(el Mundo Maya, Guatemala, etc.).* Then discuss each person's contribution, trying to use as many new expressions as you can. Be sure to note what everyone offers to do.

A: ¿Sobre qué podemos escribir este proyecto?
B: Bueno, yo deseo escribir sobre....
C: Perdón. ¿Puedes repetir lo que vas a hacer, por favor?

B Conexión con la tecnología

As an e-mail project, work in small groups of three to five students researching a group or culture that is native to your state or region. Determine the name of the group, where they lived, economic activities, number of inhabitants and where any ruins or remains may be found. Try to find out what the civilization's art was like, and try to obtain an example. Share the results with another group (a class in another region of the world, for example) and request the same information about ancient civilizations that inhabited their region of the world.

¿Qué venden en el mercado de Chichicastenango, Guatemala?

¿Qué recuerdas?

1.

2.

3.

4.

5.

6.

a leer

Estrategia

Preparación

Estrategia para leer: ***identifying the main idea of each paragraph***

When a reading is longer, consisting of several paragraphs, it helps to break it down into individual paragraphs and identify the main idea of each one. A well-written reading selection usually begins with an introductory paragraph *(párrafo introductorio)* that identifies the central idea. Following the introduction are additional paragraphs supporting the main theme. The final paragraph usually contains a conclusion summarizing the central idea.

Como preparación para la lectura, decide cuál de las siguientes ideas representa el primer párrafo, el segundo y el tercero.

A. Los Pasofinos son caballos muy populares en Norteamérica hoy.
B. Los Pasofinos tienen muchas características muy buenas.
C. Los españoles introdujeron su lengua, su religión y los caballos al nuevo mundo.

El Pasofino es un caballo superior.

Los Pasofinos: caballos de los conquistadores

Cuando los españoles **conquistaron** el imperio inca del Perú, tomaron muchos de los **recursos naturales** del nuevo mundo, como el **oro** y la **plata.** También, los españoles introdujeron entre muchas cosas el español, el catolicismo y el caballo—un animal nuevo.

El Perú está **aislado** por el Océano Pacífico y por los Andes. Por esta razón, esos caballos originales continúan con un **linaje** muy puro. Y, hoy, son los famosos caballos Pasofinos del Perú. A los peruanos les gustan mucho los Pasofinos porque son bonitos, elegantes, inteligentes y muy **mansos.** Montar un Pasofino es muy fácil porque son los caballos más **suaves** de todo el mundo. Su forma de trotar es muy suave y se llama "**el paso llano.**" Estos animales son **magníficos.**

Por todas estas razones, hoy en día los Pasofinos son muy populares en los EE.UU. En todo el mundo hay sólo 18.000 Pasofinos y más de 10.000 de ellos viven en Norteamérica. En los EE.UU. hay clubes para los **aficionados** de los Pasofinos. Si quieres saber más sobre los Pasofinos y los clubes, puedes buscarlo en el Internet.

conquistaron *conquered* **recursos naturales** *natural resources* **oro** *gold* **plata** *silver* **aislado** *isolated* **linaje** *lineage* **mansos** *gentle* **suaves** *smooth* **el paso llano** *the even step* **magníficos** *magnificent* **aficionados** *fans*

A ¿Qué comprendiste?

1. ¿Qué tomaron los españoles del nuevo mundo?
2. ¿Qué introdujeron los españoles al nuevo mundo?
3. ¿Cuáles son las características de los Pasofinos?
4. ¿Dónde hay muchos clubes para los aficionados de los Pasofinos?

B Charlando

1. ¿Sabes montar a caballo?
2. ¿Hay Pasofinos cerca de donde tú vives?
3. ¿Te gustaría montar un Pasofino?
4. ¿Qué animales te gustan? ¿Por qué?

a escribir

Estrategia

Estrategia para escribir: *defining your purpose for writing*

Before you begin a writing assignment, it is a good idea to identify your purpose. Then keep your purpose in mind throughout the writing process as you brainstorm your topic, formulate your rough draft and edit your finished product.

The purpose of this writing assignment is to describe yourself using the format of an acrostic poem. In an acrostic poem, certain letters of each line spell out the letters of a specific word the author has in mind.

Use the letters of your name or nickname, in their correct order, as your acrostic word. Design the pattern for placing a letter of your name in each line. For instance, you might choose to highlight the first letter of each line, the first letter of the last word in each line, etc.

Then, in the lines, include some personal information you have learned this year to describe your personality, your appearance and your preferences. Also, work in some information about what you are going to do in the future. Be sure to make the letters of your acrostic word stand out in the poem (as was done in the poem on this page). Finally, you may wish to accompany your poem with artwork or graphics to make it more visually appealing.

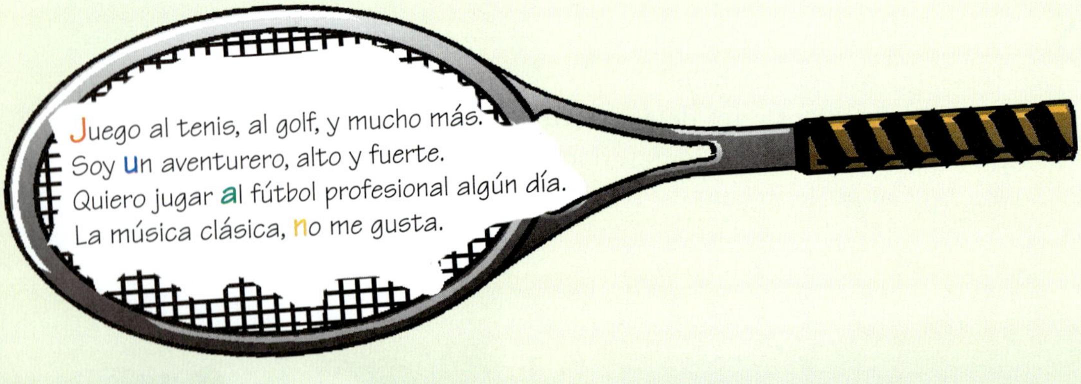

repaso

Now that I have completed this chapter, I can...

- ✓ express past actions and events.
- ✓ discuss everyday activities.
- ✓ talk about the future.
- ✓ express emotion.
- ✓ indicate wishes and preferences.
- ✓ talk about the recent past.
- ✓ make polite requests.
- ✓ describe personal characteristics.
- ✓ describe interpersonal relationships.

Puedes buscar mucha información usando el Internet.

I can also...

- ✓ tell what has to be done.
- ✓ talk about life in Peru and Guatemala.
- ✓ research a topic in the library and on the Internet.
- ✓ name some personal benefits to learning Spanish.
- ✓ recognize some benefits of reviewing what I have already learned.
- ✓ recognize the importance of reviewing what I have learned.
- ✓ discuss the importance and influence of some indigenous cultures.
- ✓ identify some careers that use Spanish.
- ✓ express myself artistically about what I have learned in Spanish class.

¿Te gustaría ser artista?

Appendices

Appendix A

Grammar Review

Definite articles

	Singular	Plural
Masculine	el	los
Feminine	la	las

Indefinite articles

	Singular	Plural
Masculine	un	unos
Feminine	una	unas

Adjective/noun agreement

	Singular	Plural
Masculine	El chico es alto.	Los chicos son altos.
Feminine	La chica es alta.	Las chicas son altas.

Pronouns

Singular	Subject	Direct object	Indirect object	Object of preposition
1st person	yo	me	me	mí
2nd person	tú Ud.	te lo/la	te le	ti Ud.
3rd person	él ella	lo la	le le	él ella
Plural				
1st person	nosotros nosotras	nos nos	nos nos	nosotros nosotras
2nd person	vosotros vosotras	os os	os os	vosotros vosotras
3rd person	Uds. ellos ellas	los/las los las	les les les	Uds. ellos ellas

Interrogatives

qué	*what*
cómo	*how*
dónde	*where*
cuándo	*when*
cuánto, -a, -os, -as	*how much, how many*
cuál/cuáles	*which (one)*
quién/quiénes	*who, whom*
por qué	*why*
para qué	*why, what for*

Demonstrative adjectives

Singular		Plural	
Masculine	**Feminine**	**Masculine**	**Feminine**
este	esta	estos	estas
ese	esa	esos	esas
aquel	aquella	aquellos	aquellas

Possessive adjectives

Singular	Singular nouns	Plural nouns
1st person	mi hermano mi hermana	mis hermanos mis hermanas
2nd person	tu hermano tu hermana	tus hermanos tus hermanas
3rd person	su hermano su hermana	sus hermanos sus hermanas
Plural	**Singular nouns**	**Plural nouns**
1st person	nuestro hermano nuestra hermana	nuestros hermanos nuestras hermanas
2nd person	vuestro hermano vuestra hermana	vuestros hermanos vuestras hermanas
3rd person	su hermano su hermana	sus hermanos sus hermanas

Appendix B

Verbs

Present tense (indicative)

Regular present tense		
hablar *(to speak)*	hablo hablas habla	hablamos habláis hablan
comer *(to eat)*	como comes come	comemos coméis comen
escribir *(to write)*	escribo escribes escribe	escribimos escribís escriben

Preterite tense (indicative)

hablar *(to speak)*	hablé hablaste habló	hablamos hablasteis hablaron
comer *(to eat)*	comí comiste comió	comimos comisteis comieron
escribir *(to write)*	escribí escribiste escribió	escribimos escribisteis escribieron

Present participle

The present participle is formed by replacing the *-ar* of the infinitive with *-ando* and the *-er* or *-ir* with *-iendo*.

hablar	hablando
comer	comiendo
vivir	viviendo

Progressive tenses

The present participle is used with the verbs *estar, continuar, seguir, andar* and some other motion verbs to produce the progressive tenses. They are reserved for recounting actions that are or were in progress at the time in question.

Present tense of stem-changing verbs

Stem-changing verbs are identified in this book by the presence of vowels in parentheses after the infinitive. If these verbs end in *-ar* or *-er,* they have only one change. If they end in *-ir,* they have two changes. The stem change of *-ar* and *-er* verbs and the first stem change of *-ir* verbs occur in all forms of the present tense, except *nosotros* and *vosotros.*

cerrar (ie) ***(to close)***	e → ie	cierro cierras cierra	cerramos cerráis cierran

Verbs like **cerrar:** calentar *(to heat),* comenzar *(to begin),* despertar *(to wake up),* despertarse *(to awaken),* empezar *(to begin),* encerrar *(to lock up),* nevar *(to snow),* pensar *(to think),* recomendar *(to recommend),* sentarse *(to sit down)*

contar (ue) ***(to tell)***	o → ue	cuento cuentas cuenta	contamos contáis cuentan

Verbs like **contar:** acordar *(to agree),* acordarse *(to remember),* almorzar *(to have lunch),* colgar *(to hang),* costar *(to cost),* demostrar *(to demonstrate),* encontrar *(to find, to meet someone),* probar *(to taste, to try),* recordar *(to remember)*

jugar (ue) ***(to play)***	u → ue	juego juegas juega	jugamos jugáis juegan

perder (ie) ***(to lose)***	e → ie	pierdo pierdes pierde	perdemos perdéis pierden

Verbs like **perder:** defender *(to defend),* descender *(to descend, to go down),* encender *(to light, to turn on),* entender *(to understand),* extender *(to extend),* tender *(to spread out)*

volver (ue) ***(to return)***	o → ue	vuelvo vuelves vuelve	volvemos volvéis vuelven

Verbs like **volver:** devolver *(to return something),* doler *(to hurt),* llover *(to rain),* morder *(to bite),* mover *(to move),* resolver *(to resolve),* soler *(to be in the habit of),* torcer *(to twist)*

pedir (i, i) ***(to ask for)***	e → i	pido pides pide	pedimos pedís piden

Verbs like **pedir:** conseguir *(to obtain, to attain, to get),* despedirse *(to say good-bye),* elegir *(to choose, to elect),* medir *(to measure),* perseguir *(to pursue),* repetir *(to repeat)*

sentir (ie, i) ***(to feel)***	e → ie	siento sientes siente	sentimos sentís sienten

Verbs like **sentir**: advertir *(to warn)*, arrepentirse *(to regret)*, convertir *(to convert)*, convertirse *(to become)*, divertirse *(to have fun)*, herir *(to wound)*, invertir *(to invest)*, mentir *(to lie)*, preferir *(to prefer)*, requerir *(to require)*, sugerir *(to suggest)*

dormir (ue, u) ***(to sleep)***	o → ue	duermo duermes duerme	dormimos dormís duermen

Another verb like **dormir**: morir *(to die)*

Present participle of stem-changing verbs

Stem-changing verbs that end in *-ir* use the second stem change in the present participle.

dormir (ue, u)	durmiendo
seguir (i, i)	siguiendo
sentir (ie, i)	sintiendo

Preterite tense of stem-changing verbs

Stem-changing verbs that end in *-ar* and *-er* are regular in the preterite tense. That is, they do not require a spelling change, and they use the regular preterite endings.

pensar (ie)	
pensé	pensamos
pensaste	pensasteis
pensó	pensaron

volver (ue)	
volví	volvimos
volviste	volvisteis
volvió	volvieron

Stem-changing verbs ending in *-ir* change their third-person forms in the preterite tense, but they still require the regular preterite endings.

sentir (ie, i)	
sentí	sentimos
sentiste	sentisteis
sintió	sintieron

dormir (ue, u)	
dormí	dormimos
dormiste	dormisteis
durmió	durmieron

Verbs with irregularities

The following charts provide some frequently used Spanish verbs with irregularities.

buscar *(to look for)*	
preterite	busqué, buscaste, buscó, buscamos, buscasteis, buscaron
Similar to:	explicar *(to explain)*, sacar *(to take out)*, tocar *(to touch, to play an instrument)*

dar *(to give)*	
present	doy, das, da, damos, dais, dan
preterite	di, diste, dio, dimos, disteis, dieron

decir *(to say, to tell)*	
present	digo, dices, dice, decimos, decís, dicen
preterite	dije, dijiste, dijo, dijimos, dijisteis, dijeron
present participle	diciendo

enviar *(to send)*	
present	envío, envías, envía, enviamos, enviáis, envían
Similar to:	esquiar *(to ski)*

estar *(to be)*	
present	estoy, estás, está, estamos, estáis, están
preterite	estuve, estuviste, estuvo, estuvimos, estuvisteis, estuvieron

hacer *(to do, to make)*	
present	hago, haces, hace, hacemos, hacéis, hacen
preterite	hice, hiciste, hizo, hicimos, hicisteis, hicieron

ir *(to go)*	
present	voy, vas, va, vamos, vais, van
preterite	fui, fuiste, fue, fuimos, fuisteis, fueron
present participle	yendo

leer *(to read)*	
preterite	leí, leíste, leyó, leímos, leísteis, leyeron
present participle	leyendo

llegar *(to arrive)*	
preterite	llegué, llegaste, llegó, llegamos, llegasteis, llegaron
Similar to:	colgar *(to hang)*, pagar *(to pay)*

oír *(to hear, to listen)*	
present	oigo, oyes, oye, oímos, oís, oyen
preterite	oí, oíste, oyó, oímos, oísteis, oyeron
present participle	oyendo

poder *(to be able)*	
present	puedo, puedes, puede, podemos, podéis, pueden
preterite	pude, pudiste, pudo, pudimos, pudisteis, pudieron
present participle	pudiendo

poner *(to put, to place, to set)*	
present	pongo, pones, pone, ponemos, ponéis, ponen
preterite	puse, pusiste, puso, pusimos, pusisteis, pusieron

querer *(to love, to want)*	
present	quiero, quieres, quiere, queremos, queréis, quieren
preterite	quise, quisiste, quiso, quisimos, quisisteis, quisieron

saber *(to know)*	
present	sé, sabes, sabe, sabemos, sabéis, saben
preterite	supe, supiste, supo, supimos, supisteis, supieron

salir *(to go out, to leave)*	
present	salgo, sales, sale, salimos, salís, salen

ser *(to be)*	
present	soy, eres, es, somos, sois, son
preterite	fui, fuiste, fue, fuimos, fuisteis, fueron

tener *(to have)*	
present	tengo, tienes, tiene, tenemos, tenéis, tienen
preterite	tuve, tuviste, tuvo, tuvimos, tuvisteis, tuvieron

traer *(to bring)*	
present	traigo, traes, trae, traemos, traéis, traen
preterite	traje, trajiste, trajo, trajimos, trajisteis, trajeron
present participle	trayendo

venir *(to come)*	
present	vengo, vienes, viene, venimos, venís, vienen
preterite	vine, viniste, vino, vinimos, vinisteis, vinieron
present participle	viniendo

ver *(to see, to watch)*	
present	veo, ves, ve, vemos, veis, ven
preterite	vi, viste, vio, vimos, visteis, vieron

Appendix C

Numbers

Cardinal numbers 0-1.000

0—cero	13—trece	26—veintiséis	90—noventa
1—uno	14—catorce	27—veintisiete	100—cien/ciento
2—dos	15—quince	28—veintiocho	200—doscientos,-as
3—tres	16—dieciséis	29—veintinueve	300—trescientos,-as
4—cuatro	17—diecisiete	30—treinta	400—cuatrocientos,-as
5—cinco	18—dieciocho	31—treinta y uno	500—quinientos,-as
6—seis	19—diecinueve	32—treinta y dos	600—seiscientos,-as
7—siete	20—veinte	33—treinta y tres, etc.	700—setecientos,-as
8—ocho	21—veintiuno	40—cuarenta	800—ochocientos,-as
9—nueve	22—veintidós	50—cincuenta	900—novecientos,-as
10—diez	23—veintitrés	60—sesenta	1.000—mil
11—once	24—veinticuatro	70—setenta	
12—doce	25—veinticinco	80—ochenta	

Ordinal numbers

1—primero,-a (primer)	6—sexto,-a
2—segundo,-a	7—séptimo,-a
3—tercero,-a (tercer)	8—octavo,-a
4—cuarto,-a	9—noveno,-a
5—quinto,-a	10—décimo,-a

Appendix D

Syllabification

Spanish vowels may be weak or strong. The vowels *a*, *e* and *o* are strong, whereas *i* (and sometimes *y*) and *u* are weak. The combination of one weak and one strong vowel or of two weak vowels produces a diphthong, two vowels pronounced as one.

A word in Spanish has as many syllables as it has vowels or diphthongs.

al gu nas
lue go
pa la bra

A single consonant (including *rr*) between two vowels accompanies the second vowel and begins a syllable.

a mi ga
fa vo ri to
ca rro

Two consonants (except for the letters combinations *ch* and *ll*) are divided, the first going with the previous vowel and the second going with the following vowel.

an tes
quin ce
ter mi nar

A consonant plus *l* or *r* is inseparable except for *rl*, *sl* and *sr*.

ma dre
pa la bra
com ple tar
Car los
is la

If three consonants occur together, the last, or any inseparable combination, accompanies the following vowel to begin another syllable.

es cri bir
som bre ro
trans por te

Prefixes should remain intact.

re es cri bir

Appendix E

Accentuation

Words that end in *a, e, i, o, u, n* or *s* are pronounced with the major stress on the next-to-the-last syllable. No accent mark is needed to show this emphasis.

octubre
refresco
señora

Words that end in any consonant except *n* or *s* are pronounced with the major stress on the last syllable. No accent mark is needed to show this emphasis.

escribir
papel
reloj

Words that are not pronounced according to the above two rules need a written accent mark.

lógico
canción
después
lápiz

An accent mark may be necessary to distinguish identical words with different meanings.

dé/de
qué/que
sí/si
sólo/solo

An accent mark is often used to divide a diphthong into two separate syllables.

día
frío
Raúl

Vocabulary Spanish/English

All active words introduced in *Somos así EN SUS MARCAS–A* and *Somos así EN SUS MARCAS–B* appear in this end vocabulary. The number or letter following an entry indicates the lesson in which an item is first actively used. Additional words and expressions are included for reference and have no number. Obvious cognates and expressions that occur as passive vocabulary for recognition only have been excluded from this end vocabulary.

Abbreviations:

d.o. direct object | *i.o.* indirect object | *pl.* plural
f. feminine | *m.* masculine | *s.* singular

A

a to, at, in *4; a caballo* on horseback *5; a crédito* on credit *18; a la(s)...* at... o'clock *4; a pie* on foot *5; a propósito* by the way *1; ¿a qué hora?* at what time? *4; a veces* sometimes, at times *10; a ver* let's see, hello (telephone greeting)
abierto,-a open *7*
abran: see *abrir*
el **abrazo** hug *12*
abre: see *abrir*
la **abreviatura** abbreviation
el **abrigo** coat *15*
abril April *10*
abrir to open *9; abran* (*Uds.* command); *abre* (*tú* command) open
la **abuela** grandmother *7*
el **abuelo** grandfather *7*
aburrido,-a bored, boring *8*
acabar to finish, to complete, to terminate *15; acabar de* (+ infinitive) to have just *15*
el **aceite** oil *11*
la **aceituna** olive
el **acento** accent *1*
la **acentuación** accentuation
aclarar to make clear, to explain
la **actividad** activity *9*, exercise
el **acuerdo** accord; *de acuerdo* agreed, okay *6*
adiós good-bye *1*
el **adjetivo** adjective; *adjetivo posesivo* possessive adjective
¿adónde? (to) where? *5*
adornar to decorate *15*
el **adverbio** adverb
los **aeróbicos** aerobics *13*
la **agencia** agency; *agencia de viajes* travel agency
agosto August *10*
el **agricultor** farmer
el **agua** *f.* water *6; agua mineral* mineral water *6*
el **aguacate** avocado *16*
ahora now *6; ahora mismo* right now *13*
ahorrar to save *18*
el **ajedrez** chess *13*
el **ajo** garlic *16*
al to the *5; al lado de* next to, beside *12*
alegre happy, merry, lively
el **alfabeto** alphabet
el **álgebra** algebra
algo something, anything *15*
el **algodón** cotton *17*
alguien someone, anyone, somebody, anybody *17*
algún, alguna some, any *17*
alguno,-a some, any *17*
allá over there *10*
allí there *4*
la **almeja** clam
el **almuerzo** lunch *4*
aló hello (telephone greeting) *4*
alquilar to rent *13*
alterna alternate (*tú* command)
alto,-a tall, high *8*
amable kind, nice *7*
amarillo,-a yellow *4*
ambiguo,-a ambiguous
la **América** America; *América Central* Central America; *América del Sur* South America
americano,-a American *13; el fútbol americano* football *13*
el **amigo, la amiga** friend *3; amigo/a por correspondencia* pen pal
el **amor** love *9*
anaranjado,-a orange (color) *17*
andino,-a Andean, of the Andes Mountains
el **anillo** ring *17*
anteayer the day before yesterday *10*
anterior preceding
antes de before *13*
añade: see *añadir*
añadir to add *16; añade* (*tú* command) add
el **año** year *10; Año Nuevo* New Year's Day *10; ¿Cuántos años tienes?* How old are you? *1; tener* (+ number)

años to be (+ number) years old *9*

apagar to turn off *13*

el **apartamento** apartment

el **apellido** last name, surname

el **apodo** nickname

aprender to learn

apropiado,-a appropriate

apunta: see *apuntar*

apuntar to point; *apunta* (*tú* command) point (at); *apunten* (*Uds.* command) point (at)

apunten: see *apuntar*

apurado,-a in a hurry *7*

aquel, aquella that (far away) *11*

aquellos, aquellas those (far away) *11*

aquí here *1; Aquí se habla español.* Spanish is spoken here.

el **árbol** tree; *árbol genealógico* family tree

el **arete** earring *18*

la **Argentina** Argentina *1*

arreglar to arrange, to straighten, to fix *15*

el **arroz** rice *16*

el **arte** art *4*

el **artículo** article

el **artista** artist

el **ascensor** elevator *18*

la **asignatura** subject

la **aspiradora** vacuum *13; pasar la aspiradora* to vacuum *15*

el **Atlántico** Atlantic Ocean

la **atracción** attraction

el **autobús** bus *5*

automático,-a automatic *18; la escalera automática* escalator *18*

la **avenida** avenue *6*

aventurero,-a adventurous

el **avión** airplane *5*

¡ay! oh! *3*

ayer yesterday *10*

la **ayuda** help

ayudar to help *11*

el **azafrán** saffron

los **aztecas** Aztecs

el **azúcar** sugar *11*

azul blue *4*

B

bailar to dance *8*

bajo,-a short (not tall), low *8; planta baja* floor level *12*

balanceado,-a balanced

el **baloncesto** basketball

el **banco** bank *5*

el **baño** bathroom *12; traje de baño* swimsuit *17*

barato,-a cheap *18*

el **barco** boat, ship *5*

barrer to sweep *15*

el **barril** barrel

basado,-a based

el **básquetbol** basketball *13*

el **basquetbolista, la basquetbolista** basketball player *14*

bastante rather, fairly, sufficiently; enough, sufficient *18*

la **basura** garbage *15*

la **bebida** drink

el **béisbol** baseball *8*

la **biblioteca** library *5*

la **bicicleta** bicycle, bike *5*

bien well *2*

bienvenido,-a welcome

la **billetera** wallet *18*

la **biología** biology *4*

blanco,-a white *4*

la **blusa** blouse *17*

la **boda** wedding

el **bolígrafo** pen *3*

Bolivia Bolivia *1*

el **bolso** handbag, purse *18*

bonito,-a pretty, good-looking, attractive *7*

borra: see *borrar*

el **borrador** eraser *3*

borrar to erase; *borra* (*tú* command) erase; *borren* (*Uds.* command) erase

borren: see *borrar*

la **bota** boot *17*

el **brazo** arm *17*

buen good (form of *bueno* before a *m., s.* noun) *14*

bueno well, okay (pause in speech) *6;* hello (telephone greeting)

bueno,-a good *8; buena suerte* good luck; *buenas noches* good night *2; buenas tardes* good afternoon *2; buenos días* good morning *2*

la **bufanda** scarf *18*

buscar to look for *9*

C

el **caballero** gentleman

el **caballo** horse *5; a caballo* on horseback *5*

la **cabeza** head *17*

cada each, every *12*

café brown (color) *17*

el **café** coffee *16*

la **cafetería** cafeteria *5*

la **caja** cashier's desk *18*

el **calcetín** sock *17*

el **calendario** calendar

la **calidad** quality *18*

caliente hot *7*

la **calle** street *6*

el **calor** heat *12; hace calor* it is hot *14; tener calor* to be hot *12*

calvo,-a bald *8*

la **cama** bed *15*

el **camarón** shrimp

el **cambio** change *14; en cambio* on the other hand *14*

caminar to walk *5*

el **camión** truck *5;* bus (Mexico); *en camión* by truck *5*

la **camisa** shirt *17*

la **canción** song *9*

canoso,-a white-haired *8*

cansado,-a tired *7*

el **cantante, la cantante** singer *6*

cantar to sing *8*

la **cantidad** quantity

la **capital** capital *14*

el **capitán** captain

el **capítulo** chapter

la **característica** characteristic, trait; *características de personalidad* personality traits; *características físicas* physical traits

¡caramba! wow! *9*

cariñoso,-a affectionate *7*

el **carnaval** carnival
la **carne** meat *16*
caro,-a expensive *18*
la **carrera** career
el **carro** car *5; en carro* by car *5*
la **carta** letter *12,* playing card *13*
la **casa** home, house *7; en casa* at home
el **casete** cassette *9*
casi almost *13*
catorce fourteen *1*
la **cebolla** onion *16*
celebrar to celebrate *10*
el **centavo** cent
el **centro** downtown, center *6; centro comercial* shopping center, mall *17*
cerca (de) near *5*
cero zero *1*
cerrado,-a closed *7*
cerrar (ie) to close *11; cierra* (*tú* command) close; *cierren (Uds.* command) close
el **cesto de papeles** wastebasket, wastepaper basket *3*
chao bye
la **chaqueta** jacket *17*
charlando talking, chatting
la **chica** girl *3*
el **chico** boy *3,* man, buddy
Chile Chile *1*
el **chisme** gossip *12*
el **chocolate** chocolate *16*
el **chorizo** sausage (seasoned with red peppers) *16*
cien one hundred *2*
la **ciencia** science
ciento one hundred (when followed by another number) *10*
cierra: see *cerrar*
cierren: see *cerrar*
cinco five *1*
cincuenta fifty *2*
el **cine** movie theater *5*
el **cinturón** belt *18*
la **ciudad** city *6*
la **civilización** civilization
¡claro! of course! *5*
la **clase** class *4*
el **clima** climate
el **coche** car; *en coche* by car
la **cocina** kitchen *11*
cocinar to cook *15*
el **cognado** cognate
el **colegio** school *4*
colgar (ue) to hang *15*
el **collar** necklace *18*
Colombia Colombia *1*
la **colonia** colony
el **color** color *4*
combinar to combine *17*
el **comedor** dining room *11*
comer to eat *6; dar de comer* to feed *15*
cómico,-a comical, funny *8*
la **comida** food *6,* dinner
como like, since, as
¿cómo? how?, what? *1; ¿Cómo?* What (did you say)? *4; ¿Cómo está (Ud.)?* How are you (formal)? *2; ¿Cómo están (Uds.)?* How are you *(pl.)? 2; ¿Cómo estás (tú)?* How are you (informal)? *2; ¡Cómo no!* Of course! *6; ¿Cómo se dice...?* How do you say...? *3; ¿Cómo se escribe...?* How do you write (spell)...? *1; ¿Cómo se llama (Ud./él/ella)?* What is (your/his/her) name? *1; ¿Cómo te llamas?* What is your name? *3*
cómodo,-a comfortable *12*
el **compañero, la compañera** classmate, partner *9*
comparando comparing
la **competencia** competition *14*
completa: see *completar*
completar to complete*; completa (tú* command) complete
la **compra** purchase *8; ir de compras* to go shopping *8*
comprar to buy *8*
comprender to understand *6; comprendo* I understand *3*
comprendo: see *comprender*
la **computadora** computer (machine) *4*
la **computación** computer science *4*
con with *1; con (mucho) gusto* I would be (very) glad to *2; con permiso* excuse me (with your permission), may I *2*
el **concierto** concert *6*
la **conjunción** conjunction
conmigo with me *18*
conseguir (i, i) to obtain, to attain, to get
la **contaminación** contamination, pollution; *contaminación ambiental* environmental pollution
contar (ue) to tell (a story) *17; cuenta* (*tú* command) tell; *cuenten* (*Uds.* command) tell
contento,-a happy, glad *7; estar contento,-a (con)* to be satisfied (with) *7*
contesta: see *contestar*
contestar to answer *8; contesta* (*tú* command) answer; *contesten* (*Uds.* command) answer
contesten: see *contestar*
el **contexto** context
contigo with you (*tú*) *18*
continúa: see *continuar*
continuar to continue *14; continúa* (*tú* command) continue; *continúen* (*Uds.* command) continue
continúen: see *continuar*
la **contracción** contraction
el **control remoto** remote control *13*
copiar to copy *14*
la **corbata** tie *17*
correcto,-a right, correct
el **corredor, la corredora** runner *14*
el **correo** mail; *correo electrónico* e-mail
correr to run *12*
la **cortesía** courtesy
corto,-a short (not long) *18*
la **cosa** thing *11*
la **costa** coast

Costa Rica Costa Rica *1*
costar (ue) to cost *13*
crear to create
el **crédito** credit *18; a crédito* on credit *18; la tarjeta de crédito* credit card *18*
creer to believe
el **crucero** cruise ship
cruzar to cross
el **cuaderno** notebook *3*
¿cuál? which?, what?, which one? *(pl. ¿cuáles?)* which ones? *4*
la **cualidad** quality
cuando when *12*
¿cuándo? when? *5*
¿cuánto,-a? how much? *4 (pl. ¿cuántos,-as?)* how many? *4; ¿Cuántos años tienes?* How old are you? *1; ¿Cuánto* (+ time expression) *hace que* (+ present tense of verb)...? How long...? *13*
cuarenta forty *2*
el **cuarto** quarter *2,* room, bedroom *12; cuarto de baño* bathroom; *menos cuarto* a quarter to, a quarter before *2; y cuarto* a quarter after, a quarter past *2*
cuarto,-a fourth *14*
cuatro four *1*
cuatrocientos,-as four hundred *10*
Cuba Cuba *1*
los **cubiertos** silverware *11*
la **cuchara** tablespoon *11*
la **cucharita** teaspoon *11*
el **cuchillo** knife *11*
cuenta: see *contar*
el **cuero** leather *18*
el **cuerpo** body *17*
cuidar to take care of
el **cumpleaños** birthday *10; ¡Feliz cumpleaños!* Happy birthday! *10*
cumplir to become, to become (+ number) years old, to reach *10; cumplir años* to have a birthday *10*

D

la **dama** lady
las **damas** checkers *13; damas* women's restroom
dar to give *13; dar de comer* to feed *15; dar un paseo* to take a walk *14; dé* (*Ud.* command) give
de from, of *1; de acuerdo* agreed, okay *6; ¿de dónde?* from where? *1; ¿De dónde eres?* Where are you from? *1; ¿De dónde es (Ud./él/ella)?* Where are you (formal) from?, Where is (he/she/it) from? *3; de la mañana* in the morning, A.M. *2; de la noche* at night, P.M. *2; de la tarde* in the afternoon, P.M. *2; de nada* you are welcome, not at all *2; de todos los días* everyday *11; ¿de veras?* really? *10; ¿Eres (tú) de...?* Are you from...? *1*
dé: see *dar*
deber should, to have to, must, ought (expressing a moral duty) *11*
décimo,-a tenth *14*
decir to tell, to say *12; ¿Cómo se dice...?* How do you say...? *3; di (tú* command) say, tell; *díganme (Uds.* command) tell me; *dime (tú* command) tell me; *¿Qué quiere decir...?* What is the meaning (of)...? *3; querer decir* to mean *12; quiere decir* it means *3; se dice* one says *3*
el **dedo** finger, toe *17*
dejar to leave *15*
del of the, from the *5*
delgado,-a thin *8*
demasiado too (much) *18*
la **democracia** democracy
el **dentista, la dentista** dentist *5*
el **departamento** department *18*
el **deporte** sport *9*
el **deportista, la deportista** athlete *14*
desaparecido,-a missing
el **desastre** disaster *15*
el **desayuno** breakfast
describe *(tú* command) describe
desde since, from *12*
desear to wish
el **deseo** wish
la **despedida** farewell
después afterwards, later, then *11; después de* after *13*
di: see *decir*
el **día** day *4; buenos días* good morning *2; de todos los días* everyday *8; todos los días* every day *9*
el **diálogo** dialog
diario,-a daily
dibuja: see *dibujar*
dibujar to draw, to sketch *13; dibuja (tú* command) draw; *dibujen (Uds.* command) draw
dibujen: see *dibujar*
el **dibujo** drawing, sketch *12*
diciembre December *10*
el **dictado** dictation
diecinueve nineteen *1*
dieciocho eighteen *1*
dieciséis sixteen *1*
diecisiete seventeen *1*
diez ten *1*
la **diferencia** difference
diferente different
difícil difficult, hard *8*
diga hello (telephone greeting)
dígame tell me, hello (telephone greeting)
díganme: see *decir*
dime: see *decir*
el **dinero** money *9*
la **dirección** address *4; dirección de correo electrónico* e-mail *4*
el **director, la directora** director
dirigir to direct *15*
el **disco** disc *4,9,* record; *disco compacto* CD-ROM *4,* audio compact disc, audio CD *9*

el **diskette** diskette *4*
divertido,-a fun *7*
doce twelve *1*
el **doctor, la doctora** doctor
el **dólar** dollar
domingo Sunday *4; el domingo* on Sunday
don title of respect used before a man's first name *5*
donde where *12*
¿dónde? where? *1; ¿de dónde?* from where?; *¿De dónde es (Ud./él/ella)?* Where are you (formal) from?, Where is (he/she/it) from? *3*
doña title of respect used before a woman's first name *5*
dormir (ue, u) to sleep *13*
dos two *1*
doscientos,-as two hundred *10*
Dr. abbreviation for *doctor*
Dra. abbreviation for *doctora*
dulce sweet *8*
durante during

E

e and (used before a word beginning with *i* or *hi*) *12*
la **ecología** ecology
el **Ecuador** Ecuador *1*
la **edad** age
el **edificio** building *6*
la **educación física** physical education
el **efectivo** cash *18; en efectivo* in cash *18*
egoísta selfish *8*
el **ejemplo** example*; por ejemplo* for example
el the *(m., s.) 3*
él he *3;* him (after a preposition) *8; Él se llama....* His name is.... *3*
eléctrico,-a electric
El Salvador El Salvador *1*
ella she *3;* her (after a preposition) *8; Ella se llama....* Her name is.... *3*
ellos,-as they *3;* them (after a preposition) *8*
empatados: see *empate*
el **empate** tie; *los partidos empatados* games tied
empezar (ie) to begin, to start *11*
en in, on, at *4; en* (+ vehicle) by (+ vehicle) *5; en cambio* on the other hand *14; en casa* at home*; en efectivo* in cash *18; en resumen* in short
encantado,-a delighted, the pleasure is mine *5*
encender (ie) to light, to turn on (a light) *11*
encontrar (ue) to find
la **encuesta** survey, poll
enero January *10*
el **énfasis** emphasis
enfermo,-a sick *7*
el **enfermera, la enfermera** nurse
la **ensalada** salad *6*
enseñar to teach, to show
entonces then *9*
entrar to go in, to come in *9*
entre between, among
la **entrevista** interview
enviar to send *14*
el **equipo** team *13*
equivocado mistaken; *número equivocado* wrong number *4*
eres: see *ser*
es: see *ser*
la **escalera** stairway, stairs *12; escalera automática* escalator *18*
la **escena** scene
escoger to choose *16; escogiendo* choosing
escogiendo: see *escoger*
escriban: see *escribir*
escribe: see *escribir*
escribir to write *12; ¿Cómo se escribe...?* How do you write (spell)...? *1; escriban* (*Uds.* command) write; *escribe* (*tú* command) write; *se escribe* it is written *1*
el **escritorio** desk *3*
escucha: see *escuchar*
escuchar to listen (to); *escucha* (*tú* command) listen; *escuchen* (*Uds.* command) listen
escuchen: see *escuchar*
la **escuela** school *5*
ese, esa that *11*
eso that (neuter form)
esos, esas those *11*
el **espacio** space
España Spain *1*
el **español** Spanish (language) *4*
español, española Spanish
especial special *11*
especializado,-a specialized
el **espectáculo** showcase
la **esposa** wife, spouse *7*
el **esposo** husband, spouse *7*
el **esquiador, la esquiadora** skier *14*
esquiar to ski *14*
está: see *estar*
la **estación** season *14*
el **estadio** stadium
el **Estado Libre Asociado** Commonwealth
los **Estados Unidos** United States of America *1*
están: see *estar*
estar to be *4; ¿Cómo está (Ud.)?* How are you (formal)? *2; ¿Cómo están (Uds.)?* How are you *(pl.)? 2; ¿Cómo estás (tú)?* How are you (informal)? *2; está* you (formal) are, he/she/it is *2; está nublado,-a* it's cloudy *14; está soleado,-a* it's sunny *14; están* they are *2; estar contento,-a (con)* to be satisfied (with) *7; estar en oferta* to be on sale *18; estar listo,-a* to be ready *14; estás* you (informal) are *2; estoy* I am *2*
estás: see *estar*
este well, so (pause in speech)
este, esta this *11; esta noche* tonight *13*
el **estéreo** stereo *9*

estos, estas these *11*
estoy: see *estar*
la estructura structure
estudia: see *estudiar*
el estudiante, la estudiante student *3*
estudiar to study *4; estudia* (*tú* command) study; *estudien* (*Uds.* command) study
estudien: see *estudiar*
el estudio study
la estufa stove *11*
estupendo,-a wonderful, marvellous *13*
el examen exam, test *9*
excelente excellent *14*
el éxito success
explica: see *explicar*
la explicación explanation
explicar to explain; *explica* (*tú* command) explain
el explorador, la exploradora explorer
la exportación exportation
exportador, exportadora exporting
expresar to express
la expresión expression
la extensión extension

F

fácil easy *8*
la falda skirt *17*
falso,-a false
la familia family *7*
famoso,-a famous
fantástico,-a fantastic, great *5*
el favor favor; *por favor* please *2*
favorito,-a favorite *6*
febrero February *10*
la fecha date *10*
felicitaciones congratulations
feliz happy *(pl. felices) 10; ¡Feliz cumpleaños!* Happy birthday! *10*
femenino,-a feminine
feo,-a ugly *8*
el ferrocarril railway, railroad
la fiesta party *5*
la filosofía philosophy
el fin end *9; fin de semana* weekend *9*
la física physics *11*
la flauta flute
la flor flower *14*
la florcita small flower
la forma form
la foto(grafía) photo *7*
la frase phrase, sentence
el fregadero sink *11*
la fresa strawberry *16*
el fresco cool *14; hace fresco* it is cool *14*
fresco,-a fresh, chilly *16*
los frijoles beans *6*
el frío cold *7; hace frío* it is cold *14; tener frío* to be cold *12*
frío,-a cold *7*
la fruta fruit *16*
fue: see *ser*
fueron: see *ser*
fuerte strong
el fútbol soccer *9; fútbol americano* football *13*
el futbolista, la futbolista soccer player *14*
el futuro future

G

la gana desire *12; tener ganas de* to feel like *12*
ganados: see *ganar*
ganar to win; *los partidos ganados* games won
el garaje garage *12*
el gato, la gata cat *9*
el género gender
generoso,-a generous *8*
la gente people *15*
la geografía geography
la geometría geometry
el gerundio present participle
el gesto gesture
el gimnasio gym
el gobernador, la gobernadora governor
gordo,-a fat *8*
la grabadora tape recorder (machine) *9*
gracias thanks *2; muchas gracias* thank you very much *2*
el grado degree *14*
gran big (form of *grande* before a *m., s.* noun)
grande big *6*
gris gray *4*
el grupo group; *grupo musical* musical group
el guante glove *17*
guapo,-a good-looking, attractive, handsome, pretty *7*
Guatemala Guatemala *1*
el guía, la guía guide
Guinea Ecuatorial Equatorial Guinea *1*
el guisante pea *16*
la guitarra guitar *9*
gusta: see *gustar*
gustar to like, to be pleasing to *8; me/te/le/nos/vos/les gustaría...* I/you/he/she/it/we/they would like... *12*
gustaría: see *gustar*
el gusto pleasure *5; con (mucho) gusto* I would be (very) glad to *2; el gusto es mío* the pleasure is mine *5; ¡Mucho gusto!* Glad to meet you! *1; Tanto gusto.* So glad to meet you. *5*

H

la habichuela green bean *16*
la habitación room, bedroom
el habitante, la habitante inhabitant
habla: see *hablar*
hablar to speak *4; habla (tú* command) speak; *hablen (Uds. command)* speak; *Se habla español.* Spanish is spoken.
hablen: see *hablar*
hace: see *hacer*
hacer to do, to make *6; ¿Cuánto* (+ time expression) *hace que* (+ present tense of verb)...? How long...? *13; hace buen (mal) tiempo* the weather is nice (bad) *14;*

hace fresco it is cool *14; hace frío (calor)* it is cold (hot) *14; hace* (+ time expression) *que* ago *13; hace sol* it is sunny *14; hace viento* it is windy *14; hacer aeróbicos* to do aerobics *13; hacer falta* to be necessary, to be lacking *16; hacer un viaje* to take a trip *9*; *hacer una pregunta* to ask a question *6; hagan* (*Uds.* command) do, make; *haz* (*tú* command) do, make; *haz el papel* play the part; *hecha* made

hagan: see *hacer*

el **hambre** *f.* hunger *12; tener hambre* to be hungry *12*

hasta until, up to, down to *1; hasta la vista* so long, see you later; *hasta luego* so long, see you later *1; hasta mañana* see you tomorrow *2; hasta pronto* see you soon *2*

hay there is, there are *4; hay neblina* it is misting *14; hay sol* it is sunny *14*

haz: see *hacer*

hecha: see *hacer*

el **helado** ice cream *16*

la **hermana** sister *7*

el **hermano** brother *7*

el **hielo** ice *14; patinar sobre hielo* to ice-skate *14*

la **hija** daughter *7*

el **hijo** son *7*

la **historia** history *4*

la **hoja** sheet*; hoja de papel* sheet of paper

hola hi, hello *1*

el **hombre** man *17*

Honduras Honduras *1*

la **hora** hour *2; ¿a qué hora?* at what time? *4; ¿Qué hora es?* What time is it? *2*

el **horario** schedule *4*

horrible horrible *8*

el **hotel** hotel *5*

hoy today *6*

el **huevo** egg *16*

I

la **idea** idea *10*

ideal ideal *8*

ignorar to not know

imagina: see *imaginar*

la **imaginación** imagination

imaginar to imagine; *imagina* (*tú* command) imagine

el **impermeable** raincoat *17*

importante important *8*

importar to be important, to matter *16*

la **impresora (láser)** (laser) printer *4*

los **incas** Incas

incluir to include

indefinido,-a indefinite

la **independencia** independence

indica: see *indicar*

la **indicación** cue

indicado,-a indicated

indicar to indicate; *indica* (*tú* command) indicate

indígena native

el **informe** report

el **inglés** English (language) *4*

el **ingrediente** ingredient *16*

inicial initial

inmenso,-a immense

la **inspiración** inspiration

inteligente intelligent *8*

interesante interesting *8*

interrogativo,-a interrogative

el **invierno** winter *14*

la **invitación** invitation

invitar to invite

ir to go *5; ir a* (+ infinitive) to be going to (do something) *6; ir de compras* to go shopping *8; ¡vamos!* let's go! *5; ¡vamos a* (+ infinitive)! let's (+ infinitive)! *6; vayan* (*Uds.* command) go to; *ve* (*tú* command) go to

la **isla** island

J

el **jamón** ham *16*

la **jirafa** giraffe

joven young *10*

el **juego** game

jueves Thursday *4; el jueves* on Thursday

el **jugador, la jugadora** player *14*

jugar (ue) to play *8, 13; jugar a* (+ sport/game) *8*

el **jugo** juice *6*

julio July *10*

junio June *10*

junto,-a together *15*

L

la the *(f., s.) 3;* her, it, you *(d.o.) 9; a la...* at...o'clock *4*

el **lado** side *12; al lado (de)* next to, beside *12; por todos lados* everywhere *14*

la **lámpara** lamp *11*

la **lana** wool *17*

la **langosta** lobster

el **lápiz** pencil *(pl. lápices) 3*

largo,-a long *18*

las the *(f., pl.) 3;* them, you *(d.o.) 9; a las...* at...o'clock *4*

la **lástima** shame; *¡Qué lástima!* What a shame! *9*

la **lata** can *16*

el **lavaplatos** dishwasher (machine) *11*

lavar to wash *15*

le (to, for) him, (to, for) her, (to, for) it, (to, for) you (formal)(*i.o.*) *5*

lean: see *leer*

la **lección** lesson

la **leche** milk *15*

la **lechuga** lettuce *16*

la **lectura** reading

lee: see *leer*

leer to read *6; lean* (*Uds.* command) read; *lee* (*tú* command) read

lejos (de) far (from) *5*

la **lengua** language

lento,-a slow *8*

les (to, for) them, (to, for) you *(pl.)(i.o.) 5*

la **letra** letter

levantarse to get up, to rise; *levántate* (*tú* command)

get up; *levántense* (*Uds.* command) get up
levántate: see *levantarse*
levántense: see *levantarse*
la **libertad** liberty, freedom
la **libra** pound *16*
libre free *7*
la **librería** bookstore *9*
el **libro** book *3*
el **líder** leader
limitar to limit
limpiar to clean *15*
limpio,-a clean *7*
lindo,-a pretty *18*
la **lista** list *13*
listo,-a ready *14,* smart *15; estar listo,-a* to be ready *14; ser listo,-a* to be smart *15*
la **literatura** literature
llama: see *llamar*
llamar to call, to telephone *9; ¿Cómo se llama (Ud./él/ella)?* What is (your/his/her) name? *3; ¿Cómo te llamas?* What is your name? *1; llamaron* they called (preterite of *llamar*); *me llamo* my name is *1; se llaman* their names are; *te llamas* your name is *1; (Ud./Él/Ella) se llama....* (Your [formal]/His/Her) name is.... *3*
llamaron: see *llamar*
llamas: see *llamar*
llamo: see *llamar*
llegar to arrive *15; llegó* arrived (preterite of *llegar*)
llegó: see *llegar*
llevar to take, to carry *16;* to wear *17*
llover (ue) to rain *14*
la **lluvia** rain *14*
lo him, it, you *(d.o.) 9; lo que* what, that which *12; lo siento* I am sorry *2*
loco,-a crazy *7*
lógicamente logically
lógico,-a logical
los the *(m., pl.) 3;* them, you *(d.o.) 9*
luego then, later, soon *1; hasta luego* so long, see you later *1*
el **lugar** place *14*
lunes Monday *4; el lunes* on Monday
la **luz** light *(pl. luces) 11*

M

la **madre** mother *7*
maduro,-a ripe *16*
el **maestro** teacher, master; *La práctica hace al maestro.* Practice makes perfect.
el **maíz** corn *16*
mal badly *2;* bad *14*
la **maleta** suitcase *9*
malo,-a bad *8*
la **mamá** mother, mom
la **manera** manner, way
la **mano** hand *17*
el **mantel** tablecloth *11*
la **mantequilla** butter *11*
la **manzana** apple *16*
mañana tomorrow *2; hasta mañana* see you tomorrow *2; pasado mañana* the day after tomorrow *10*
la **mañana** morning *2; de la mañana* A.M., in the morning *2; por la mañana* in the morning *13*
el **mapa** map *3*
la **maquinita** little machine, video game *13*
mariachi popular Mexican music and orchestra
el **marisco** seafood, shellfish
martes Tuesday *4; el martes* on Tuesday
marzo March *10*
más more, else *7; el/la/los/las* (+ noun) *más* (+ adjective) the most (+ adjective) *16; lo más* (+ adverb) *posible* as (+ adverb) as possible *16; más* (+ noun/adjective/adverb) *que* more (+ noun/adjective/adverb) than *16*
masculino,-a masculine
las **matemáticas** mathematics *4*
el **material** material *18*
máximo,-a maximum *14*
maya Mayan
los **mayas** Mayans
mayo May *10*
mayor older, oldest *10,* greater, greatest *16*
la **mayúscula** capital letter *1*
me (to, for) me *(i.o.) 8;* me *(d.o.) 9; me llaman* they call me; *me llamo* my name is *1*
la **medianoche** *Es medianoche.* It is midnight. *2*
el **médico, la médica** doctor *5*
medio,-a half*; y media* half past *2*
el **medio** means
el **mediodía** noon*; Es mediodía.* It is noon. *2*
mejor better *16; el/la/los/las mejor/mejores* (+ noun) the best (+ noun) *16*
menor younger, youngest *10,* lesser, least *16*
menos minus, until, before, to (to express time) *2,* less *11; el/la/los/las* (+ noun) *menos* (+ adjective) the least (+ adjective + noun) *16; lo menos* (+ adverb) *posible* as (+ adverb) as possible *16; menos* (+ noun/ adjective/adverb) *que* less (+ noun/ adjective/adverb) than *16; por lo menos* at least
mentir (ie, i) to lie
la **mentira** lie *12*
el **menú** menu *6*
el **mercado** market *16*
el **merengue** merengue (dance music)
el **mes** month *10*
la **mesa** table *11; poner la mesa* to set the table *11; recoger la mesa* to clear the table *15*
el **mesero, la mesara** food server *6*

el **metro** subway *5*
mexicano,-a Mexican
México Mexico *1*
mi my *3; (pl. mis)* my *7*
mí me *8;* (after a preposition) *8*
el **miedo** fear *12; tener miedo de* to be afraid of *12*
el **miembro** member, part
mientras que while
miércoles Wednesday *4; el miércoles* on Wednesday
mil thousand *10*
mínimo,-a minimum *14*
la **minúscula** lowercase
el **minuto** minute *13*
mío,-a my, mine; *el gusto es mío* the pleasure is mine *5*
mira: see *mirar*
mirar to look (at) *8; mira* (*tú* command) look *4; mira* hey, look (pause in speech); *miren* (*Uds.* command) look; *miren* hey, look (pause in speech)
miren: see *mirar*
mismo right (in the very moment, place, etc.) *13; ahora mismo* right now *13*
mismo,-a same *13*
el **misterio** mystery
la **mochila** backpack *3*
el **modelo** model
moderno,-a modern
el **momento** moment *6*
el **mono** monkey
montar to ride *9*
moreno,-a brunet, brunette, dark-haired, dark-skinned *8*
la **moto(cicleta)** motorcycle *5*
la **muchacha** girl, young woman *5*
el **muchacho** boy, guy *5*
muchísimo very much, a lot
mucho much, a lot, very, very much *3*
mucho,-a much, a lot of, very *6; (pl. muchos,-as)* many *6; con (mucho) gusto* I would be (very) glad to *2; muchas gracias* thank you very much *2; ¡Mucho gusto!* Glad to meet you! *1*
la **mujer** woman *17*
el **mundo** world*; todo el mundo* everyone, everybody
la **muralla** wall
el **museo** museum *6*
la **música** music *4*
muy very *2*

N

la **nación** nation
nacional national
nada nothing *17; de nada* you are welcome, not at all *2*
nadar to swim *8*
nadie nobody *17*
la **naranja** orange *6*
la **Navidad** Christmas *10*
la **neblina** mist *14; hay neblina* it is misting *14*
necesitar to need *4*
negativo,-a negative
el **negocio** business; *hombre de negocios* businessman; *mujer de negocios* businesswoman
negro,-a black *4*
nervioso,-a nervous *7*
nevar (ie) to snow *14*
ni not even *10; ni...ni* neither...nor *17*
Nicaragua Nicaragua *1*
la **nieta** granddaughter *7*
el **nieto** grandson *7*
la **nieve** snow *14*
ningún, ninguna none, not any *17*
ninguno,-a none, not any *17*
no no *1*
la **noche** night *2; buenas noches* good night *2; de la noche* P.M., at night *2; esta noche* tonight *13; por la noche* at night *12*
el **nombre** name
el **norte** north
nos (to, for) us *(i.o.) 8;* us *(d.o.) 9*
nosotros,-as we *3;* us (after a preposition) *8*
la **noticia** news
novecientos,-as nine hundred *10*
noveno,-a ninth *14*
noventa ninety *2*
la **novia** girlfriend
noviembre November *10*
el **novio** boyfriend
nublado,-a cloudy *14; está nublado* it is cloudy *14*
nuestro,-a our *7*
nueve nine *1*
nuevo,-a new *3; el Año Nuevo* New Year's Day *10*
el **número** number *4; número de teléfono/de fax/de teléfono celular* telephone/fax/cellular telephone number *4, número equivocado* wrong number *4*
nunca never *3*

O

o or *4; o...o* either...or *17*
la **obra** work, play
ochenta eighty *2*
ocho eight *1*
ochocientos,-as eight hundred *10*
octavo,-a eighth *14*
octubre October *10*
ocupado,-a busy, occupied *7*
ocupar to occupy
la **odisea** odyssey
la **oferta** sale *18; estar en oferta* to be on sale *18*
oficial official
la **oficina** office *5*
oigan hey, listen (pause in speech)
oigo hello (telephone greeting)
oír to hear, to listen (to) *8; oigan* hey, listen (pause in speech); *oigo* hello (telephone greeting); *oye* hey, listen (pause in speech) *6*
la **olla** pot, saucepan *15*

olvidar to forget 16
la **omisión** omission
once eleven 1
el **opuesto** opposite
la **oración** sentence
el **orden** order
la **organización** organization
el **órgano** organ
el **oro** gold 18
os (to, for) you (Spain, informal, *pl., i.o.),* you (Spain, informal, *pl., d.o.)*
el **otoño** autumn 14
otro,-a other, another *(pl. otros,-as)* 7; *otra vez* again, another time 11
oye hey, listen (pause in speech) 6

P

el **Pacífico** Pacific Ocean
el **padre** father 7; *(pl. padres)* parents
la **paella** paella (traditional Spanish dish with rice, meat, seafood and vegetables) 15
pagar to pay 18
la **página** page 3
el **país** country
la **palabra** word 3; *palabra interrogativa* question word; *palabras antónimas* antonyms, opposite words
el **pan** bread 11
Panamá Panama 1
la **pantalla** screen 4
el **pantalón** pants 17
las **pantimedias** pantyhose, nylons 17
el **pañuelo** handkerchief, hanky 18
la **papa** potato 16
el **papá** father, dad
los **papás** parents
el **papel** paper 3, role; *haz el papel* play the role; *la hoja de papel* sheet of paper
para for, to, in order to 7
el **paraguas** umbrella 18
el **Paraguay** Paraguay 1
parecer to seem 16
la **pared** wall 3
la **pareja** pair, couple
el **pariente, la pariente** relative 7
el **parque** park 5
el **párrafo** paragraph
la **parte** part
el **partido** game, match 8; *partidos empatados* games tied; *partidos ganados* games won; *partidos perdidos* games lost
pasado,-a past, last 10; *pasado mañana* the day after tomorrow 10
pásame: see *pasar*
pasar to pass, to spend (time) 9, to happen, to occur; *pásame* pass me 11; *pasar la aspiradora* to vacuum 15; *¿Qué te pasa?* What is wrong with you?
el **pasatiempo** pastime, leisure activity 13
la **Pascua** Easter
el **paseo** walk, ride, trip 14; *dar un paseo* to take a walk 14
el **patinador, la patinadora** skater 14
patinar to skate 14; *patinar sobre ruedas* to in-line skate 8; *patinar sobre hielo* to ice-skate 14
el **patio** courtyard, patio, yard 12
pedir (i, i) to ask for, to order, to request 12; *pedir perdón* to say you are sorry 12; *pedir permiso (para)* to ask for permission (to do something) 12; *pedir prestado,-a* to borrow 12
la **película** movie, film 9
pelirrojo,-a red-haired 8
pensar (ie) to think, to intend, to plan 11; *pensar de* to think about (i.e., to have an opinion) 11; *pensar en* to think about (i.e., to focus one's thoughts on) 11; *pensar en* (+ infinitive) to think about (doing something)
peor worse 16; *el/la/los/las peor/peores* (+ noun) the worst (+ noun) 16
pequeño,-a small 12
perder (ie) to lose; *los partidos perdidos* games lost
perdidos: see *perder*
perdón excuse me, pardon me 2; *pedir perdón* to say you are sorry 12
perezoso,-a lazy
perfecto,-a perfect 18
el **perfume** perfume 18
el **periódico** newspaper 3
el **periodista, la periodista** journalist, reporter
el **período** period
la **perla** pearl 18
el **permiso** permission, permit 13; *con permiso* excuse me (with your permission), may I 2; *pedir permiso (para)* to ask for permission (to do something) 12
permitir to permit 13
pero but 6
el **perro, la perra** dog 9
la **persona** person 15
personal personal 18; *el pronombre personal* subject pronoun
el **Perú** Peru 1
el **pescado** fish 6
el **petróleo** oil
el **piano** piano 8
el **pie** foot 17; *a pie* on foot 5
la **pierna** leg 17
el **pijama** pajamas 18
la **pimienta** pepper (seasoning) 11
el **pimiento** bell pepper 16
pintar to paint
la **pirámide** pyramid
la **piscina** swimming pool 12
el **piso** floor 12; *el primer piso* first floor 12
la **pista** clue
la **pizarra** blackboard 3
la **planta** plant 12; *planta baja* ground floor 12

la **plata** silver *18*
el **plátano** banana *16*
el **plato** dish, plate *11; plato de sopa* soup bowl *11*
la **playa** beach *7*
la **plaza** plaza, public square *6*
poco,-a not very, little *12; un poco* a little (bit) *9*
poder (ue) to be able *13*
políticamente politically
el **pollo** chicken *6*
poner to put, to place, to turn on (an appliance) *13; poner la mesa* to set the table *11*
popular popular *7*
un **poquito** a very little (bit) *11*
por for *7,* through, by *12,* in *13,* along *14; por ejemplo* for example*; por favor* please *2; por la mañana* in the morning *13; por la noche* at night *12; por la tarde* in the afternoon *13; por teléfono* by telephone, on the telephone *12; por todos lados* everywhere *14*
¿por qué? why? *5*
porque because *5*
la **posibilidad** possibility
la **posición** position, place
el **póster** poster
el **postre** dessert *11*
la **práctica** practice *9; La práctica hace al maestro.* Practice makes perfect.
el **precio** price *16*
preferir (ie, i) to prefer *11*
la **pregunta** question *6; hacer una pregunta* to ask a question *6*
preguntar to ask *6*
la **preparación** preparation
preparar to prepare *15*
el **preparativo** preparation
la **preposición** preposition
la **presentación** introduction
presentar to introduce, to present*; le presento a* let me introduce you (formal, *s.*) to *5; les presento a* let me introduce you *(pl.)* to *5; te presento a* let me introduce you (informal, *s.*) to *5*
presente present
presento: see *presentar*
prestado,-a on loan *12; pedir prestado,-a* to borrow *12*
prestar to lend *15*
la **primavera** spring *14*
primer first (form of *primero* before a *m., s.* noun) *12; el primer piso* first floor *12*
primero,-a first *10*
primero first (adverb) *9*
el **primo, la prima** cousin *7*
principal main
la **prisa** rush, hurry, haste *12; tener prisa* to be in a hurry *12*
el **problema** problem *5*
produce produces
el **producto** product
el **profesor, la profesora** teacher *3; el profe* teacher
el **programa** program, show *13*
prometer to promise *17*
el **pronombre** pronoun; *pronombre personal* subject pronoun
el **pronóstico** forecast
pronto soon, quickly *2; hasta pronto* see you soon *2*
la **pronunciación** pronunciation
el **propósito** aim, purpose; *a propósito* by the way *1*
próximo,-a next
la **publicidad** publicity
público,-a public
la **puerta** door *3*
Puerto Rico Puerto Rico *1*
pues thus, well, so, then (pause in speech) *6*
la **pulsera** bracelet *18*
el **punto** point
la **puntuación** punctuation
el **pupitre** desk *3*

Q

que that, which *9; lo que* what, that which *12; más* (+ noun/adjective/ adverb) *que* more (+ noun/adjective/ adverb) than *16; que viene* upcoming, next *9*
¡qué (+ adjective)! how (+ adjective)! *7*
¡qué (+ noun)! what a (+ noun)! *9*
¿qué? what? *3; ¿a qué hora?* at what time? *4; ¿Qué comprendiste?* What did you understand?; *¿Qué hora es?* What time is it? *2; ¿Qué quiere decir...?* What is the meaning (of)...? *3; ¿Qué tal?* How are you? *2; ¿Qué te pasa?* What is wrong with you?; *¿Qué temperatura hace?* What is the temperature? *14; ¿Qué (+ tener)?* What is wrong with (someone)? *12; ¿Qué tiempo hace?* How is the weather? *14*
quedar to remain, to stay *17; quedarle bien a uno* to fit, to be becoming *17*
el **quehacer** chore *15*
querer (ie) to love, to want, to like *11; ¿Qué quiere decir...?* What is the meaning (of)...? *3; querer decir* to mean *12; quiere decir* it means *3; quiero* I love *7;* I want *5*
querido,-a dear *10*
el **queso** cheese *16*
¿quién? who? *3; (pl. ¿quiénes?)* who? *5*
quiere: see *querer*
quiero: see *querer*
la **química** chemistry
quince fifteen *1*
quinientos,-as five hundred *10*
quinto,-a fifth *14*
quisiera would like
quizás perhaps *15*

R

la **radio** radio (broadcast) *8; el radio* radio (apparatus)
rápidamente rapidly *10*

rápido,-a rapid, fast *8*
el **rascacielos** skyscraper
el **ratón** mouse (*pl. ratones*) *4*
la **razón** reason
real royal
la **realidad** reality
la **receta** recipe *15*
recibir to receive *18*
recoger to pick up *15; recoger la mesa* to clear the table *15*
recordar (ue) to remember *13*
redondo,-a round
el **refresco** soft drink, refreshment *6*
el **refrigerador** refrigerator *11*
el **regalo** gift *18*
regañar to scold
regatear to bargain, to haggle
la **regla** ruler *3*
regresar to return, to go back
regular average, okay, so-so, regular *2*
relacionado,-a related
el **reloj** clock, watch *3*
remoto,-a remote *13*
repasar to reexamine, to review
el **repaso** review
repetir (i, i) to repeat *12; repitan* (*Uds.* command) repeat; *repite* (*tú* command) repeat
repitan: see *repetir*
repite: see *repetir*
reportando reporting
la **República Dominicana** Dominican Republic *1*
resolver (ue) to resolve, to solve
responder to answer
la **respuesta** answer
el **restaurante** restaurant *6*
el **resultado** result
el **resumen** summary; *en resumen* in short
la **reunión** meeting
la **revista** magazine *3*
rico,-a rich
el **riel** rail
el **ritmo** rhythm
rojo,-a red *4*
la **ropa** clothing *15; ropa interior* underwear *17*
rosado,-a pink *17*
rubio,-a blond, blonde *8*
la **rutina** routine

S

sábado Saturday *4; el sábado* on Saturday
saber to know *6; sabes* you know *6; sé* I know *3*
sabes: see *saber*
el **sacapuntas** pencil sharpener *3*
sacar to take out *15*; *sacar fotos* to take photographs
la **sal** salt *11*
la **sala** living room *12*
salir to go out *7*
la **salsa** salsa (dance music)
el **saludo** greeting
el **salvavidas** lifeguard
la **sangre** blood
el **santo** saint's day; *Todos los Santos* All Saints' Day
el **saxofón** saxophone
se *¿Cómo se dice...?* How do you say...? *3; ¿Cómo se escribe...?* How do you write (spell)...? *1; ¿Cómo se llama (Ud./él/ella)?* What is (your/his/her) name? *3; se considera* it is considered; *se dice* one says *3; se escribe* it is written *1; Se habla español.* Spanish is spoken.; *se llaman* their names are; *(Ud./Él/Ella) se llama....* (Your [formal]/His/Her) name is.... *3*
sé: see *saber*
sea: see *ser*
la **sed** thirst *12; tener sed* to be thirsty *12*
la **seda** silk *17*
seguir (i, i) to follow, to continue, to keep on; *sigan* (*Uds.* command) follow; *sigue* (*tú* command) follow
según according to
el **segundo** second *14*
segundo,-a second *13*
seis six *1*
seiscientos,-as six hundred *10*
selecciona select (*tú* command)
la **selva** jungle; *selva tropical* tropical rain forest
la **semana** week *9; el fin de semana* weekend *9; Semana Santa* Holy Week
sentarse (ie) to sit (down); *siéntate* (*tú* command) sit (down); *siéntense* (*Uds.* command) sit (down)
sentir (ie, i) to be sorry, to feel sorry, to regret *11; lo siento* I am sorry *2*
señalar to point to, to point at, to point out; *señalen* (*Uds.* command) point to
señalen: see *señalar*
el **señor** gentleman, sir, Mr. *2*
la **señora** lady, madame, Mrs. *2*
la **señorita** young lady, Miss *2*
septiembre September *10*
séptimo,-a seventh *14*
ser to be *3; eres* you are *1; ¿Eres (tú) de...?* Are you from...? *1; es* you (formal) are, he/she/it is *2; es la una* it is one o'clock *2; Es medianoche.* It is midnight. *2; Es mediodía.* It is noon. *2; fue* you (formal) were, he/she/it was (preterite of *ser*) *10; ¿Qué hora es?* What time is it? *2; sea* it is; *son* they are *2; son las* (+ number) it is (+ number) o'clock *2; soy* I am *1*
serio,-a serious
la **servilleta** napkin *11*
sesenta sixty *2*
setecientos,-as seven hundred *10*
setenta seventy *2*
sexto,-a sixth *14*
si if *9*
sí yes *1*
siempre always *6*
siéntate: see *sentarse*
siéntense: see *sentarse*
siento: see *sentir*
siete seven *1*
sigan: see *seguir*
el **siglo** century *13*
los **signos de puntuación** punctuation marks

sigue: see *seguir*
siguiente following; *lo siguiente* the following
la **silabificación** syllabification
el **silencio** silence
la **silla** chair *3*
el **símbolo** symbol
similar alike, similar
simpático,-a nice, pleasant *5*
sin without *16*
sintético,-a synthetic *18*
la **situación** situation
sobre on, over *4,* about*; patinar sobre hielo* to ice-skate *14; patinar sobre ruedas* to in-line skate *8*
la **sobrina** niece *7*
el **sobrino** nephew *7*
el **sol** sun *14; hace sol, hay sol* it is sunny *14*
solamente only
soleado,-a sunny *14; está soleado* it is sunny *14*
solo,-a alone
sólo only, just *15*
el **sombrero** hat *17*
son: see *ser*
el **sondeo** poll
el **sonido** sound
la **sopa** soup *11*
la **sorpresa** surprise *9*
soy: see *ser*
Sr. abbreviation for *señor 2*
Sra. abbreviation for *señora 2*
Srta. abbreviation for *señorita 2*
su, sus his, her, its, your *(Ud./Uds.),* their *7*
suave smooth, soft
el **subdesarrollo** underdevelopment
subir to climb, to go up, to go upstairs, to take up, to bring up, to carry up *15*
el **suceso** happening
sucio,-a dirty *7*
el **sueño** sleep *12; tener sueño* to be sleepy *12*
el **suéter** sweater *17*
el **supermercado** supermarket *15*
el **sur** south
el **sustantivo** noun

T

tal such, as, so; *¿Qué tal?* How are you? *2*
el **tamal** tamale
el **tamaño** size *18*
también also, too *5*
el **tambor** drum
tampoco either, neither *4*
tan so *9; tan* (+ adjective/adverb) *como* (+ person/item) as (+ adjective/adverb) as (+ person/item) *16*
tanto,-a so much *5; tanto,-a* (+ noun) *como* (+ person/item) as much/many (+ noun) as (+ person/item) *16; tanto como* as much as *16; Tanto gusto.* So glad to meet you. *5*
la **tapa** tidbit, appetizer
la **tarde** afternoon *2; buenas tardes* good afternoon *1; de la tarde* P.M., in the afternoon *2; por la tarde* in the afternoon *13*
la **tarea** homework *8*
la **tarjeta** card *18; tarjeta de crédito* credit card *18*
el **taxi** taxi *5*
la **taza** cup *11*
te (to, for) you *(i.o.) 5;* you *(d.o.) 9; ¿Cómo te llamas?* What is your name? *1; te llamas* your name is *1*
el **teatro** theater *6*
el **teclado** keyboard *4*
el **teléfono** telephone *4; el número de teléfono* telephone number *4; por teléfono* by the telephone, on the telephone *12*
la **telenovela** soap opera *13*
la **televisión** television *8; ver (la) televisión* to watch television *8*
el **televisor** television set *13*
el **tema** theme, topic
la **temperatura** temperature *14; ¿Qué temperatura hace?* What is the temperature? *14*
temprano early *10*
el **tenedor** fork *11*
tener to have *9; ¿Cuántos años tienes?* How old are you? *1; ¿Qué (+ tener)?* What is wrong with (person)? *12; tener calor* to be hot *12; tener frío* to be cold *12; tener ganas de* to feel like *12; tener hambre* to be hungry *12; tener miedo de* to be afraid *12*; *tener* (+ number) *años* to be (+ number) years old *9; tener prisa* to be in a hurry *12; tener que* to have to *11; tener sed* to be thirsty *12; tener sueño* to be sleepy *12; tengo* I have *1; tengo* (+ number) *años* I am (+ number) years old *1; tiene* it has; *tienes* you have *1*
tengo: see *tener*
el **tenis** tennis *8*
el **tenista, la tenista** tennis player *14*
tercer third (form of *tercero* before a *m., s.* noun) *14*
tercero,-a third *14*
terminar to end, to finish *4*
ti you (after a preposition) *8*
la **tía** aunt *7*
el **tiempo** time *7;* weather *14,* verb tense; *Hace buen (mal) tiempo.* The weather is nice (bad). *14; ¿Qué tiempo hace?* How is the weather? *14*
la **tienda** store *6*
tiene: see *tener*
tienes: see *tener*
el **tío** uncle *7*
típico,-a typical
el **tipo** type, kind
la **tiza** chalk *3*
toca: see *tocar*
el **tocadiscos** audio compact disc player *9*

tocar to play (a musical instrument) *8,* to touch; *toca* (*tú* command) touch; *toquen* (*Uds.* command) touch
todavía yet *13,* still *14*
todo,-a all, every, whole, entire *7; de todos los días* everyday *11; por todos lados* everywhere *14; todo el mundo* everyone, everybody*; todos los días* every day *9*
todos,-as everyone, everybody
tolerante tolerant
tomar to take *5,* to drink, to have *6*
el **tomate** tomato *16*
tonto,-a silly *8*
el **tópico** theme
toquen: see *tocar*
trabajar to work *15; trabajando en parejas* working in pairs
el **trabajo** work *15*
traer to bring *15*
el **traje** suit *17; traje de baño* swimsuit *17*
el **transporte** transportation *5*
tratar (de) to try (to do something)
trece thirteen *1*
treinta thirty *2*
el **tren** train *5*
tres three *1*
trescientos,-as three hundred *10*
triste sad *7*
el **trombón** trombone
la **trompeta** trumpet
tu your (informal) *4; (pl. tus)* your (informal) *7*
tú you (informal) *1*
la **tumba** tomb
el **turista, la turista** tourist

U

u or (used before a word that starts with *o* or *ho*) *12*
Ud. you (abbreviation of *usted*) *2;* you (after a preposition) *8; Ud. se llama....* Your name is.... *3*
Uds. you (abbreviation of *ustedes*) *2;* you (after a preposition) *8*
último,-a last
un, una a, an, one *3*
único,-a only, unique *7*
la **universidad** university
uno one *1*
unos, unas some, any, a few *3*
el **Uruguay** Uruguay *1*
usar to use *18*
usted you (formal, *s.*) *2;* you (after a preposition) *8*
ustedes you *(pl.) 2;* you (after a preposition) *8*
la **uva** grape *16*

V

las **vacaciones** vacation *17*
¡vamos! let's go! *5; ¡vamos a* (+ infinitive)*!* let's (+ infinitive)! *6*
varios,-as several
el **vaso** glass *11*
vayan: see *ir*
ve: see *ir*
veinte twenty *1*
veinticinco twenty-five *2*
veinticuatro twenty-four *2*
veintidós twenty-two *2*
veintinueve twenty-nine *2*
veintiocho twenty-eight *2*
veintiséis twenty-six *2*
veintisiete twenty-seven *2*
veintitrés twenty-three *2*
veintiuno twenty-one *2*
vender to sell *17*
Venezuela Venezuela *1*
vengan: see *venir*
venir to come *10; vengan (Uds.* command) come
la **ventana** window *3*
ver to see, to watch *6; a ver* let's see, hello (telephone greeting) *ver (la) televisión* to watch television *8*
el **verano** summer *7*
el **verbo** verb
verdad true
la **verdad** truth *12*
¿verdad? right? *5*
verde green *4*
la **verdura** greens, vegetables *16*
ves: see *ver*
el **vestido** dress *17*
la **vez** time *(pl. veces) 10; a veces* at times, sometimes *10;* (number +) *vez/veces al/a la* (+ time expression) (number +) time(s) per (+ time expression) *13; otra vez* again, another time *11*
viajar to travel *11*
el **viaje** trip *9; hacer un viaje* to take a trip *9*; *la agencia de viajes* travel agency
la **vida** life *13*
viejo,-a old *10*
el **viento** wind *14; hace viento* it is windy *14*
viernes Friday *4; el viernes* on Friday
el **vinagre** vinegar *16*
la **vista** view; *hasta la vista* so long, see you later
vivir to live *7*
el **vocabulario** vocabulary
la **vocal** vowel; *vocales abiertas* open vowels; *vocales cerradas* closed vowels
el **volibol** volleyball *13*
volver (ue) to return, to go back, to come back *13*
vosotros,-as you (Spain, informal, *pl.*) *2*
la **voz** voice *(pl. voces) 8*
vuestro,-a,-os,-as your (Spain, informal, *pl.*)

Y

y and *1; y cuarto* a quarter past, a quarter after *2; y media* half past *2*
ya already *11; ¡ya lo veo!* I see it!
yo I *1*

Z

la **zanahoria** carrot *16*
el **zapato** shoe *17; zapato bajo* flats *17; zapato de tacón* high-heel shoe *17*

Vocabulary English/Spanish

A

a un, una *2*; *a few* unos, unas *2*; *a lot (of)* mucho *6*, muchísimo
about sobre
accent el acento *1*
activity actividad *9*
to **add** añadir *16*
address la dirección *4*
aerobics los aeróbicos *13*; *to do aerobics* hacer aeróbicos *13*
affectionate cariñoso,-a *7*
afraid asustado,-a; *to be afraid of* tener miedo de *12*
after después de *13*
afternoon la tarde *2*; *good afternoon* buenas tardes *1*; *in the afternoon* de la tarde *2*; por la tarde *9*
afterwards después *13*
again otra vez *11*
age la edad
agency la agencia; *travel agency* agencia de viajes
ago hace *(+ time expression)* que *13*
agreed de acuerdo *6*
airplane el avión *5*; *by airplane* en avión *5*
algebra el álgebra
all todo,-a *7*
almost casi *13*
alone solo,-a
along por *14*
already ya *11*
also también *5*
always siempre *6*
American americano,-a *13*
an un, una *3*
and y *1*; e *(used before a word beginning with* i *or* hi*) 12*
another otro,-a *3*; *another time* otra vez *8*
answer la respuesta
to **answer** contestar *8*
any unos, unas *3*; alguno,-a, algún, alguna *15*
anybody alguien *17*
anyone alguien *17*
anything algo *17*
apartment el apartamento
apple la manzana *16*
April abril *10*
Argentina la Argentina *1*
arm el brazo *17*
to **arrange** arreglar *15*
to **arrive** llegar *15*
art el arte *4*
artist el artista, la artista
as tal *2*, como; *as (+ adverb) as possible* lo más/menos *(+ adverb)* posible *16*; *as (+ adjective/adverb) as (+ person/item)* tan *(+ adjective/adverb)* como *(+ person/item) 16*; *as much/many (+ noun) as (+ person/item)* tanto,-a *(+ noun)* como *(+ person/item) 16*; *as much as* tanto como *16*
to **ask** preguntar *6*; *to ask a question* hacer una pregunta *6*; *to ask for* pedir *(i, i) 12*; pedir permiso (para) *to ask for permission (to do something) 12*
at en; *at home* en casa *18*; *at night* de la noche *2*, por la noche *12*; *at...o'clock* a la(s)... *4*; *at times* a veces *10*; *at what time?* ¿a qué hora? *4*
athlete el deportista, la deportista *14*
to **attain** conseguir *(i, i)*
attractive bonito,-a, guapo,-a *7*
August agosto *10*
aunt la tía *7*
automatic automático,-a *18*
autumn el otoño *14*
avenue la avenida *6*
average regular *2*
avocado el aguacate *16*

B

backpack la mochila *3*
bad malo,-a *8*
bald calvo,-a *8*
banana el plátano *16*
bank el banco *5*
to **bargain** regatear
baseball el béisbol *8*
basketball el básquetbol *13*, el baloncesto; *basketball player* el basquetbolista, la basquetbolista *14*
bathroom el baño *12*, el cuarto de baño
to **be** ser *3*; *to be able to* poder *(ue) 13*; *to be afraid of* tener miedo de *12*; *to be hot* tener calor *12*; *to be hungry* tener hambre *12*; *to be important* importar *16*; *to be in a hurry* tener prisa *12*; *to be lacking* hacer falta *16*; *to be necessary* hacer falta *16*; *to be (+ number) years old* tener *(+ number)* años *9*; *to be pleasing to* gustar *8*; *to be ready* estar listo,-a *14*; *to be satisfied (with)* estar contento,-a (con) *7*; *to be sleepy* tener sueño

12; *to be smart* ser listo,-a *15*; *to be sorry* sentir *11*; *to be thirsty* tener sed *12*
beach la playa *7*
beans los frijoles *6*
because porque *5*
to **become** cumplir *10*; *to become (+ number) years old* cumplir *10*
bed la cama *15*
bedroom el cuarto *12*, la habitación
before antes de *13*
to **begin** empezar *(ie) 11*
to **believe** creer
belt el cinturón *18*
beside al lado (de) *12*
best mejor *16*; *the best (+noun)* el/la/los/las mejor/mejores *(+ noun) 16*
better mejor *16*
between entre
bicycle la bicicleta *5*
big grande *6*, gran *(form of* grande *before a m., s. noun)*
bike la bicicleta *5*
biology la biología *4*
birthday el cumpleaños *10*; *Happy birthday!* ¡Feliz cumpleaños! *10*; *to have a birthday* cumplir años *10*
black negro,-a *4*
blackboard la pizarra *3*
blond, blonde rubio,-a *8*
blouse la blusa *17*
blue azul *4*
boat el barco *5*
body el cuerpo *17*
Bolivia Bolivia *1*
book el libro *3*
bookstore la librería *9*
boot la bota *17*
bored aburrido,-a *8*
boring aburrido,-a *8*
to **borrow** pedir prestado,-a *12*
boy el chico *3*, el muchacho *5*
boyfriend el novio
bracelet la pulsera *18*
bread el pan *11*
breakfast el desayuno
to **bring** traer *15*
to **bring up** subir *15*
brother el hermano *7*
brown café *(color) 17*
brunet, brunette moreno,-a *8*
building el edificio *6*
bus el autobús *5*
busy ocupado,-a *7*
but pero *6*
butter la mantequilla *11*
to **buy** comprar *8*
by por *7*; *by (+ vehicle)* en *(+ vehicle) 5*; *by telephone* por teléfono *12*; *by the way* a propósito

C

cafeteria la cafetería *5*
calendar el calendario
to **call** llamar *9*
can la lata *16*
capital la capital *14*
car el carro *5*, el coche; *by car* en carro *5*, en coche
card la tarjeta *18*; *credit card* tarjeta de crédito *18*; *playing card* la carta *13*
carrot la zanahoria *16*
to **carry** llevar *16*; *to carry up* subir *15*
cash el efectivo *18*; *in cash* en efectivo *18*
cassette el casete *9*
cat el gato, la gata *9*
CD-ROM disco compacto
to **celebrate** celebrar *10*
center el centro *6*; *shopping center* centro comercial *17*
century el siglo *13*
chair la silla *3*
chalk la tiza *3*
change el cambio *14*
cheap barato,-a *18*
checkers las damas *13*
cheese el queso *16*
chemistry la química
chess el ajedrez *13*
chicken el pollo *6*
Chile Chile *1*
chilly fresco,-a *14*
chocolate el chocolate *16*
to **choose** escoger *16*
chore el quehacer *15*
Christmas la Navidad *10*
city la ciudad *6*
clam la almeja
class la clase *4*
classmate el compañero, la compañera *9*
clean limpio,-a *7*
to **clean** limpiar *15*
to **climb** subir *15*
clock el reloj *3*
to **close** cerrar *(ie) 11*
closed cerrado,-a *7*
clothing la ropa *15*
cloudy nublado,-a *14*; *it is cloudy* está nublado *14*
coat el abrigo *15*
coffee el café *16*
cold frío,-a *7*; el frío *7*; *it is cold* hace frío *14*; *to be cold* tener frío *12*
Colombia Colombia *1*
color el color *14*
to **combine** combinar *17*
to **come** venir *10*; *to come back* volver *(ue) 13*; *to come in* entrar *9*
comfortable cómodo,-a *12*
comical cómico,-a *8*
compact disc el disco compacto *4*; *audio compact disc, audio CD 9*; *CD-ROM 4*; *audio compact disc player* el tocadiscos *9*
competition la competencia *14*

to **complete** completar, acabar *15*
computer la computadora *4*
computer science la computación *4*
concert el concierto *6*
congratulations felicitaciones
to **continue** continuar *14*, seguir *(i, i)*
to **cook** cocinar *15*
cool el fresco *14*; *it is cool* hace fresco *14*
to **copy** copiar *14*
corn el maíz *16*
to **cost** costar *(ue) 13*
Costa Rica Costa Rica *1*
cotton el algodón *17*
country el país
couple la pareja
courtyard el patio *12*
cousin el primo, la prima *7*
crazy loco,-a *7*
to **create** crear
credit el crédito *18*; *credit card* la tarjeta de crédito *18*; *on credit* a crédito *18*
to **cross** cruzar
Cuba Cuba *1*
cup la taza *11*

D

dad el papá
to **dance** bailar *8*
dark obscuro,-a; *dark-haired, dark-skinned* moreno,-a *8*
date la fecha *10*
daughter la hija *7*
day el día *4*; *every day* todos los días *11*; *the day after tomorrow* pasado mañana *10*; *the day before yesterday* anteayer *10*
dear querido,-a *10*
December diciembre *10*
to **decorate** adornar *15*
degree el grado *14*
delighted encantado,-a *5*
dentist el dentista, la dentista *5*
department el departamento *18*
desire la gana *12*
desk el escritorio, el pupitre *3*; *cashier's desk* la caja *18*
dessert el postre *11*
difficult difícil *8*
dinner la comida
to **direct** dirigir *15*
director el director, la directora
dirty sucio,-a *7*
disaster el desastre *15*
disc el disco *4, 7*
dish el plato *11*
dishwasher el lavaplatos *11*
diskette el diskette *4*
to **do** hacer *6*; *to do aerobics* hacer aeróbicos *13*
doctor el médico, la médica *5*, el doctor, la doctora
dog el perro, la perra *9*
dollar el dólar
Dominican Republic la República Dominicana *1*
door la puerta *3*
downtown el centro *6*
to **draw** dibujar *13*
drawing el dibujo *12*
dress el vestido *17*
drink el refresco *6*, la bebida
to **drink** tomar *6*
drum el tambor
during durante

E

e-mail dirección de correo electrónico *4*
each cada *12*
early temprano *10*
earring el arete *4*
Easter la Pascua
easy fácil *8*
to **eat** comer *6*
Ecuador el Ecuador *1*
egg el huevo *16*
eight ocho *1*
eight hundred ochocientos,-as *10*
eighteen dieciocho *1*
eighth octavo,-a *14*
eighty ochenta *2*
either tampoco *4*; *either...or* o...o *17*
electric eléctrico,-a *11*
elevator el ascensor *18*
eleven once *1*
El Salvador El Salvador *1*
else más *7*
end el fin *9*
to **end** terminar *4*
English el inglés *(language) 4*
enough bastante *18*
to **erase** borrar
eraser el borrador *3*
escalator la escalera automática *12*
every todo,-a *7*, cada *12*; *every day* todos los días *9*
everybody todo el mundo, todos,-as
everyday de todos los días *11*
everyone todo el mundo, todos,-as
everywhere por todos lados *14*
exam el examen *9*
example el ejemplo; *for example* por ejemplo
excellent excelente *14*
excuse me perdón, con permiso *2*
expensive caro,-a *18*
to **explain** explicar, aclarar
explanation la explicación

F

fairly bastante
family la familia *7*; *family tree* el árbol genealógico
famous famoso,-a
fantastic fántastico,-a *5*
far (from) lejos (de) *5*
fast rápido,-a *8*
fat gordo,-a *8*

father el padre *7*
favorite favorito,-a *6*
fear el miedo *12*; *to be afraid of* tener miedo de *12*
February febrero *10*
to **feed** dar de comer *15*
to **feel like** tener ganas de *12*
to **feel sorry** sentir (*ie*) *11*
fifteen quince *1*
fifth quinto,-a *14*
fifty cincuenta *2*
film la película *9*
to **find** encontrar (*ue*)
finger el dedo *17*
to **finish** terminar *4*, acabar *15*
first primero,-a *10*, primer *(form of* primero *before a m., s. noun) 12*, primero *(adverb) 10*; *first floor* el primer piso *12*
fish el pescado *6*
to **fit** quedarle bien a uno *17*
five cinco *1*
five hundred quinientos,-as *10*
to **fix** arreglar *15*
floor el piso *12*; *first floor* el primer piso *12*; *ground floor* la planta baja *12*
flower la flor *14*
flute la flauta
to **follow** seguir (*i, i*); *the following* lo siguiente
food la comida *6*; *food server* el mesero, la mesera *6*
foot el pie *17*; *on foot* a pie *5*
football el fútbol americano *13*
for por, para *7*; *for example* por ejemplo *2*
to **forget** olvidar *16*
fork el tenedor *11*
forty cuarenta *2*
four cuatro *1*
four hundred cuatrocientos,-as *10*
fourteen catorce *1*
fourth cuarto,-a *14*
free libre *7*
fresh fresco,-a *16*
Friday viernes *4*; *on Friday* el viernes
friend el amigo, la amiga *3*
from de *1*, desde *12*; *from the* de la/del (de + el) *5*; *from where?* ¿de dónde? *1*
fruit la fruta *16*
fun divertido,-a *7*
funny cómico,-a *8*

G

game el partido *8*, el juego
garage el garaje *12*
garbage la basura *15*
garlic el ajo *16*
generous generoso,-a *8*
geography la geografía
geometry la geometría
to **get** conseguir *(i, i)*
gift el regalo *18*
girl la chica *3*, la muchacha *5*
girlfriend la novia
to **give** dar *13*
glad contento,-a *3*; *Glad to meet you!* ¡Mucho gusto! *1*; *I would be (very) glad to* con (mucho) gusto *1*; *So glad to meet you.* Tanto gusto. *1*
glass el vaso *8*
glove el guante *17*
to **go** ir *5*; *let's go!* ¡vamos! *5*; *to be going to (do something)* ir a *(+ infinitive) 6*; *to go back* regresar, volver *(ue) 13*; *to go in* entrar *9*; *to go out* salir *7*; *to go shopping* ir de compras *8*; *to go up* subir *15*; *to go upstairs* subir *15*
gold el oro *18*
good bueno,-a *8*, buen (*form of* bueno *before a m., s. noun*) *14*; *good afternoon* buenas tardes *2*; *good luck* buena suerte; *good morning* buenos días *2*; *good night* buenas noches *2*
good-bye adiós *1*
good-looking guapo,-a *7*, bonito,-a *7*
gossip el chisme *12*
granddaughter la nieta *7*
grandfather el abuelo *7*
grandmother la abuela *7*
grandson el nieto *7*
grape la uva *16*
gray gris *4*
great fantástico,-a *5*
greater mayor *16*
greatest mayor *16*
green verde *4*
green bean la habichuela *16*
greens la verdura *16*
group el grupo; *musical group* grupo musical
Guatemala Guatemala *1*
guitar la guitarra *9*
guy el muchacho *5*
gym el gimnasio

H

half medio,-a; *half past* y media *2*
ham el jamón *16*
hand la mano *17*; *on the other hand* en cambio *14*
handbag el bolso *18*
handkerchief el pañuelo *18*
handsome guapo,-a *7*
to **hang** colgar *(ue) 15*
to **happen** pasar
happy contento,-a *7*, feliz (*pl.* felices) *10*, alegre; *Happy birthday!* ¡Feliz cumpleaños! *10*
hard difícil *8*
hat el sombrero *17*
to **have** tomar *6*, tener *9*; *to have a birthday* cumplir años *10*; *to have just* acabar de *(+ infinitive) 15*; *to have to* deber, tener que *11*
he él *3*
head la cabeza *17*

to **hear** oír *8*
heat el calor *12*
hello hola *1*; *hello (telephone greeting)* aló *4*, diga, oigo
help la ayuda
to **help** ayudar *11*
her su, sus *7*; la *(d.o.) 9*; le *(i.o.) 1*; *(after a preposition)* ella *8*
here aquí *1*
hey mira, miren, oye, oigan
hi hola *1*
him lo *(d.o.) 9*; le *(i.o.) 5*; *(after a preposition)* él *8*
his su, sus *7*
history la historia *4*
hockey el hockey
home la casa *7*; *at home* en casa
homework la tarea *8*
Honduras Honduras *1*
horrible horrible *8*
horse el caballo *5*; *on horseback* a caballo *5*
hot caliente *7*; *it is hot* hace calor *14*; *to be hot* tener calor *12*
hotel hotel *5*
hour la hora *2*
house la casa *7*
how? ¿cómo? *1*; *How are you?* ¿Qué tal? *2*; *How are you (formal)?* ¿Cómo está (Ud.)? *2*; *How are you (informal)?* ¿Cómo estás (tú)? *2*; *How are you (pl.)?* ¿Cómo están (Uds.)? *2*; *How do you say...?* ¿Cómo se dice...? *3*; *How do you write (spell)...?* ¿Cómo se escribe...? *1*; *How is the weather?* ¿Qué tiempo hace? *14*; *How long...?* ¿Cuánto *(+ time expression)* hace que *(+ present tense of verb)...? 13*; *how many?* ¿cuántos,-as? *4*; *how much?* ¿cuánto,-a? *4*; *How old are you?* ¿Cuántos años tienes? *1*
how (+ adjective)! ¡qué *(+ adjective)*! *7*
hug el abrazo *12*
hunger el hambre *f. 12*
hungry: to be hungry tener hambre *12*
hurry la prisa *12*; *in a hurry* apurado,-a *7*; *to be in a hurry* tener prisa *12*
husband el esposo *7*

I

I yo *1*
ice el hielo *14*; *to ice-skate* patinar sobre hielo *14*
ice cream el helado *16*
idea la idea *10*
ideal ideal *8*
if si *9*
to **imagine** imaginar
important importante *8*
in en *4*, por *7*
ingredient el ingrediente *16*
in order to para *7*
intelligent inteligente *8*
to **intend** pensar *(ie) 11*
interesting interesante *8*
to **introduce** presentar *5*; *let me introduce you (formal, s.) to* le presento a *5*; *let me introduce you (informal, s.) to* te presento a *5*; *let me introduce you (pl.) to* les presento a *5*
invitation la invitación
to **invite** invitar
island la isla
it la *(d.o.)*, lo *(d.o.) 9*
its su, sus *7*

J

jacket la chaqueta *17*
January enero *10*
juice jugo *6*
July julio *10*
June junio *10*
just sólo

K

to **keep on** seguir *(i,i)*
keyboard el teclado *4*
kind amable *7*, el tipo
kitchen la cocina *11*
knife el cuchillo *11*
to **know** saber *6*

L

lady la señora, Sra. *2*, la dama; *young lady* la señorita *2*
lamp la lámpara *11*
language la lengua, el idioma
last pasado,-a *10*, último,-a
later luego *1*, después *11*; *see you later* hasta luego *1*, hasta la vista
lazy perezoso,-a
to **learn** aprender
leather el cuero *18*
to **leave** dejar *15*
leg la pierna *17*
to **lend** prestar *15*
less menos *11*; *less (+ noun/adjective/adverb) than* menos *(+ noun/adjective/adverb)* que *16*; *the least (+ adjective + noun)* el/la/los/las *(+ noun)* menos *(+ adjective) 16*
let's (+ infinitive)! ¡vamos a *(+ infinitive)*! *6*
let's go! ¡vamos! *5*
letter la carta *12*, la letra; *capital letter* la mayúscula *1*; *lowercase letter* la minúscula

lettuce la lechuga *16*
library la biblioteca *5*
lie la mentira *12*
to **lie** mentir *(ie, i)*
life la vida *13*
light la luz *(pl. luces) 11*
to **light** encender *(ie) 11*
like como
to **like** gustar *8*; querer *11*; *I/you/he/she/it/we/they would like...* me/te/le/nos/os/les gustaría... *12*
list la lista *13*
to **listen (to)** oír *8*, escuchar
little poco,-a *12*; *a little (bit)* un poco *5*; *a very little (bit)* un poquito *9*
to **live** vivir *7*
living room la sala *12*
lobster la langosta
long largo,-a *18*
to **look (at)** mirar *8*; *to look for* buscar *5*
to **lose** perder *(ie)*
love el amor *9*
to **love** querer *11*
lunch el almuerzo *4*

M

machine la máquina; *little machine* la maquinita *13*
magazine la revista *3*
to **make** hacer *6*
mall el centro comercial *17*
man el hombre *17*
many mucho,-a *6*
map el mapa *3*
March marzo *10*
market el mercado *16*
match el partido *8*
material el material *18*
mathematics las matemáticas *4*
to **matter** importar *16*
maximum máximo,-a *14*
May mayo *10*
me me *(i.o.) 8*; me *(d.o.) 9*; *they call me* me llaman; *(after a preposition)* mí
to **mean** querer decir *12*; *it means* quiere decir *3*; *What is the meaning (of)...?* ¿Qué quiere decir...? *3*
meat la carne *16*
menu el menú *6*
Mexico México *1*
midnight la medianoche *2*; *It is midnight.* Es medianoche. *2*
milk la leche *15*
mine mío,-a; *the pleasure is mine* el gusto es mío *5*
minimum mínimo,-a *14*
minus menos *2*
minute el minuto *13*
Miss la señorita, Srta. *2*
mist la neblina *14*
mistaken equivocado
modern moderno,-a
mom la mamá
moment el momento *6*
Monday lunes *4*; *on Monday* el lunes
money el dinero *9*
month el mes *10*
more más *7*; *more (+ noun/adjective/adverb) than* más (+ noun/adjective/adverb) que *16*
morning la mañana *2*; *good morning* buenos días *2*; *in the morning* de la mañana *2*, por la mañana *13*
most: the most (+ adjective + noun) el/la/los/las *(+ noun)* más *(+ adjective) 16*
mother la madre *7*
motorcycle la moto(cicleta) *5*
mouse ratón (*pl.* ratones) *4*
movie la película *9*; *movie theater* el cine *5*
Mr. el señor, Sr. *2*
Mrs. la señora, Sra. *2*
much mucho,-a, mucho *6*; *very much* muchísimo
museum el museo *6*
music la música *4*
must deber *11*
my mi *3*, *(pl. my)* mis *7*; *my name is* me llamo *1*

N

name el nombre; *last name* el apellido; *my name is* me llamo *1*; *their names are* se llaman; *What is your name?* ¿Cómo te llamas? *3*; *What is (your/his/her) name?* ¿Cómo se llama (Ud./él/ella)? *1*; *(Your [formal]/His/Her) name is....* (Ud./Él/Ella) se llama.... *3*; *your name is* te llamas *1*
napkin la servilleta *11*
near cerca (de) *5*
necklace el collar *18*
to **need** necesitar *4*
neither tampoco *4*; *neither...nor* ni...ni *17*
nephew el sobrino *7*
nervous nervioso,-a *7*
never nunca *3*
new nuevo,-a *3*; *New Year's Day* el Año Nuevo *10*
news la noticia
newspaper el periódico *3*
next próximo,-a, que viene *9*; *next to* al lado (de) *12*
Nicaragua Nicaragua *1*
nice simpático,-a *5*, amable *7*; *the weather is nice* hace buen tiempo *14*
nickname el apodo
niece la sobrina *7*
night la noche *2*; *at night* de la noche *2*, por la noche *12*; *good night* buenas noches *2*

nine nueve *1*
nine hundred novecientos,-as *10*
nineteen diecinueve *1*
ninety noventa *2*
ninth noveno,-a *14*
no no *1*
nobody nadie *17*
none ninguno,-a, ningún, ninguna *17*
noon el mediodía; *It is noon.* Es mediodía. *2*
north el norte
not: not any ninguno,-a, ningún, ninguna *17*; *not even* ni *10*; *not very* poco,-a *12*
notebook el cuaderno *3*
nothing nada *17*
November noviembre *10*
now ahora *4*; *right now* ahora mismo *13*
number el número *4*; *telephone/fax/cellular telephone number* número de teléfono/de fax/de teléfono celular *4*; *wrong number* número equivocado *4*

O

to **obtain** conseguir *(i, i)*
occupied ocupado,-a *7*
to **occur** pasar
o'clock a la(s)... *4*; *it is (+number) o'clock* son las *(+number) 2*; *it is one o'clock* es la una *2*
October octubre *10*
of de *1*; *of the* de la/del (de + el) *1*
of course! ¡claro! *5*, ¡Cómo no! *6*
office la oficina *5*
official oficial
oh! ¡ay! *3*
oil el aceite *11*, el petróleo
okay de acuerdo *6*, regular *2*; *(pause in speech)* bueno *6*
old viejo,-a *10*; *How old are you?* ¿Cuántos años tienes? *1*; *to be (+ number) years old* tener *(+ number)* años *9*
older mayor *10*
oldest el/la mayor *10*
on en *4*, sobre *4*; *on credit* a crédito *18*; *on foot* a pie *5*; *on loan* prestado,-a *12*; *on the other hand* en cambio *14*; *on the telephone* por teléfono *12*
one un, una, uno *3*
one hundred cien *2*; *(when followed by another number)* ciento *10*
onion la cebolla *16*
only único,-a *7*, sólo *15*, solamente
open abierto,-a *7*
to **open** abrir *9*
or o *4*, u *(used before a word that starts with o or ho) 12*; *either...or* o...o *17*
orange la naranja *6*; anaranjado,-a *(color) 17*
to **order** pedir *(i, i) 12*
organ el órgano
other otro,-a *7*
ought deber *11*
our nuestro,-a *7*
over sobre *4*; *over there* allá *10*

P

paella la paella *15*
page la página *3*
pair la pareja
pajamas el pijama *18*
Panama Panamá *1*
pants el pantalón *17*
pantyhose las pantimedias *17*
paper el papel *3*; *sheet of paper* la hoja de papel
Paraguay el Paraguay *1*
pardon me perdón *2*
parents los padres *3*, los papás
park el parque *5*
partner el compañero, la compañera *9*
party la fiesta *5*
to **pass** pasar *9*; *pass me* pásame *11*
past pasado,-a *10*; *half past* y media *2*
pastime el pasatiempo *13*
patio el patio *12*
to **pay** pagar *18*
pea el guisante *16*
pearl la perla *18*
pen el bolígrafo *3*
pencil el lápiz (*pl.* lápices) *3*; *pencil sharpener* el sacapuntas *3*
people la gente *15*
pepper la pimienta *(seasoning) 11*; *bell pepper* el pimiento *16*
perfect perfecto,-a *18*
perfume el perfume *18*
perhaps quizás *15*
permission el permiso *13*; *to ask for permission (to do something)* pedir permiso (para) *12*
permit el permiso *13*
to **permit** permitir *13*
person la persona *13*
personal personal *18*
Peru el Perú *1*
philosophy la filosofía
photo la foto(grafía) *7*
physics la física *11*
piano el piano *8*
to **pick up** recoger *15*
pink rosado,-a *17*
place el lugar *14*, la posición
to **place** poner *13*
to **plan** pensar (*ie*) *11*
plant la planta *12*
plate el plato *11*
to **play** jugar *(ue) 8*, *13*; *(a musical instrument)* tocar *8*; *(+ a sport/game)* jugar a *8*

player el jugador, la jugadora *14*
playing card la carta *13*
plaza la plaza *6*
pleasant simpático,-a *5*
please por favor *2*
pleasure el gusto *5*; *the pleasure is mine* encantado,-a, el gusto es mío *5*
plural el plural
point el punto
to **point** apuntar; *to point to (at, out)* señalar
politically políticamente
pollution la contaminación ambiental
popular popular *7*
pot la olla *15*
potato la papa *16*
pound la libra *16*
practice la práctica *9*
to **prefer** preferir *(ie, i) 11*
to **prepare** preparar *15*
pretty bonito,-a *3*, guapo,-a *3*, lindo,-a *16*
price el precio *16*
printer (laser) la impresora (láser) *4*
problem el problema *5*
program el programa *13*
to **promise** prometer *17*
public público,-a; *public square* la plaza *6*
Puerto Rico Puerto Rico *1*
purchase la compra *8*
purpose el propósito
purse el bolso *18*
to **put** poner *11*

Q

quality la calidad *18*
quarter el cuarto *2*; *a quarter after, a quarter past* y cuarto *2*; *a quarter to, a quarter before* menos cuarto *2*
question la pregunta *6*; *to ask a question* hacer una pregunta *6*
quickly pronto *2*

R

radio (broadcast) la radio *8*; *radio (apparatus)* el radio
rain la lluvia *14*
to **rain** llover *(ue) 14*
raincoat el impermeable *17*
rapid rápido *8*
rapidly rápidamente *10*
rather bastante *18*
to **reach** cumplir *10*
to **read** leer *6*
reading la lectura
ready listo,-a *14*; *to be ready* estar listo,-a *14*
really? ¿de veras? *10*
to **receive** recibir *18*
recipe la receta *15*
record el disco; *record player* el tocadiscos *9*
red rojo,-a *4*
red-haired pelirrojo,-a *8*
refreshment el refresco *6*
refrigerator el refrigerador *4*
to **regret** sentir *(ie, i) 11*
regular regular *2*
relative el pariente, la pariente *7*
to **remain** quedar *17*
to **remember** recordar *(ue) 13*
remote remoto,-a *13*; *remote control* el control remoto *13*
to **rent** alquilar *13*
to **repeat** repetir *(i, i) 12*
report el informe
reporter el periodista, la periodista
to **request** pedir *(i, i) 12*
to **resolve** resolver *(ue)*
restaurant el restaurante *6*
to **return** volver *(ue) 7*, regresar
to **review** repasar
rice el arroz *16*
ride el paseo *14*
to **ride** montar *9*
right correcto,-a; *right now* ahora mismo *13*
right? ¿verdad? *5*
ring el anillo *17*
ripe maduro,-a *16*
room el cuarto *12*; *dining room* el comedor *11*; *living room* la sala *12*
ruler la regla *3*
to **run** correr *12*
runner el corredor, la corredora *14*
rush la prisa *12*

S

sad triste *7*
saint's day día del santo; *All Saints' Day* Día de todos los Santos
salad la ensalada *6*
sale la oferta *18*; *to be on sale* estar en oferta *18*
salt la sal *11*
same mismo,-a *13*
satisfied: to be satisfied (with) estar contento,-a (con) *7*
Saturday sábado *4*; *on Saturday* el sábado
saucepan la olla *15*
sausage el chorizo *(seasoned with red peppers) 16*
to **save** ahorrar *18*
saxophone el saxofón
to **say** decir *12*; *How do you say...?* ¿Cómo se dice...? *3*; *one says* se dice *3*; *to say you are sorry* pedir perdón *12*
scarf la bufanda *18*
schedule el horario *4*
school el colegio *4*, la escuela *5*
science la ciencia
to **scold** regañar

screen la pantalla *4*
season la estación *14*
second el segundo *14*; segundo,-a *13*
to **see** ver *6*; *I see it!* ¡ya lo veo!; *let's see* a ver; *see you later* hasta la vista, hasta luego *1*; *see you soon* hasta pronto *2*; *see you tomorrow* hasta mañana *2*; *you see* ves
to **seem** parecer *16*
selfish egoísta *8*
to **sell** vender *17*
to **send** enviar *14*
sentence la oración, la frase
September septiembre *10*
seven siete *1*
seven hundred setecientos,-as *10*
seventeen diecisiete *1*
seventh séptimo,-a *14*
seventy setenta *2*
several varios,-as
shame la lástima; *What a shame!* ¡Qué lástima! *9*
she ella *3*
sheet la hoja; *sheet of paper* hoja de papel
ship el barco *5*
shirt la camisa *17*
shoe el zapato *17*; *high-heel shoe* zapato de tacón *17*; *low-heel shoe* zapato bajo *15*
short bajo,-a *(not tall) 8*, corto,-a *(not long) 18*; *in short* en resumen
should deber *11*
show el programa *13*
to **show** enseñar
shrimp el camarón
sick enfermo,-a *7*
side el lado *12*
silk la seda *17*
silly tonto,-a *8*
silver la plata *18*
silverware los cubiertos *11*
since desde *12*, como
to **sing** cantar *8*
singer el cantante, la cantante *6*
sink el fregadero *11*
sir el señor, Sr. *2*
sister la hermana *7*
six seis *1*
six hundred seiscientos,-as *10*
sixteen dieciséis *1*
sixth sexto,-a *14*
sixty sesenta *2*
size el tamaño *18*
to **skate** patinar *14*; *to ice-skate* patinar sobre hielo *14*; *to in-line skate* patinar sobre ruedas *8*
skater el patinador, la patinadora *14*
sketch el dibujo *12*
to **sketch** dibujar *13*
to **ski** esquiar *14*
skier el esquiador, la esquiadora *14*
skirt la falda *17*
skyscraper el rascacielos
sleep el sueño *12*
to **sleep** dormir *(ue, u) 13*
slow lento,-a *8*
small pequeño,-a *12*
smart listo,-a *15*; *to be smart* ser listo,-a *15*
smooth suave
snow la nieve *14*
to **snow** nevar *(ie) 14*
so tal, tan *9*
soap opera la telenovela *13*
soccer el fútbol *9*; *soccer player* el futbolista, la futbolista *14*
sock el calcetín *17*
soft suave; *soft drink* el refresco *6*
so long hasta luego *1*
to **solve** resolver *(ue)*
some unos, unas *3*; alguno,-a, algún, alguna *17*
somebody alguien *17*
someone alguien *17*
something algo *17*
sometimes a veces *10*
son el hijo *7*
song la canción *9*
soon luego *1*, pronto *2*; *see you soon* hasta pronto *2*
sorry: I am sorry lo siento *2*; *to feel sorry* sentir *(ie, i) 11*; *to say you are sorry* pedir perdón *12*
so-so regular *2*
soup la sopa *11*; *soup bowl* el plato de sopa *11*
south el sur
Spain España *1*
Spanish el español *(language) 4*, español, española
to **speak** hablar *4*
special especial *11*
to **spend (time)** pasar *9*
sport el deporte *9*
spouse esposo,-a *7*
spring la primavera *14*
stadium el estadio
stairway la escalera *12*
to **start** empezar *(ie) 11*
to **stay** quedar *17*
stereo el estéreo *9*
still todavía *14*
store la tienda *6*
stove la estufa *11*
to **straighten** arreglar *15*
strawberry la fresa *16*
street la calle *6*
strong fuerte
student el estudiante, la estudiante *3*
study el estudio
to **study** estudiar *4*
subject la asignatura *15*
subway el metro *5*
such tal
sufficient bastante *18*
sufficiently bastante

sugar el azúcar *11*
suit el traje *17*
suitcase la maleta *9*
summer el verano *7*
sun el sol *14*
Sunday domingo *4*; *on Sunday* el domingo
sunny soleado,-a *14*; *it is sunny* está soleado *14*, hay sol *14*, hace sol *14*
supermarket el supermercado *15*
surprise la sorpresa *9*
sweater el suéter *17*
to **sweep** barrer *15*
sweet dulce *8*
to **swim** nadar *8*
swimming pool la piscina *12*
swimsuit el traje de baño *17*
synthetic sintético,-a *18*

T

table la mesa *11*; *to clear the table* recoger la mesa *15*; *to set the table* poner la mesa *11*
tablecloth el mantel *11*
tablespoon la cuchara *11*
to **take** tomar *5*, llevar *16*; *to take a trip* hacer un viaje *9; to take out* sacar *15*; *to take up* subir *15*
tall alto,-a *8*
tape recorder la grabadora *9*
to **teach** enseñar
teacher el profesor, la profesora *3*
team el equipo *13*
teaspoon la cucharita *11*
telephone el teléfono *4*; *by the telephone, on the telephone* por teléfono *12*; *telephone number* el número de teléfono *4*; *cellular telephone number* el número de teléfono celular
to **telephone** llamar *9*
television la televisión *8*; *to watch television* ver (la) televisión *8*
television set el televisor *13*
to **tell** decir *12*; *(a story)* contar *(ue) 17*; *tell me* dígame (Ud. *command*)
temperature la temperatura *14*; *What is the temperature?* ¿Qué temperatura hace? *14*
ten diez *1*
tennis el tenis *8*
tennis player el tenista, la tenista *14*
tenth décimo,-a *14*
to **terminate** acabar *15*
test el examen *9*
than: more (+ **noun/adjective/adverb**) **than** más *(+ noun/adjective/adverb)* que *16*
thanks gracias *2*; *thank you very much* muchas gracias *2*
that que *9*, ese, esa *11*, *(far away)* aquel, aquella *11*, *(neuter form)* eso; *that which* lo que *12*
the el *(m., s.) 3*, la *(f., s.) 3*, las *(f., pl.) 3*, los *(m., pl.) 3*; *to the* al *5*
theater el teatro *6*
their su, sus *7*
them les *(i.o.) 5*; los/las *(d.o.) 9*; *(after a preposition)* ellos,-as *8*
theme el tema, el tópico
then luego *1*, después *11*, entonces *9*; *(pause in speech)* pues *6*
there allí *4*; *there is, there are* hay *4*; *over there* allá *10*
these estos, estas *11*
they ellos,-as *3*; *they are* son *3*; *they were* fueron
thin delgado,-a *8*
thing la cosa *11*
to **think** pensar *(ie) 11*; *to think about (i.e., to have an opinion)* pensar de *11*; *to think about (i.e., to focus one's thoughts)* pensar en *11*; *to think about (doing something)* pensar en *(+ infinitive)*
third tercero,-a, tercer *(form of* tercero *before a m., s. noun) 14*
thirst la sed *12*; *to be thirsty* tener sed *12*
thirteen trece *1*
thirty treinta *2*
this este *(m., s.)*, esta *(f., s.) 11*
those esos, esas *11*, *(far away)* aquellos, aquellas *11*
thousand mil *10*
three tres *1*
three hundred trescientos,-as *10*
through por *12*
Thursday jueves *4*; *on Thursday* el jueves
thus pues *6*
tie la corbata *17*
time el tiempo *7*, la vez (*pl.* veces) *10*; *at times, sometimes* a veces *10*; *at what time?* ¿a qué hora? *4*; *(number +) time(s) per (+ time expression) (number +)* vez/veces al/a la *(+ time expression) 13*; *What time is it?* ¿Qué hora es? *2*
tired cansado,-a *7*
to a *4*
today hoy *6*
toe el dedo *17*
together junto,-a
tomato el tomate *16*
tomorrow mañana *2*; *see you tomorrow* hasta mañana *2*; *the day after tomorrow*

pasado mañana *10*
tonight esta noche *13*
too también *5*, *too (much)* demasiado *18*
to **touch** tocar
train el tren *5*
transportation el transporte *5*
to **travel** viajar *11*
tree el árbol; *family tree* árbol genealógico
trip el paseo *14*, el viaje *9*; *to take a trip* hacer un viaje *9*
trombone el trombón
truck el camión
trumpet la trompeta
truth la verdad *12*
to **try (to do something)** tratar (de)
Tuesday martes *4*; *on Tuesday* el martes
to **turn off** apagar *13*
to **turn on** encender *(ie) 11*; *to turn on (an appliance)* poner *13*
twelve doce *1*
twenty veinte *1*
twenty-eight veintiocho *2*
twenty-five veinticinco *2*
twenty-four veinticuatro *2*
twenty-nine veintinueve *2*
twenty-one veintiuno *2*
twenty-seven veintisiete *2*
twenty-six veintiséis *2*
twenty-three veintitrés *2*
twenty-two veintidós *2*
two dos *1*
two hundred doscientos,-as *10*

U

ugly feo,-a *8*
umbrella el paraguas *18*
uncle el tío *7*
to **understand** comprender *6*
underwear la ropa interior *17*
unique único,-a *7*
United States of America los Estados Unidos *1*
university la universidad
until hasta *1*, *(to express time)* menos *2*
upcoming que viene *9*
Uruguay el Uruguay *1*
us nos *(i.o.) 8*; nos *(d.o.) 9*; *(after a preposition)* nosotros *8*
to **use** usar *18*

V

vacation las vacaciones *17*
vacuum la aspiradora *13*; *to vacuum* pasar la aspiradora *15*
vegetable la verdura *16*
Venezuela Venezuela *1*
verb el verbo
very muy, mucho,-a *6*; *not very* poco,-a *12*; *very much* muchísimo
video game la maquinita *13*
vinegar el vinagre *16*
voice la voz (*pl.* voces) *8*
volleyball el volibol *13*

W

walk el paseo *14*; *to take a walk* dar un paseo *14*; *to walk* caminar *5*
wall la pared *3*, la muralla
wallet la billetera *18*
to **want** querer *11*
to **wash** lavar *15*
wastebasket el cesto de papeles *3*; *wastepaper basket* el cesto de papeles *3*
watch el reloj *3*
to **watch** ver *6*; *to watch television* ver (la) televisión
water el agua *f. 8*; *mineral water* agua mineral *6*
way la manera; *by the way* a propósito *1*
we nosotros *3*
to **wear** llevar *17*
weather el tiempo *14*; *How is the weather?* ¿Qué tiempo hace? *14*; *the weather is nice (bad)* hace buen (mal) tiempo *14*
Wednesday miércoles *4*; *on Wednesday* el miércoles
week la semana *9*
weekend el fin de semana *9*
welcome bienvenido,-a; *you are welcome* de nada *2*
well bien *2*; *(pause in speech)* bueno, este, pues *6*
what a (+ noun)! ¡qué (+ *noun*)! *9*
what? ¿qué? *3*, ¿cuál? *4*; *at what time?* ¿a qué hora? *4*; *What is the meaning (of)...?* ¿Qué quiere decir...? *3*; *What is the temperature?* ¿Qué temperatura hace? *14*; *What is wrong with (someone)?* ¿Qué (+ tener)? *12*; *What is wrong with you?* ¿Qué te pasa?; *What is your name?* ¿Cómo te llamas? *3*; *What is (your/his/her) name?* ¿Cómo se llama (Ud./él/ella)? *1*; *What time is it?* ¿Qué hora es? *2*
when cuando *12*
when? ¿cuándo? *5*
where donde *12*
where? ¿dónde? *1*; *from where?* ¿de dónde? *1*; *(to) where?* ¿adónde? *5*; *Where are you (formal) from?, Where is (he/she/it) from?* ¿De dónde es (Ud./él/ella)? *3*
which que *9*; *that which* lo que *12*
which? ¿cuál? *4*; *which one?* ¿cuál? *4*; *which ones?* ¿cuáles? *4*

white blanco,-a *4*
white-haired canoso,-a *8*
who? ¿quién? *3*, *(pl.)* ¿quiénes? *5*
why? ¿por qué? *5*
wife la esposa *7*
to **win** ganar; *games won* los partidos ganados
wind el viento *14*; *it is windy* hace viento *14*
window la ventana *3*
winter el invierno *14*
to **wish** desear
with con *1*; *with me* conmigo *18*; *with you* (tú) contigo *18*
without sin *16*
woman la mujer *17*; *women's restroom* damas
wonderful estupendo,-a *13*
wool la lana *17*
word la palabra *3*
work el trabajo *15*, la obra
to **work** trabajar *15*
world el mundo
worse peor *16*
worst: the worst (+ noun) el/la/los/las peor/peores *16*
wow! ¡caramba! *9*
to **write** escribir *12*; *How do you write...?* ¿Cómo se escribe...? *1*; *it is written* se escribe *1*

Y

yard el patio *12*
year el año *10*; *New Year's Day* el Año Nuevo *10*; *to be (+ number) years old* tener *(+ number)* años *9*
yellow amarillo,-a *15*
yes sí *1*
yesterday ayer 10; *the day before yesterday* anteayer 10
yet todavía *13*
you tú *(informal) 1*, usted (Ud.) *(formal, s.) 2*, ustedes (Uds.)*(pl.) 2*, vosotros,-as *(Spain, informal, pl.) 2*; *(after a preposition)* ti *8*, usted (Ud.), ustedes (Uds.), vosotros,-as *2*; la, lo, *(d.o.) 9*, las, los, *(d.o.) 9*, te *(d.o.) 11*, os *(Spain, informal, pl., d.o.)*, le *(formal, i.o.)*, les *(pl., i.o.) 1*, os *(Spain, informal, pl., i.o.)*, te *(i.o.) 5*; *Are you from...?* ¿Eres (tú) de...? *1*; *you are* eres *1*; *you (formal) are* es *2*; *you (pl.) were* fueron
young joven *10*; *young lady* la señorita *2*; *young woman* la muchacha *5*
younger menor *10*
youngest el/la menor *10*
your tu (*informal*) *4*, tus (*informal, pl.*) *7*, su, sus (Ud./Uds.) *7*, vuestro,-a, -os,-as *(Spain, informal, pl.)*

Z

zero cero *1*

Index

Page references followed by "A" refer to *Somos así EN SUS MARCAS–A*; those followed by "B" refer to *Somos así EN SUS MARCAS–B*; those both preceded and followed by "B" refer to the Bridge Program of *Somos así EN SUS MARCAS–B.*

a
- after *empezar* and before infinitive 7B
- after *vamos* and before infinitive 118A
- before definite article 91A
- for telling time 69A
- personal 185A, 146B
- used with *ir* to express future time 110A

abbreviations 20A, 26A
acabar de + infinitive 94B
accent marks 53A, 97A, 120A, 61B, 72B, 78B, 95B, 153B
adjectives
- after *¡qué!* 146A, 179A, B38B
- agreement 64A, 135A, 137A, 142A, B18B, 16B, 36B, 79B, 134B
- comparative forms 112B, 113B
- demonstrative 16B, 17B
- descriptive 142A, 162A, B18B
- of quantity 209A, 15B
- position 64A, 135A, 137A
- possessive 137A, B18B
- superlative forms 112B, 113B
- used as nouns 134B
- used with *estar* 142A, 166A

adverbs
- comparative forms 112B, 113B
- superlative forms 112B, 113B

affirmative expressions 145B
alphabet 8A
-ar verbs (see *verbs*)
articles
- contractions with 91A, 100A
- definite 49A, 53A, 54A, 91A, 134B
- indefinite 54A

classroom expressions 9A
cognates 12A, 32A, 34A, 56A, 162A, B4B, 126B
comparative forms 112B, 113B
conjunctions *e* and *u* 23B
contractions *al* and *del* 91A, 100A
dar
- present tense 70B
- preterite tense 122B

dates 210A, 212A
days of the week 187A, 203A
de
- before definite article 91A
- uses 61A, 137A

deber + infinitive 6B
decir
- present tense 25B, 32B
- preterite tense 153B

definite articles 49A, 53A, 54A, 91A, 134B
demonstrative adjectives 16B, 17B
diminutives 151B
direct object pronouns
- forms 182A, 185A, B45B, 60B, 93B, 95B, 146B
- position 183A, 60B, 61B, 93B
- with infinitives 61B, 93B
- with negative expressions 183A
- with present participles 61B, 93B

dirigir, present tense 98B
emphatic forms 159A, 192A, 99B, 159B
-er verbs (see *verbs*)
estar
- present tense 72A, B6B, B46B
- preterite tense 122B
- uses 72A, 142A, 166A, B6B
- vs. *ser* 166A, B6B
- with a present participle 57B

exclamations
- punctuation 8A
- *¡qué* + adjective*!* 146A, 179A, B38B
- *¡qué* + noun*!* 179A, B38B

expressions
- affirmative 145B
- classroom 9A
- negative 52A, 155A, 183A, 95B, 145B, 146B
- of quantity 15B
- time 55B
- with *tener* 180A, 36B

formal vs. informal 20A
future tense
- expressed by the present tense 200A
- with *ir a* + infinitive 110A, 200A

greetings 7A, 18A, 22A, 77A, B4B
gustar
- used with emphatic forms 159A
- used with indirect object pronouns 155A, 159A, 192A, B6B, 95B

hace + time + *que* + present tense 54B
hacer
- present tense 120A, B29B, B46B, 70B
- preterite tense 153B

-iar verbs 72B
indefinite articles 54A
indirect object pronouns
- forms 192A, B8B, B20B, 95B, 111B
- position 95B
- with emphatic forms 159A, 99B
- with infinitives 95B
- with present participles 95B

infinitives
- after *acabar de* 94B
- after *deber* 6B
- after *empezar a* 7B
- after *ir a* 110A
- after *pensar* 9B
- after *tener que* 6B, 176B
- after *vamos a* 118A
- definition 67A
- with direct object pronouns 61B, 93B
- with indirect object pronouns 95B

informal vs. formal 20A
interrogative words 96A, 97A, B27B
introductions 90A, B20B
ir
- followed by *a* (or *al*) + destination 100A
- *ir a* + infinitive 110A, B19B
- present participle 59B
- present tense 100A, B19B, B46B
- preterite tense 143B

-ir verbs (see *verbs*)
jugar, present tense 49B
leer
- present participle 59B
- preterite tense 153B

mentir, preterite tense 141B
mirar vs. *ver* 158A
negative expressions 52A, 155A, 183A, 95B, 145B, 146B
nominalization of adjectives 134B
nouns
- after *¡que!* 179A, B38B
- after *tener* 36B
- diminutive forms 151B
- feminine used with masculine article 65B
- gender 49A, 53A, 63A, 64A, 135A, 137A, 36B, 65B, 79B
- plural 53A, 63A, 64A, 134A, 135A, 137A, 155A, 79B

numbers
- cardinal 12A, 25A, 210A
- ordinal B27B, 79B

object pronouns
- direct 182A, 185A, B45B, 60B, 61B, 93B, 95B, 146B
- indirect 192A, B8B, B20B, 95B, 111B
- used with infinitives 61B, 95B
- used with present participles 61B, 95B

oír
- present participle 59B
- present tense 100B
- preterite tense 153B

ordinal numbers B27B, 79B
pedir
- present tense 32B, 33B
- preterite tense 141B
- vs. *preguntar* 33B

pensar
- present tense 7B
- uses 9B

personal *a* 185A, 146B
poder
present participle 59B
present tense 49B
poner, present tense 70B
possession with *de* 61A, 137A
possessive adjectives 137A, B18B
preferir
present participle 59B
present tense 7B
preterite tense 141B
preguntar vs. *pedir* 33B
prepositional pronouns 159A, 192A, 159B
prepositions
after infinitives 100A
after *pensar* 9B
before prepositional pronouns 159A, 192A, 159B
present participle
formation 57B, 59B
with direct object pronouns 61B, 93B
with indirect object pronouns 95B
present progressive tense 57B
present tense
dar 70B
decir 25B, 32B
estar 72A, B6B, B46B, 57B
gustar 155A, 159A, 192A
hacer 120A, B29B, B46B, 70B
hay 78A
-iar verbs 72B
ir 100A, B19B, B46B
irregular verbs (see individual verbs or Appendices)
jugar 49B
oír 100B
pedir 32B, 33B
pensar 7B, 9B
poder 49B
poner 70B
preferir 7B
querer 7B
regular *-ar* verbs 67A, B9B, B39B, 37B
regular *-er* verbs 116A, B28B, B39B, 37B
regular *-ir* verbs 133A, B28B, B39B, 37B, 141B
saber 120A, B46B, 70B
salir 133A, B29B, B46B, 70B
ser 44A, B6B, B46B
stem-changing verbs 7B, 32B, 49B
tener 180A, B29B, B46B, 7B
to indicate future time 110A, 200A
traer 100B
-uar verbs 72B
used with *hace* to express time 54B
venir 199A, B29B, B46B, 7B
ver 120A, B46B, 70B
verbs with spelling changes 7B, 98B
preterite tense
-car verbs 102B
dar 122B
decir 153B
estar 122B
-gar verbs 102B
hacer 153B
ir 143B
irregular verbs (see individual verbs or Appendices)
leer 153B
mentir 141B
oír 153B
pedir 141B
preferir 141B
regular *-ar* verbs 102B, 121B
regular *-er* verbs 140B
regular *-ir* verbs 140B, 141B
repetir 141B
sentir 141B
ser 143B
stem-changing verbs 140B, 141B
tener 153B
ver 153B
verbs with spelling changes 102B, 121B, 153B
-zar verbs 102B
pronouns
direct object 182A, 185A, B45B, 60B, 61B, 93B, 95B, 146B
indirect object 192A, B8B, B20B, 95B, 111B
position in a sentence 41A, 183A, 61B, 95B
prepositional 159A, 192A, 159B
subject 41A, 42A, 67A, 116A, 133A
used with infinitives 95B
used with present participles 61B, 95B
punctuation 8A
que, to connect two phrases 9B, 26B
¡qué!
¡qué + adjectives*!* 146A, 179A, B38B
¡qué + nouns*!* 179A, B38B
querer, present tense 7B, 24B
question formation
punctuation 8A
question words 96A
tag questions 97A
word order 97A
repetir
present tense 32B
preterite tense 141B
saber, present tense 120A, B46B, 70B
salir, present tense 133A, B29B, B46B, 70B
sentir
present participle 59B
present tense 7B
preterite tense 141B
ser
present tense 44A, B6B, B46B
preterite tense 143B
uses 142A, 166A, 212A, B6B
vs. *estar* 166A, B6B
spelling changes in verbs 49B, 98B, 102B, 121B, 153B
stem-changing verbs
e → i 32B, 49B
e → ie 7B, 32B, 49B
o → ue 49B
present participle 59B
preterite tense 141B
u → ue 49B
subject pronouns 41A, 42A, 67A, 116A, 133A
superlative forms 112B
tener
expressions with *tener* 180A, 36B
+ nouns 36B
present tense 180A, B29B, B46B, 7B
preterite tense 153B
tener que + infinitive 6B, 176B
time
A.M. and P.M. 26A
asking for and telling 26A, 69A, B5B
expressions 55B
with *hace* 54B
todo 135A
traer, present tense 100B
tú vs. *Ud.* 12A
-uar verbs 72B
Ud. vs. *tú* 12A
vamos a + infinitive 118A
venir
present participle 59B
present tense 199A, B29B, B46B, 7B
ver
present tense 120A, B46B, 70B
preterite tense 153B
vs. *mirar* 158A
verbs
-iar 72B
irregular (see individual verbs or Appendices)
present participle 57B, 93B, 95B
present progressive tense 57B
present tense 44A, 67A, 72A, 100A, 110A, 116A, 120A, 133A, 155A, 159A, 166A, 180A, 192A, 199A, 200A, B6B, B9B, B19B, B28B, B29B, B39B, B46B, 7B, 9B, 25B, 32B, 33B, 37B, 49B, 54B, 70B, 98B, 100B, 141B
preterite tense 102B, 121B, 122B, 140B, 141B, 143B, 153B
regular *-ar* 67A, B9B, B39B, 37B, 57B, 102B, 121B, 140B
regular *-er* 116A, B28B, B39B, 37B, 57B, 140B
regular *-ir* 133A, B28B, B39B, 37B, 57B, 140B
similar to *gustar* 111B
stem-changing 7B, 32B, 49B, 59B, 141B
-uar 72B
with spelling changes 49B, 98B, 102B, 121B, 153B
volver, present participle 59B
word order
in exclamations 146A, 179A
in negative sentences 52A, 155A, 183A
in questions 97A, 54B
with adjectives 64A, 112B, 113B
with *gustar* 155A, 192A, 95B
with *hace* + time + *que* + present tense 54B
with object pronouns 183A, 61B, 95B

Credits

Acknowledgments

The authors wish to thank the many people of the Caribbean Islands, Central America, South America, Spain and the United States who assisted in the photography used in the textbook and videos. Also helpful in providing photos and materials were the Argentina Government Tourist Office, *Servicio Nacional de Turismo-Chile (SERNATUR),* Consulate General of Costa Rica, *Corporación nacional de turismo-Colombia, Corporación Ecuatoriana Turismo (CETUR),* Guatemala Tourist Office, Consulate General of the Dominican Republic, Dominican Republic Tourist Office, Mexican Government Tourism Offices, *Ministerio de Turismo de Nicaragua,* Peruvian Tourist Board (FOPTUR), Puerto Rico Tourism Company, the Tourist Office of Spain and the Consulate General of Venezuela. The authors also express their gratitude to Michael C. Kustermann for assistance with obtaining pictures of license plates that appear in the textbook.

The following focus group participants and survey respondants contributed insights, comments and suggestions that served as a foundation for the publication of *Somos así EN SUS MARCAS:*

Pamela Alspach, Triad Local High School, North Lewisburg, Ohio; *Louis Amici*, Kennedy-Kenrick Catholic High School, Norristown, Pennsylvania; *Konnie K. Anderson*, Canby High School, Canby, Minnesota; *Amy C. Badger*, Drayton Hall Middle School, Charleston, South Carolina; *Jane Taylor Bartram*, Buffalo High School, Kenova, West Virginia; *Victor D. Bastek*, Ridgefield Memorial High School, Ridgefield, New Jersey; *Elizabeth Beckmann*, Guthrie Center High School, Guthrie Center, Iowa; *Maria T. Benivegna*, Belleville East High School, Belleville, Illinois; *Wallis S. Berry*, Wando High School, Mt. Pleasant, South Carolina; *Matthew L. Blake*, Porter-Gaud School, Charleston, South Carolina; *Diane Blue*, Pemberton Township High School, Pemberton, New Jersey; *Desiree Boeck*, Columbus High School, Waterloo, Iowa; *Clare A. Bohannon*, Jersey Community High School, Jerseyville, Illinois; *Matt Boyd*, Porter-Gaud School, Charleston, South Carolina; *Ronald Butler*, Miami Sunset Senior High School, Miami, Florida; *Merri-Sue Cardwell*, East Jordan High School, East Jordan, Michigan; *Kristie Carlson*, Prospect High School, Mt. Prospect, Illinois; *Selmira Carvajal*, Glades Middle School, Miami, Florida; *Katherine Catterton*, Wando High School, Mt. Pleasant, South Carolina; *Vikki Caudill*, St. Teresa High School, Decatur, Illinois; *Thomas A. Chaffee*, Portville Central School, Portville, New York; *Diana Chase,* Howell High School, Farmingdale, New Jersey; *Leila A. Chun*, Northeast Middle School, Baltimore, Maryland; *Alfred R. Crudale*, Toll Gate High School, Warwick, Rhode Island; *Eileen K. Denstad*, Caledonia High School, Caledonia, Minnesota; *Daniel DeVries*, Miami Killian Senior High School, Miami, Florida; *Donna Timmel Díaz*, St. Martin's School, Buffalo, New York; *Karen Dibiase*, Pilgrim High School, Warwick, Rhode Island; *Victoria Dilorenzo*, Amherst Central School, Amherst, New York; *Cecilia Doris*, Northern Highlands Regional High School, Allendale, New Jersey; *Magaly Ehmann*, Amherst Central High School, Amherst, New York; *Barbara Fagan*, Claysburg-Kimmel High School, Claysburg, Pennsylvania; *Rosemary Farioli*, Central Academy, Springfield, Massachusetts; *Greg Farlow*, Alvirne High School, Hudson, New Hampshire; *Rick A. Fenstermaker*, Brookville Area High School, Brookville, Pennsylvania; *Mary G. Fisher*, Cornell High School, Cornell, Wisconsin; *John Fitzer*, Delano High School, Delano, Minnesota; *Jane Friedland*, C. J. Hooker Middle School, Goshen, New York; *Ann P. Gage*, Amherst High School, Buffalo, New York; *Lila J. Gidley*, Chester High School, Chester, Illinois; *Susan D. Goldey*, South Plainfield High School, South Plainfield, New Jersey; *Gretchen Gonzalez*, Sheridan High School, Thornville, Ohio; *Carol Gutke*, Antioch Upper Grade School, Antioch, Illinois; *Betty Halsey*, Oceana High School, Oceana, West Virginia; *Michelyn Barkman Hatch*, Williamsburg High School, Williamsburg, Pennsylvania; *Nancy S. Hernández*, Simsbury High School, Simsbury, Connecticut; *Sebastian Hernández*, R. B. Stall High School, North Charleston, South Carolina; *Gregory Hevey*, Alvirne High School, Hudson, New Hampshire; *Jeanna Hill*, Paradise High School, Paradise, California; *Karen Hodge*, North Pemiscot High School, Wardell, Missouri; *Marilyn Jackson*, Freshwater Education District, Staples, Minnesota; *LaDona Jergerson*, Panorama High School, Panora, Iowa; *Anita Johnson*, Knoxville Junior High School, Knoxville, Illinois; *Cynthia Johnson*, South Range High School, North Lima, Ohio; *Rosemary Johnson*, Miller High School, Miller, Missouri; *Rich Jonas*, T. F. South High School, Lansing, Illinois; *Aimee Kinder*, Wando High School, Mt. Pleasant, South Carolina; *Nancy A. Kinder*, Wando High School, Mt. Pleasant, South Carolina; *Mary King*, James Island High School, Charleston, South Carolina; *Kristin Kissock*, La Quinta High School, La Quinta, California; *Philip J. LaBella*, Smethport Area High School, Smethport, Pennsylvania; *Pedro Ledesma* Miami Carol City Senior High School, Carol City, Florida; *Sebastian Leon*, Freehold Township High School, Freehold, New Jersey; *Herbert Le Shay*, St. John's High School, John's Island, South Carolina; *DaShannon Lovin*, Barbourville Independent High School, Barbourville, Kentucky; *Sally Masone*, Jefferson TWP High School, Oak Ridge, New

Jersey; *Janet Mau*, Herscher High School, Herscher, Illinois; *Kiva McEwen*, Carbondale Community High School, Carbondale, Illinois; *Alice M. McNaught*, Cumberland High School, Cumberland, Rhode Island; *Denise Nelson*, Clark County Road-1 High School, Kahoka, Missouri; *Maria Nelson*, Peoria High School, Peoria, Illinois; *Donald J. Nicole*, Saint Andrew's School, Boca Raton, Florida; *Rita Novello*, Liberty High School, Youngstown, Ohio; *Patricia Olderr*, Hinsdale South High School, Darien, Illinois; *Linda Ortiz*, Labrae High School, Leavittsburg, Ohio; *Edella Pagán*, North Charleston High School, North Charleston, South Carolina; *Natascha Patino Ferguson*, Ashley River Elementary, Charleston, South Carolina; *Arlen Pawchyk*, North Branford High School, North Branford, Connecticut; *Dolores Pescador*, La Quinta High School, La Quinta, California; *Barbara Pine*, MES Middle School, Yorktown, New York; *Gail M. Pilgram*, Porter-Gaud School, Charleston, South Carolina; *Mary Lu Pingitore*, Monmouth Beach Elementary School, Monmouth Beach, New Jersey; *Lisa Polito*, MES Middle School, Yorktown, New York; *Helen L. Poulin*, North Country Union High School, Newport, Vermont; *Natalie L. Prasch*, Sauk Centre High School, Sauk Centre, Minnesota; *Joan Prezioso*, Matawan Avenue Middle School, Cliffwood, New Jersey; *Caroline Radcliffe*, North Charleston High School, North Charleston, South Carolina; *Thomas Ralston*, James Buchanan High School, Mercersburg, Pennsylvania; *Ed S. Rife*, Julian Junior High School, Oak Park, Illinois; *Angela Ross*, Arnett J. Brown, Jr. Middle School, Balto, Maryland; *Mary Scheithauer*, Westland High School, Galloway, Ohio; *Anita Schroeder*, Totino-Grace High School, Fridley, Minnesota; *María Segura*, The Green Vale School, Glen Head, New York; *John Shepherd*, Shenandoah High School, Sarahsville, Ohio; *Donna Simon*, Farmington High School, Farmington, Minnesota; *Kelly Smielecki*, Batavia High School, Batavia, New York; *Julie St. Leger*, Port Clinton High School, Port Clinton, Ohio; *Cynthia Smith*, Buist Academy, Charleston, South Carolina; *Daphne Sherman*, James Island High School, Charleston, South Carolina; *Willa L. Steele*, Highview Baptist School, Louisville, Kentucky; *Dawn Stephens*, Oakland High School, Oakland, Illinois; *Sister Carole Tabano*, Academy of the Holy Angels, Demarest, New Jersey; *Joan Tashman*, The Green Vale School, Glen Head, New York; *Dolores Tavkar*, Westlake Middle School, Thornwood, New York; *Joyce Galo Teggart*, Shrewsbury High School, Shrewsbury, Massachusetts; *Janice Thomas*, Wando High School, Mt. Pleasant, South Carolina; *Ralph Toro*, Carteret High School, Carteret, New Jersey; *George R. Valley*, Otter Valley Union High School, Brandon, Vermont; *Nydia L. Vélez-Therminy*, Chatsworth High School, Chatsworth, California; *Michelle Vogl*, Pekin High School, Packwood, Iowa; *William J. West*, Westport Middle School, Westport, Massachusetts; *Linda Wickre*, Shiloh Christian School, Bismarck, North Dakota; *Justine Wills*, Herscher High School, Herscher, Illinois; *Catherine Wilson*, R. B. Stall High School, North Charleston, South Carolina; *Kate Wilson*, East Leyden High School, Franklin Park, Illinois; *Mary Jane Wilson*, De Soto County High School, Arcadia, Florida; *Kimberly Yensan*, Barker Central School District, Lockport, New York; *Linda York*, Lebanon Junior High School, Lebanon, Missouri; *Sharon Zangrilli*, Poland Central School, Poland, New York; *Debby Zarate*, Culver City High School, Culver City, California; *Bruce Zeunle*, Union Catholic High School, Scotch Plains, New Jersey; *Maria Zoch*, George Washington Middle School, Ridgewood, New Jersey

Photo Credits

Balthis, Frank: 48 (br), 153 (b), 174 (b)
Black, Sally/Blacklight Photography: 49 (b), 168
Cass, Maxine: 135 (b), 143 (t)
Chatterton, Carolyn: 41 (c), 153 (t), 188 (r)
Cohen, Stuart: 1 (t), 7 (r), 39 (tl), 49 (t), 54, 100 (l), 110 (t, b), 112, 117, 120, 125 (c), 129 (b), 131 (t), 143 (b), 147 (l, r), 187 (t), 193 (#1, 5)
D'Antonio, Nancy: viii (l), 21 (t), 50, 96 (b), 118 (r), 131 (b), 162
Daemmrich, Robert E./Tony Stone Images: 88 (t), 92
Daemmrich, Robert: 6 (t, b), 29, 32, 44 (tr), 51 (b), 63 (r), 65, 89 (c), 125 (l), 130 (tr), 134, 165 (cr), 197 (t, b)
Degginger, E. R./Color-Pic, Inc.: ix (r), 23 (b), 135 (t), 181 (#3 t, b), 192
Dekovic, Gene: 0 (tr), 4, 17, 41 (b), 43 (t), 101, 109 (t), 119
Dorn-Fernández, Amy: 98
Englebert, Victor: 12, 95
Flipper, Florent/Unicorn Stock Photos: 63 (l), 78 (b)
Fried, Robert: vi (t), B22, B25, B42, B43, B48, 18, 26, 43 (b), 44 (tl, b), 45 (b), 48 (bl), 51 (t), 55, 58, 61, 62 (t, bl), 68 (t, b), 69 (t, c), 70, 77 (t), 78 (t), 83 (c, b), 99 (t), 104 (b), 113 (t), 115 (tr, br), 118 (l), 123, 130 (tl), 136 (t), 145, 146 (b), 152 (b), 160, 161 (l), 165 (t), 169 (b), 170 (b), 171 (b), 175 (br), 178 (l), 179, 180, 181 (#1), 183 (bl), 189 (r), 193 (#2)
Garg, Arvind: 109 (b), 111 (t), 170 (tr), 189 (tl, bl), 193 (#4)
Goldberg, Beryl: v (c), 0 (tl), 15 (b), 33, 91, 125 (r), 140, 141, 146 (t), 190
Golding, Kim/Tony Stone Images: ix (l), 130 (b)
Gregg, Peter/Color-Pic, Inc.: 178 (r)
Grill, Tom/Comstock: vii (t), 88 (b), 129 (t)
Harvey, Mark: 48 (t)
Hersch, H. Huntly: iv, 14, 39 (tr), 41 (t), 45 (t), 149 (bl)
Hill, Justine: 62 (br), 82 (r), 83 (t)
Hodge, Shirley/Root Resources: 174 (t)
Holmes, Robert/Robert Holmes Photography: 159 (t)
Humberto, Carlos/The Stock Market: v (b), 24
Johnson, Markham/Robert Holmes Photography: 184 (c)

Klein, Don: 5 (t), 23 (t, c), 47, 193 (#3)
Larson, June: 74 (l)
Lee, Rick/SuperStock: 89 (t)
Leo de Wys, Inc./Ben Blankenburg: vi (b), 68 (c)
Leo de Wys, Inc./Bill Bachmann: B1, 87 (t), 107 (br), 186 (l), 187 (bl)
Leo de Wys, Inc./Bob Krist: 116
Leo de Wys, Inc./Fridmar Damm: 87 (b), 175 (t)
Leo de Wys, Inc./J. Messerschmidt: 181 (#4)
Leo de Wys, Inc./Jeff Greenberg: 159 (b), 169 (t)
Leo de Wys, Inc./Ken Haas: 59 (t)
Leo de Wys, Inc./Sipa/Derisborg: 165 (cl)
Leo de Wys, Inc./Steve Vidler: 115 (c)
Leo de Wys, Inc./Sunstar: 139 (l)
Leo de Wys, Inc./W. Hille: 27
Lewine, Rob/The Stock Market: 0 (b)
Mayer, Saul: 181 (#2), 183 (br)
Morgan, W. D.: 135 (c), 136 (b), 151 (t), 181 (#5)
Mullen, Karen Holsinger/Unicorn Stock Photos: 59 (b)
Paso Fino Horse Association: 194
Peterson, Chip, and Rosa María de la Cueva: 5 (b), 25 (r), 38 (b), 82 (l), 151 (c)
Place, Chuck: B34, 170 (tl)
Prince, Norman: 183 (tl)
Rangel, Francisco: 143 (c), 187 (br), 191
Root, Mary A./Root Resources: 183 (tr), 184 (t, b), 193 (#6)
Rubin, Lior: 186 (c), 188 (c)
Sanger, David: 38 (t)
Schaefer, Larry/Root Resources: vii (b), 104 (c)
Shaw, Kay: 154
Simson, David: 15 (t), 21 (br), 25 (l), 34 (l, r), 39 (b), 59 (c), 62 (c), 64, 72, 74 (r), 77 (b), 89 (b), 96 (t), 99 (b), 100 (r), 106, 111 (b), 113 (b), 122, 127, 138, 139 (r), 149 (t, br), 151 (b), 163, 165 (b), 173, 175 (bl), 185, 186 (r)
Stewart, Scot: 188 (l)
Stuckey, Michael/Comstock: 1 (b)
Teague, Graeme: 171 (t)
Tellus Vision: 161 (r)
Till, Tom: 69 (b)
Tourist Office of Spain: 104 (t), 105, 107 (t)
UPI (United Press International): B7, 10
Vautier, Mireille: B21
Villalba, Carlos: viii (r), 152 (t)
Weigand, Sally: 7 (l), 21 (bl), 80, 107 (bl), 121
Young-Wolff, David/Tony Stone Images: 88 (tl)